COMMUNAL PIETISM AMONG
EARLY AMERICAN MORAVIANS

AMS PRESS
NEW YORK

COMMUNAL PIETISM AMONG
EARLY AMERICAN MORAVIANS

BY

JACOB JOHN SESSLER

SUBMITTED IN PARTIAL FULFILMENT OF
THE REQUIREMENTS FOR THE DEGREE OF
DOCTOR OF PHILOSOPHY, IN THE FACULTY
OF PHILOSOPHY, COLUMBIA UNIVERSITY.

NEW YORK
HENRY HOLT AND COMPANY

Reprinted from the edition of 1933, New York
First AMS EDITION published 1971
Manufactured in the United States of America

International Standard Book Number: 0-404-08430-3

Library of Congress Catalog Number: 70-134387

AMS PRESS INC.
NEW YORK, N. Y. 10003

TO MY WIFE

PREFACE

THIS treatise is concerned primarily with the pioneer Moravians in America, especially with the settlements in and around Bethlehem, Pa. Enough of the European history of the Moravians is necessarily introduced to make the American situation intelligible to the reader, but I make no claim to original research on matters relating to the European background.

I gratefully acknowledge my indebtedness to the authorities of the Moravian Archives at Bethlehem, particularly to Prof. William N. Schwarze, the Archivist and President of the Moravian College and Theological Seminary, for his assistance in consulting the manuscript records. My thanks are also due to the Rev. Dr. S. H. Gapp, president of the Provincial Elders' Conference, for a critical reading of the manuscript and for helpful suggestions.

I owe much to the constant encouragement and inspiration of my wife, Gela M. Sessler, who has made it possible for me to undertake this work and has also spent many hours of tedious work on the manuscript and the proof. Above all, I am grateful to Herbert Wallace Schneider, Professor of Religion at Columbia University, for his helpful and critical comments on the subject and the organization of the materials.

All the translations from the German are by the writer with a few exceptions which are otherwise credited.

J. J. S.

Middletown, N. J.
March 1, 1933.

CONTENTS

ILLUSTRATIONS

COMMUNAL PIETISM AMONG
EARLY AMERICAN MORAVIANS

CHAPTER I

THE MORAVIAN HERITAGE

IN the torture chamber in the university town of Prague, Bohemia, the bones of the feeble, hoary-headed saint, Gregory the Patriarch, were cracking as he lay stretched upon the rack to force from him a recantation of his heresies. As he lapsed into unconsciousness and was taken from the rack for dead, he had a vision of the glorious future of the Church of the Brethren, whom both the King and the Pope had resolved to exterminate.[1]

Gregory the Patriarch had come some eighty miles for a visit to Prague from the village of Kunwald, near an old castle called Lititz, in the northeastern part of Bohemia, where such as were dissatisfied with the Roman Church had gathered around him. Some had come from the larger cities like Prague; some from Moravia; others from the Bohemian National Church, called the Utraquist Church, which was as corrupt as the Roman Church; and still others had come from the small Waldensian [2] groups that lived in the valleys.

These were all known as followers of John Hus, for after he was burned at the stake in 1415 by the Council of Constance, they led the Nationalists of Bohemia in the revolt, which was the beginning of the Hussite war.

In the course of time, the admirers of Hus split into two factions: the Utraquists and the Taborites; the purpose of the former was restricted to restoring the cup of communion to the laity, whereas that of the latter was a reformation of the entire

[1] J. E. Hutton: *History of the Moravian Church,* pp. 48, 49.

[2] Persecutions of the Waldenses in Italy and France compelled them to wander over southern Europe in search of freedom of conscience. They rebelled against the corruption of the Church and dead ecclesiasticism. They entered Bohemia and Moravia and endured persecutions in common with the Brethren. A colony of Waldenses from the Margravate of Brandenberg moved into the Kunwald valley. Bohemians, Moravians and Waldenses were absorbed in the general movement of the Reformation.

Church. War between these two parties resulted in the establishment of the Utraquists as the National Church of Bohemia. However, in Prague a band of Utraquists, under the preaching of Rokycana, and others, especially from among the Taborites, pledged themselves to practise purity and piety according to the ideals of Hus. These in 1456 retreated to Kunwald, with Gregory the Patriarch as their leader and teacher, and in the following year they adopted a formal statement of their principles. The history of the Moravian Church, also called the United Brethren or *Unitas Fratrum,* begins with this date.

When King George Podiebrad saw how rapidly these heterodox Brethren were increasing, he issued an edict that all his subjects must join either the Utraquist or the Roman Church. Some were brutally murdered and burned at the stake, and the remainder fled for their lives. It is said that "for two full years they lived the life of hunted deer in the forest," and "when snow lay on the ground they trailed behind them a pine-tree branch, so that folk would think a wild beast had been prowling around." When the King finally grew tired of this "hide and seek" contest, the persecutions ceased for a period. Thus, while the enemy was off guard, these Brethren strengthened their foothold, and in 1467 at the Synod of Lhota, three were chosen to establish a ministry of their own. The episcopacy was conferred upon these three by a Waldensian bishop named Stephen. They grew so rapidly in numbers that when the Reformation began, they had four hundred places of worship with a membership of about two hundred thousand.

The Bohemians refused to take part in the Smalcaldic war between the Protestants and Catholics, and in 1548 Ferdinand sought vengeance by demanding that all who lived on royal estates must either join the Utraquist or the Roman Church or leave the country within forty-two days. As a consequence many went to Prussia, and when they were persecuted there by the Lutherans, they moved to Poland, where the Brethren already had some churches. In 1609, Emperor Rudolph II in the Bohemian Charter granted liberty to the evangelical party, and the Brethren had rest from persecution for a few years.

But in the Counter-Reformation beginning in 1621, under Ferdinand II, thousands of families preferred to leave the country, rather than to give up their faith.[3]   The evangelical party of Bohemia and Moravia was now apparently completely destroyed.   After the destruction of Lissa in Poland in 1656, the Brethren there united with the Reformed Church.   This victory of the Catholics concludes the first era of the history of the Moravian Church.

The next period is called the "Hidden Seed," and the man around whom the events of these years center is John Amos Comenius.   In 1627 he had gone to Poland, where at a Synod of the Brethren in 1632 at Lissa, he was made a bishop.   But when Lissa was destroyed by the Poles in 1656, the Brethren fled, Comenius going to Amsterdam where he died in 1671. After leaving Lissa, he was busy in literary and educational work.   He published the doctrines of the Brethren in the form of a catechism, and in another work, *Ratio Disciplinæ Ordinisque Ecclesiasticæ in Unitate Fratrum Behemorum,* he set forth their discipline and church order, together with a history of their church.

During these years of the "Hidden Seed," he predicted the re-establishment of the Brethren's Church, and urged the consecration of new bishops lest the line of succession should be broken.   At his request Nicholas, the court Chaplain of the Duke of Liegnitz, and Peter Jablonsky, a minister in Danzig, were consecrated in 1662.   These two ordained Christian Sitkovius and Daniel Ernst Jablonsky,[4] and the latter with the consent of the former consecrated David Nitschmann,[5] thus

[3] "In 1617 Bohemia had seven hundred and thirty-two cities, and thirty-four thousand seven hundred villages; when Ferdinand II died in 1637, there remained one hundred and thirty cities and six thousand villages, and its three millions of inhabitants were reduced to seven hundred and eighty thousand."   Comenius, *School of Infancy,* p. 161.

[4] Daniel Ernst Jablonsky, the court preacher in Berlin, was a son of Peter Jablonsky, who was a son-in-law of Amos Comenius.   Christian Sitkovius was the Superintendent of the United Reformed and Brethren's Churches of Poland.

[5] "Documents of the ordination of David Nitschmann as Senior and Antistis of the Moravian Church in March 13, 1735, given by Jablonsky, June 14, 1737."   Ms. Beth. Arch.

carrying forward the Apostolic Succession unbroken into the Renewed Church. In these years of obscurity, those who had belonged to the Brethren's Church were compelled to submit to the Roman Church, but in spite of this external compulsion, they secretly cherished the traditions and ideals of the Brethren.

The third and present stage of the Brethren is called the "Renewed Church," extending from 1722 to the present. Although the Thirty Years' War had apparently annihilated the *Unitas Fratrum*, the ideals of purity and piety to which they had clung so tenaciously could not be stamped out. The Hidden Seed awaited fertile soil from the days of Comenius until the days of Philip Jacob Spener (1635-1705), who prepared the soil in Germany out of which grew the Renewed Church. Spener instituted the pietistic movement in Germany, emphasizing *"ecclesiolæ in ecclesia"* (little churches within the church) to promote a revival of practical and devout Christianity. August Hermann Francke, who had founded the famous orphanage at Halle, was Spener's most sympathetic pupil. Under the leadership of Spener, the University of Halle was founded, and the appointments to the professorships were made under his influence. Halle was now the center of the pietistic movement, and one of its achievements was the reorganizing of the Bohemian-Moravian Church, under Count Zinzendorf, who had studied at Halle and was Spener's godson.[6]

By the Peace of Westphalia the central authority of the Emperor and the Diet was now vested in many princes. The governments were bound to allow at least private worship, liberty of conscience, and the right of emigration. But these measures of toleration were not extended to the hereditary lands of the House of Hapsburg. Thus all ecclesiastical life in Bohemia and Moravia which was not Roman Catholic could be suppressed by the Austrian Hapsburgs. The result was that thousands left their homes for the sake of religious freedom. Of all these emigrants, we are particularly interested in those

[6] Although Zinzendorf soon broke with the Halle pietists, he was an exponent of the pietistic movement.

Brethren of the Ancient Church who were led to Bethelsdorf by Christian David and were allowed to settle there by its proprietor, Count Zinzendorf.

Almost forty years of the Renewed Church are inextricably interwoven with the dominating personality of Count Nicholas Ludwig von Zinzendorf, who succeeded in collecting the few scattered remnants of the Ancient Church. It is said of him that when he was yet a boy he wrote messages to God on small pieces of paper and threw them out of the window. "At the age of six he regarded Christ as his brother, would talk with him for hours as with a familiar friend and was often found wrapped in thought, like Socrates in the market place at Athens." [7] At the age of ten he was taken to Halle by his mother, where he came under the influence of Professor Francke, the pietist. The story goes that "by mistake he overheard a conversation between her and the pious professor. She described him as a lad of parts, but full of pride, and in need of the curbing rein. . . . He was proud of his noble birth; he was rather officious in his manner; he had his meals at Francke's private table; he had private lodgings a few minutes' walk from the school; he had plenty of money in his purse; and therefore, on the whole, he was as well detested as the son of a lord can be. . . . He had no sense of sin whatever, and no sense of any need of pardon. . . . For two years he lived in a moral purgatory. The masters gave him the fire of their wrath, and the boys the cold shoulder of contempt. The masters called him a malicious rebel and the boys called him a snob. As the little fellow set off for morning school, with his pile of books upon his arm, the others waylaid him, jostled him to and fro, knocked him into the gutter, scattered his books on the street, and then officiously reported him late for school. He was clever, and therefore the masters called him idle; and when he did not know his lesson they made him stand in the street, with a pair of ass's ears on his head, and a placard on his back proclaiming to the public that the culprit was a 'lazy donkey.' " [8]

[7] Hutton: *History of the Moravian Church*, p. 178.
[8] *Ibid.*, pp. 180, 181.

At Halle, the young Count and a group of fellow pietists formed the "Order of the Grain of Mustard Seed," the rules of which were that its members should steadfastly maintain the doctrine of Jesus, walk worthily in it, exercise charity towards their neighbors, and especially endeavor to promote the conversion of Jews and heathen. His uncle did not favor the pietists, and through him, Zinzendorf was removed from Halle, and in his seventeenth year he was sent to Wittenberg where he stayed two years. Then to finish his education, he traveled in Holland, Switzerland, and France. When he had become of age he accepted a position as King's Councilor at Dresden, at the Court of Augustus the Strong, King of Saxony; it is said that he did so contrary to his desire, in compliance with the wishes of his relatives. Because of his pietistic views and his bold declarations about prejudice and vice, he did not find much favor in Dresden nor at the Saxon Court.

In 1722, under the pressure of persecution in Bohemia and Moravia, fugitives came to his estate where the community of Herrnhut was established. Here Zinzendorf's characteristic doctrine of free redemption, justification, and salvation through the Blood of Christ, found fertile soil in the hearts of these exiles; it was held in so great estimation by them, that for many years it was the only topic insisted upon in their preaching. The Herrnhut community is the source from which Moravianism received its renewed vitality, and whence it was imported directly to America.

The congregation at Herrnhut consisted of two strains, the Slavonic and the German. The first were Czech fugitives from Bohemia and Moravia. The second group were Germans, some of whom had fled from Bohemia and Moravia and some from Germany, members of the Lutheran and Reformed Churches who were of a pietistic nature and desired a more inward religion than their churches could offer them.

Although Zinzendorf welcomed these exiles to his estates, he can hardly be spoken of as the founder of Moravianism. It was contrary to his purpose to erect a separate Moravian Church. He tried to prevent the settlers on his estate from organizing into such a church, for his aim was that the Herrnhuters should be a group of pious people within the Lutheran Church, influencing others within that church toward a more vital religion.   At first these exiles attended the services in the Lutheran Church in Bethelsdorf, but later for sentimental reasons and on the grounds that the constitution of their Ancient Church was older than any other Protestant form of religion, they desired to renew the Ancient Church and be free from the Lutherans.   This whole tendency Zinzendorf strenuously opposed, but when he failed, he threw in his own lot with the Moravians.[9]

The Count could not have had in mind the founding of a new church system.   "The arrival of the first Moravian emigrants, and their subsequent settlement on his estate at Bethelsdorf, to which Herrnhut belongs, took place during his absence, and almost without his knowledge; and according to his own declaration, his only object was to provide an asylum for these oppressed people, hoping that by their pious example, they might be useful to his other tenants."[10]   Various motives can be hidden in this statement that "his only object was to provide an asylum for oppressed people," and that "they might be useful to his other tenants."   Since during this pietistic movement there were many *"ecclesiolæ in ecclesia,"* the Count was probably anxious to establish such "a church within a church."   He was attracted by the piety of these exiles from Moravia and Bohemia, and the thought of making his estate a pietistic center appealed to him.   Then too, Zinzendorf was making no economic sacrifice in welcoming these fugitives; on the contrary, such a settlement on his estate was to his material advantage, especially when we consider that their place of refuge "was an unclaimed wilderness."[11]   The place where these pilgrims built their homes "was an extremely wild and marshy spot overgrown with bushes and briers, at the declivity of the

[9] "The Count granted them a conditional refuge, but did not himself remove to his new home until after the first Moravians had settled there.   There was no intention on his part to espouse their course." J. T. Hamilton: *American Church History*, vol. VIII, p. 435.

[10] J. Holmes: *History of the Protestant Church of the United Brethren,* p. 177.

[11] Hamilton: *American Church History*, vol. VIII, p. 435.

hill, called the Hutberg, and the high road between Löbau and
Zittau was at times almost impassible for carts or wagons.
Augustin Neisser's wife therefore, when first viewing it, could
not help asking the question, 'Where shall we find bread in this
wilderness?' " [12]   These new tenants were poor, although some
of them had forsaken large estates in Moravia, and their livelihood had to be made from the soil.   Increased population and
their efforts in tilling the soil would mean increased wealth for
the Count.

Five years after their settlement, there was dissension between these Brethren and the Lutherans concerning doctrine
and the preservation of the church order and discipline of the
Ancient Brethren.   Many were ready to quit Herrnhut in
search of another place where they might model their conduct
after the church of their ancestors.   Christian David, who had
brought the first exiles to this estate, was among the seceders
and moved some distance out of Herrnhut, where he built a
small cottage for himself.   He writes: "Of what use is it to us
to have ventured our lives if the souls are now to be entangled
in the trammels of common Lutheranism, and thus are led into
miserable delusion, while they are made to believe that they
have found the sure ground, and are extolled even to the skies
on that account; though, as yet, they are unacquainted with
the real conversion of the heart, and being kept from this essential point, they become twofold more the children of hell,
than they were before." [13]

When Zinzendorf, who was in Dresden at the time, heard
of the dissension and of the threats of some to leave, he obtained leave of absence from the Saxon Court to investigate
the trouble.   Harmony was restored by a number of resolutions drawn up by the Count, Mr. Rothe, the Lutheran minister, and some others.

In the following year, 1728, when Zinzendorf was on a visit
at the University of Jena, the Lutheran minister, Mr. Rothe,
"endeavored to persuade the Brethren at Herrnhut to drop
the name of Bohemian and Moravian Brethren, and to call

[12] *The Memorial Days of the Renewed Church of the Brethren,* p. 28.
[13] *Ibid.,* p. 82.

themselves Lutherans. By doing this, it was urged, they would avoid many difficulties, and escape from the machinations of their persecutors; they would moreover gain universal love, and be enabled to do much good." [14] When the Count heard this he became alarmed at these renewed discussions of the question. "He foresaw that the consequence of the proposed alterations, which evidently sprang from the fear of man, and a desire to please man, could be none other than the total separation of a great part of the Moravian Brethren from the Lutheran Church. On that account both he and those of the Moravian Brethren who were with him, protested in their own, as well as in the name of the absent elders, against all such innovations. And he hastened to return to Herrnhut, where he again succeeded in his earnest endeavors to settle and obviate these new dissensions and errors." [15] The Count feared their withdrawal, and in a discourse with them, he pacified them as he had done the year before. The result of the discourse was that it was unanimously resolved to retain the name "Brethren" and their former constitution.

For religious and economic reasons, the two strains of which the Herrnhuters were composed were most useful for the realization of Zinzendorf's aims. The Slavonic strain was largely represented by peasants whose past training fitted them for the manual labor required to fructify this "unclaimed wilderness." From among the Germans there were men with liberal educations, of whom Spangenberg and Peter Böhler were notable examples. The former served the Church in Europe and America for nearly forty years, and the latter, next to Spangenberg, was the most influential man in the early history of the American Moravian Church.

Although Zinzendorf at first may not have espoused their aim to renew the Ancient Church, with the passing of the years, their number having increased to about six hundred by 1730, he was compelled to further their ends. Because of the persistence on the part of these exiles to be separate from the Lutheran Church, which plea was again renewed in 1731, Zinzendorf was forced to promote Moravianism. And because

[14] *Ibid.*, p. 193.   [15] *Ibid.*

he tried persistently to instill his own ideas into the Brethren, he caused many of the serious divisions and disturbances which were a hindrance to the progress and widening of the activities of Moravianism both in Europe and America.

With the year 1727, complications between the Count and the Saxon government began to be increasingly serious and the relationship more strained.[16] In 1727 he had been allowed a leave of absence from Court to deal with the trouble among his tenants, to which we have already referred. He left his duties at Court permanently in 1727, but his official break with the Saxon government did not occur until later. The leave of absence made his withdrawal appear temporary, but he could have had no intention of resuming his official work. Whenever he was on his estate he lived in Bethelsdorf, but now he had a house built for himself in Herrnhut, and two months after his leave of absence was granted, he moved into it.

While his attention to the controversies on his estate was one reason for his absence from Court, another was his strained relationship with the Saxon government. Saxony was reduced to the verge of ruin by her minister Bruhl, who had already burdened her with a debt of a hundred million dollars, and for two years had withheld the public salaries, and had sold Saxon troops to the Dutch and English for the defense of their colonies. "The deep dungeons of the Köningstein, the Sonnenstein, and the Pleissenburg were crowded with malcontents. These horrors occasioned the retreat of Count Zinzendorf from the world, and in 1722, his offer of an asylum in Herrnhut to persons equally piously disposed. He termed himself the 'assembler of souls.' He was banished as a rebel by Bruhl, but was in 1747, permitted to return and to continue his pious labors." [17]

To say that Zinzendorf had as his only avowed purpose to give himself and all his time to the cause of religion, and that

[16] Not only had the conduct of these Moravians and Zinzendorf aroused public suspicion, but he had given shelter to the Schwenkfelders from Silesia, who disagreed with the Lutherans respecting the Lord's Supper.

[17] Wolfgang Menzel: *History of Germany*, translated from the 4th German edition by Mrs. George Horrocks, Bohn's *Standard Library*, vol. III, p. 1278.

therefore he resigned his office, is claiming more for him than he would honestly have dared to claim for himself. The immediate circumstance which prompted him to leave the Court in 1727 was the increasing opposition to him there, which would have forced him to leave shortly thereafter. The same spirit of stubbornness, pride, and sentimentalism, which were already in evidence in his boyhood days, he carried over into manhood.

Zinzendorf anticipated this trouble with the government, for previous to his resignation he sold his estate by a regular contract to his wife. One reason for this act must have been to safeguard his property in case his enemies at Court should press him. This transfer of his property to his wife relieved him from the duties of magistrate,[18] and his enemies could not compel him to take action against his tenants, who by this time had come to the attention of civil authorities. Zinzendorf was now free to be merely the patron of the Herrnhuters. In November of 1732, the expected happened when the Saxon Court ordered him to alienate his property, but fortunately the Count had made ample provisions for such an emergency.

However, he was not yet ready to confine his energies to the interests of the Moravians but regarded himself as a free volunteer in the service of Christ—*"ein freier Knecht des Herrn."* In 1731 Zinzendorf was present at the coronation of Christian VI of Denmark, hoping that the King would grant him the office of court preacher or some other position. He made a lengthy visit at the court and was kindly received. Instead of being favored with an office, the King merely decorated him with the Order of the Danebrog in token of his zealousness in the service of God.

Meanwhile his enemies among the theologians and royal families at the courts were increasing.[19] But with the failure

[18] "In this and many other parts of Germany a nobleman as Lord of the manor, exercises a judicial authority over his tenantry, who are in a state of vassalage. He as a magistrate, can publish injunctions and prohibitions, and has his own courts for the trial of civil, and sometimes even of criminal causes." Holmes: *History,* p. 223.

[19] In 1744 Christian VI issued a Danish royal edict against the Brethren and their heresies, warning against their subtle ways of taking young

'of his trip to Denmark and the growing hostility at home, his only avenue of escape from his enemies was to revive his interest in the "Order of the Grain of Mustard Seed."

Another governmental commission investigated conditions at Herrnhut in 1736. The Count was suspected of harboring fanatics and promoting a Separatist Movement with views and practices contrary to the Lutheran Church.[20] The result of this investigation was the banishment of the Count for ten years.

Count Zinzendorf's exile from Saxony was followed by many important consequences to himself and to the Brethren's Church, as this compulsory absence became the occasion of extending the boundaries of the Church and increasing the number of its congregations in different countries. On hearing of his banishment, Count Ysenburg-Wächtersbach gave Zinzendorf an invitation to occupy Ronneburg in Wetterau. The lords of this estate were deeply in debt and for this reason welcomed settlers. Ronneburg was a half-ruined castle of the Middle Ages. The place was forbidding, but Zinzendorf accepted the offer and commenced preaching to the people of mixed nationalities who were near the castle; he formed schools and gave food and clothing to the poor.

At Ronneburg the "Congregation of Pilgrims" was instituted. It was called a Pilgrim Congregation because from this group individuals went out from place to place to preach the gospel. This body stood at the head of the Brethren's affairs during the Count's exile. In this group, Zinzendorf and the Elders

persons out of the land to Herrnhut and Marienborn under pretenses of educating them, but in reality to indoctrinate them with their tenets, which in time could mean nothing but schisms and unrest in the churches. Fresenius: *Bewährte Nachrichten von Herrnhutischen Sachen*, vol. II, pp. 635-637. Among his other enemies are to be reckoned Anthon and the younger Francke at Halle, Court Preacher Marferger at Dresden, Chaplain Winkler at Abersdorf, Magister Urlsberger at Augsberg, Court Preacher Ziegenthagen in London, Count von Bruhl at Dresden, Baron Huldenberg of Neukirch, Count Christian Ernest of Stallberg-Wernigerode, and his aunt Henrietta of the nobility. J. T. Hamilton: *History of the Moravian Church*, p. 71.

[20] Zinzendorf claimed to have been examined for his orthodoxy by the Theological Faculty at Copenhagen in 1735. This is denied by Fresenius. See *Bewährte Nachrichten von Herrnhutischen Sachen*, vol. II, p. 153 f.

were the administrative and executive board for the Brethren everywhere. Since Zinzendorf could not remain in Herrnhut to direct affairs, the "Pilgrim Congregation" scheme made it possible for the governing board to accompany him in his exile. By this method he still controlled affairs in Herrnhut, through the ruling board with him, who did his bidding.

Ten years after the arrival of the first settlers at Herrnhut, there was a decided movement to spread their wings and settle in foreign lands. It is generally understood that this eagerness to colonize was due to their missionary zeal. When one considers the large percentage of missionaries sent out in comparison with other denominations, it would seem that the missionary endeavor must have been the chief aim behind the colonization movement. The Brethren started their mission work at a time when the churches of Europe had no interest in foreign missions. However, the question that forces itself upon the critical historian is: Was the missionary effort an end in itself or a means to an end? Was the establishment of settlements the end, or missions? It is not necessary for the inquirer to decide in favor of one or the other. It is not an "either-or" problem. Both were present in their thoughts, but the question remains: Were these settlements the result of their missionary zeal, or were their missionary accomplishments a product of their need to form free settlements? Facts seem to point to the latter.[21]

In view of the fact that external and political pressure was brought to bear upon the dwellers at Herrnhut, settlements in foreign parts were rapidly becoming a necessity. "Most of these settlements were formed in the middle of the eighteenth century and may be viewed as the fruit of the exceedingly numerous and bitter tears which persecution wrung from the eyes of the venerable Brethren, in their native country of

[21] What C. A. Pescheck writes about the Moravians at Herrnhut throws light upon our question. In speaking about the decisions of the Saxon government, after the commission had investigated matters at Herrnhut in 1733, he writes: "New-comers were, however, not to be received, it being contrary to the will of the Bohemian authorities; this led to the idea of establishing colonies in other parts." *The Reformation and the Anti-reformation in Bohemia*, vol. II, p. 379.

Bohemia and Moravia. . . . But the formation of these congregations was not only the result of the persecution of the Brethren, it also led to their successful missions among the heathen." [22]   Persecution, in other words, led to the need for settlements in foreign parts, and this need in turn gave impetus to the theory of missionary work, which then grew to such proportions that it is easy to confuse it with the purpose behind the settlements.

The situation is summed up by a Moravian historian who writes: "It seemed not unlikely, that just as the Saxon government withdrew its protection from the Schwenkfelders in 1733, so also the Moravian and Bohemian emigrants might be ordered to leave the land. . . . To be prepared for just such an emergency, Moravian colonies were settled in various parts of the world, according to the leading of providence." [23]   The government, to be sure, after its investigation in 1732, promised them protection, "as long as they should demean themselves quietly and peaceably," but such terms were obviously not satisfactory, since their enemies might readily accuse them of disturbing the peace of the church. The inhabitants of Herrnhut now divided themselves into two groups. The one was composed of those who were natives of Germany and educated in the national church. These resolved to stay. The other was composed of the Moravian emigrants. These prepared themselves to emigrate if necessary and form colonies in other countries.

This deep-seated feeling of political and economic insecurity kindled their imaginations and they applied to themselves the words: "When they persecute you in this city, flee into the next, for verily I say unto you, ye shall not have gone through the cities of Israel, till the Son of Man be come." Were they not persecuted? Then, might it not also be their task to "go through the cities of Israel"?

The direct result of this was that even before settlements in foreign parts were begun, individual missionaries went out to

[22] *The Reformation and the Anti-reformation in Bohemia*, vol. II, p. 382.

[23] L. T. Reichel: *Early History of the Church of the United Brethren*, p. 63.

go "through the towns of Israel" in foreign lands. In the very years of the restrictive measures by the Saxon Court, this work in foreign lands began: in the West Indies in 1732, Greenland in 1733, North America in 1734, Surinam in 1735, and South Africa in 1736. Thus even before settlements in other lands were established, missionaries had gone out by twos and threes, and as they went forth into new worlds, this song, which had accompanied them in their exile from Bohemia and Moravia, was upon their lips:

> Blessed be the day when I must roam,
> Far from my country, friends, and home,
> An exile poor and mean;
> My Father's God will be my guide,—
> Will angel guards for me provide,—
> My soul from dangers screen.
> Himself will lead me to a spot,
> Where all my cares and griefs forgot,
> I shall enjoy sweet rest.
> As pants the hart for water-brooks,—
> My thirsting soul, with longing looks
> To God, my refuge blest.[24]

In short, they went forth into distant parts for the same reason that the Pilgrim Fathers came to America. They were practically forced to. We need not belittle their missionary urge, for it was there from the beginning, and their zeal increased as time went on. The missionary fame of the Moravians has been increased by the fact that their settlements were made in such regions as were inhabited by people still almost or entirely uncivilized, with whom they worked effectively. Wherever possible the Church bought land for these missionaries to form settlements. These colonies were societies or communities of missionaries.

When we turn to the life of Zinzendorf, we find that the original impulse to begin missions in an age when such work was unpopular was the same as that which we have found in

[24] *An Epitome of the History of the Church of the United Brethren in the way of questions and answer for the information of young persons*, p. 31.

the lives of the Herrnhuters as a whole. It is true that in his youth he showed an interest in missions, for it was in his early years at Halle that he founded the "Order of the Grain of Mustard Seed." But not until he was thirty-three, when he resigned his duties in the Saxon Court, was he ready to devote himself to it. We could concede to Zinzendorf the benefit of the doubt and allow the traditional view that all that was needed was the external occasion to bring out the missionary purpose he had cherished since his youth. However, it seems certain that his political ostracism was the direct cause which forced him to accept the missionary challenge when he did. The fact that three years after he had left the Saxon Court he sought a position as Court preacher in the Danish Court indicates that as late as eight years after the arrival of the exiles he had not yet decided to unite with them.

Finally, the decree of banishment against Zinzendorf left little else for him to do but to undertake this work of spreading the gospel in foreign parts. Being at Cassel when he received the royal mandate of banishment, he remarked after reading it: "At all events it will require ten years before I can permanently fix my residence in Herrnhut, for now we must collect a congregation of Pilgrims, and train laborers to go forth into all the world, to preach Christ and his salvation." [25]

After the Count had left the Court and had taken up his residence at Herrnhut, the Brethren rapidly developed an exclusive social and economic structure. In Herrnhut as in the other settlements formed later, the form of government was a theocracy. The secular and religious affairs were regulated by a meeting of the inhabitants and a church council. A community court of justice had general oversight and arbitrated civil disputes, and Elders whose numbers varied from time to time, had oversight in spiritual matters.

When the Brethren formed other centers the name "settlement" was applied only to such exclusively Moravian colonies. Such settlements were founded at Herrnhut, Herrnhaag, and Marienborn on the continent; Fairfield, Fulneck, and Okrook

[25] Reichel: *Historic Sketch of the Church and Missions of the United Brethren,* p. 61.

in England. Gracehill in Ireland, and Bethlehem, Nazareth, Lititz, and Salem in America. They had family houses, chapels, Single Brethren houses, Single Sisters houses, similar ones for the widows and widowers, and schools for the boys and girls according to the different "Choir" divisions.

With the exception of the twenty years of the General Economy at Bethlehem, all the members followed their own occupations. And at no time in any of the settlements was there a real community of goods. With the increase of lands and settlements a General Diacony was created, which held all the lands, buildings, and industries under its control and direction.

CHAPTER II

THE CHURCH OF GOD IN THE SPIRIT

COUNT ZINZENDORF, accompanied by his daughter Benigna, arrived in America in December 1741 and remained here for over a year. The Moravians were then only a small group who had just built a log house at Bethlehem. The house was dedicated on Christmas Eve, with Zinzendorf present. A prolific sectarianism flourished at the time in Pennsylvania. Speaking of the deplorable religious conditions the Count said: "All shades of sectarians exist here down to open infidelity. Besides the English, Swedish and German Lutherans, and the Scotch, Dutch and German Reformed, there were Arminians, Baptists, 'Vereinigte Vlaaminger en Waterlander,' Mennonites from Danzig, Arians, Socinians, Schwenckfelders, German Old Tunkers, New Tunkers, New Lights, Inspired, Sabbatarians or Seventh-day Baptists, Hermits, Independents, and Free Thinkers." [1] "Thousands who had been nominal members of the church in the fatherland were now without worship, and had little or no desire for it. . . . There were hermits along the Wissahickon, and Protestant monks and nuns at Ephrata. The Organized German Lutheran parishes were only three or four in number, and even these were without pastors much of the time. Though the Swedes along the Delaware were somewhat better off, the supply of ministers was inadequate in their case also. Nor was the condition of the Reformed Church much superior. In neither case was there the co-operative action of a synod or any systematic provision for general oversight. . . . It had become a proverbial expression, that a man who was utterly indifferent to revealed religion belonged to 'The Pennsylvania Church.' " [2]

[1] Sachse: *The German Sectarians in Penn., 1708-1742,* p. 442.
[2] Hamilton: *History,* p. 103.

NICHOLAUS LUDWIG VON ZINZENDORF

It was into such a state of religious confusion that Count Zinzendorf came upon his visit to America. The original purpose of his coming to America was threefold. The first was colonization. As the patron of the Moravians, he was concerned about taking up land for the faithful in the New World. The second was the missionary purpose. This included the Christianizing of his fellow countrymen as well as the Indians. Although he spent much time in Philadelphia, Bethlehem, and Germantown, he made several extensive trips among the Indians and was the first white man to go into the Wyoming Valley.[3]   Another reason for his visit to America was to organize the Germans of all sects into some form of evangelical religion, which he called the Church of God in the Spirit. He came, thinking that all these sects were eager to be emancipated from their present religious confusion. Instead he found the sects firm in their prejudices and not at all anxious to compromise.

This third purpose was put into effect immediately upon his arrival in America. The idea sprouted in the mind of Henry Antes, who was first to welcome the Count. He was a member of the Skippack Brethren (*Vereinigte Skippack Brüder*). There were about twenty-five in this association, among whom were Henry Antes, John Bechtel, John Gruber, and Christopher Wiegner.[4]   These Skippack Brethren were largely Separatists, having broken their relations with the orthodox churches, who met at the home of Christopher Wiegner for worship. A closer harmony among all the sects in Pennsylvania was an ever-recurring topic at these meetings. The

[3] For a full account of Zinzendorf's travels among the American Indians, see Loskiel's *History of the Mission Among the Indians,* vol. II.

[4] Henry Antes was a mechanic belonging to the German Reformed Church. Although he was not a licensed minister, he frequently preached. John Bechtel, although not ordained, had a license from the University of Heidelberg and preached in Germantown where many German Reformed had settled. He was dismissed from his church because of intimacy with Antes and Zinzendorf. John Gruber was a Separatist belonging to the Inspired. Christopher Wiegner was a Schwenkfelder and one of three leaders who accompanied the first colony of Schwenkfelders to America, when they were commissioned by the Saxon government to leave Zinzendorf's estate where they had taken refuge.

success with which the Skippack Brethren formed a union, although being of different creeds, encouraged Zinzendorf's idea of bringing together all the German sects in Pennsylvania.

Another factor aided the Count. He had harbored on his estate in Germany a group of exiles who were followers of Casper Schwenkfeld.[5] Being accused of soliciting these exiles from other countries, the Count made provision for the Schwenkfelders to go to Georgia. When the Schwenkfelders set out for America, three leaders, George Böhnisch, a Moravian, Christopher Baus, a Hungarian who had joined the Brethren, and Christopher Wiegner of Silesia, of the same faith as the Schwenkfelders, accompanied them. The Moravian missionary August G. Spangenberg was to have accompanied them, but at the last moment these Schwenkfelders decided to sail for Pennsylvania instead of Georgia, thus completely upsetting the calculations of the Count. Instead, Spangenberg was commissioned to establish a Moravian colony on the land bought in Georgia. After he had established the colony there, he left Georgia on March 15, 1736, being commissioned to work among the Schwenkfelders in Pennsylvania.

"The object of the coming of Spangenberg, as of Wiegner, Baus and Böhnish, was in part at least to bring the Schwenkfelders over to the Moravian faith."[6] Difficulties soon arose between Spangenberg and the Schwenkfelders, perhaps due to hard feelings of a long standing, which may have induced the Schwenkfelders to go to Pennsylvania instead of to Georgia as the Count had planned. Spangenberg at this time was lodged by Christopher Wiegner, who in turn was living on a Schwenkfelder estate, seems to have become estranged from them. The Schwenkfelders, however, held aloof from Wiegner, especially since he tolerated the Skippack Brethren at his home, with

[5] Casper Schwenkfeld von Ossing was a Silesian nobleman in sympathy with the Reformation. He corresponded with Luther, but the latter broke relationships with him due to disagreements about the doctrine of Holy Communion. For a full account of the Schwenkfelders, see *Erläuterung für Casper Schwenkfeld und die Zugethanen seiner Lehre* and *Historical Sketch* by C. Heyduck. Both works in the library of the Historical Society of Pa.

[6] *Pennsylvania German Society,* vol. XIII, p. 105.

whose doctrines they did not agree. These Skippack Brethren "vexed the souls of earnest Schwenkfelders." [7] George Weiss [8] told Wiegner and Spangenberg "to let the Schwenkfelders alone, saying that they could and would not agree, and that it would be useless to try to make Moravians of them." [9]

The relations between Spangenberg and Wiegner on the one hand, and the Schwenkfelders on the other, rapidly took a critical turn. "Wiegner made the following entry in his diary January 19, 1738: 'Attended services at M. Kriebel's. George Weiss said the Bible was a closed book and was only for the saints (*Heilig-recommandirte*), hence his 1,500 hymns and other literature. This affected me so much that I made a loud exclamation and Br. Sp. [Spangenberg] did the same which stirred up considerable uproar. George Weiss wrote a letter to which we replied again.' This stormy meeting meant much. An extensive correspondence followed. It was more than a mere clashing between Weiss and Spangenberg. It was rather a clashing between two great systems of thought—Weiss defending Casper Schwenkfeld and Spangenberg representing Zinzendorf, a professed adherent of the Lutheran faith, although the great defender of the Moravians. The following April, Wiegner wrote: 'George Weiss rejects us,' and Spangenberg wrote: 'The Schwenkfelders form themselves wholly into a sect and completely close themselves against all others who do not approve of their cause, whereby consciences are bound and the spirit of Christ is quenched. I can reject no brother nor separate myself from him to win others and be a means of salvation to them. The Lord will show what the outcome will be. We do not say much, but have expressed ourselves both orally and in writing.' " [10]

During this time Spangenberg was in correspondence with Zinzendorf in Germany and kept him informed of his failure among the Schwenkfelders. This failure and the successful formation of the Associated Brethren at Skippack, whose meet-

[7] *Ibid.*, p. 57.
[8] George Weiss was the pastor of this colony of Schwenkfelders.
[9] *Pa. Ger. Soc.*, vol. XIII, p. 59.
[10] *Pa. Ger. Soc.*, vol. XIII, pp. 107, 108.

ings Spangenberg now attended, gave hope of some kind of church unity among the Germans in Pennsylvania. In the association at Skippack Zinzendorf saw in embryo a unity between men of various sects, and in it he saw possibilities of developing a similar unity between larger bodies from many creeds. These men at Wiegner's house stressed their resemblances and similarities in creed and doctrine and formed "a church in the Spirit." Could it not be enlarged to include all the sects of Pennsylvania? Thus arose Zinzendorf's grand idea of the Church of God in the Spirit.

What Zinzendorf meant by this Church of God in the Spirit was a league of members of every sect who could be bound together by spiritual ties instead of by an externally formulated association. In this league the denominational doctrines were not to be stressed, but rather the Spirit that gave rise to these convictions. It was not his idea to unite all the German sects into a single corporate body, but merely to agree in essentials and thus form one Congregation of God in the Spirit.

Zinzendorf's Church of God in the Spirit was not as novel an idea with him as the name might imply. It was a new name for the "Diaspora" which the Brethren conducted in Europe, forming societies in the various denominations after Spener's idea of "little churches within the church." "The word 'Diaspora' embraces all the awakened or believing souls dispersed among the great body of professing Christians." [11] Those who united with the Brethren by means of the "Diaspora" work, and those who came on their own accord, gave rise to the Trope plan. This was a novel plan by means of which those from other confessions could join the Brethren without surrendering their peculiar church traditions and beliefs. Thus there was a Lutheran, a Reformed, and a Moravian Trope. Each Trope could best train and educate souls in the peculiar church tendencies and traditions in which the members were reared. This was the underlying idea of the Trope plan, which Zinzendorf expounded as early as 1736 at a Synod in Marienborn, Germany.[12]

[11] *Church Miscellany*, Jan. 1850.
[12] See his *General Regeln vors Volk des Herrn*, in the conclusions of

The members of the Brethren must accept the orders and regulations peculiar to the different Tropes. "When a brother of the Lutheran or Reformed 'tropus' has his abode in a congregation which properly belongs to the Episcopal Brethren's Church, then he assents to the orders, regulations and ceremonies which are customary there. If a brother of the Episcopal (Moravian) church comes to a congregation where the Lutheran 'tropus' is used, he takes no umbrage at the orders, ceremonies and regulation, but looks upon himself in duty bound to observe them as long as he is in that congregation-place." [13]   Ordination in the Lutheran and Reformed Church was accepted by the Brethren without reordination.   If a minister was raised to the rank of bishop, it was done by the bishops of the Brethren.

The Diaspora in Europe was the Invisible Church, and the Brethren's Church was a visible instance of the Invisible Church Universal. Members of the "Societies" of the Diaspora and the Brethren were the enlightened and awakened. Now, the Church of God in the Spirit was the name applied to the Pennsylvania section of the Invisible Church. The members from every sect in Pennsylvania, gathering in what were called the "Pennsylvania Synods," were to be another instance of the Invisible Church in visible form.

The Trope innovation also served as a convenient policy by means of which Zinzendorf could remain consistent with himself as a Lutheran clergyman and at the same time be the champion of the Moravians. In 1737 he was made a bishop in the Moravian Church, but just before his coming to Pennsylvania he announced that he had laid aside for the present his office of bishop among the Moravians and wished to be known simply as a Lutheran clergyman. He also publicly renounced his title as Count and wished to be known as Dominie de Thürnstein. This he did to avoid any barriers in his work in Pennsylvania which such titles might raise, due

the Marienborn and Ebersdorf Synods of 1744. Ms. Beth. Arch. Also see his *Syllabus von des Herrn Bishops Evang. Luth. Tropi Behörde Büdingische Sammlung*, vol. III, pp. 903-908.

[13] *Publication of the North Carolina Historical Commission*, vol. III, p. 996.

to suspicion and prejudices.[14]   In the fourth Pennsylvania Synod, he even expressed his strong preference for the Lutheran Church.[15]   No doubt a reason for such an expression on his part was to ingratiate himself with the Lutheran element in Pennsylvania.   He also consistently claimed to be a Lutheran in Europe for the added prestige it would give him, as a Count, to belong to the State Church.   In fact it was a stroke of diplomacy on his part to claim allegiance to Lutheranism in the early years of the Renewed Church, when the Brethren were being suspected and persecuted.   Under the Trope plan he could be a Lutheran as well as patron of the Moravians.   He belonged to the Lutheran Trope in the Brethren's Church. While in America, he even became a regular pastor of the Lutheran Church in Philadelphia.[16]   Zinzendorf himself said: "My Lutheran fellow-religionists persuaded me to preach to them; this I did willingly, since I am indebted to them first of all." [17]

In view of Zinzendorf's attempt to gather those of the Invisible Church in the many sects into a harmonious unit, we must inquire what his conception of the church was.   He was in sympathy with the doctrines and theories of Lutheranism, but he considered Moravianism far superior in the sense that its practice was consistent with its doctrine.   For Zinzendorf all of Protestantism could unite in the Lutheran Church, so long as the "cross-theology" of the atonement in Christ remained the central doctrine.   He thought of the Moravians as the group who most eagerly held to this Christo-centric the-

[14] He surrendered his title in a Latin oration before Governor Thomas and others. *Büdingische Sammlungen*, vol. III, pp. 330 f.   Also see *Pa. Magazine of History and Biography*, vol. VI, p. 150.   De Thürnstein was one of his lesser titles.   His full title was Nicholas Lewis, Count and Lord of Zinzendorf and Pottendorf; Lord of the Baronies of Freydeck, Schöneck, Thürnstein and the vale of Wachovia; Lord of the Manor of Upper, Middle and Lower Berthelsdorf; Hereditary Warden of the Chase to his Imperial Roman Majesty in the Duchy of Austria, below the Ems; late Aulic and Justicial Counsellor to his Majesty, Augustus II, King of Poland, for the Electorate of Saxony.   Levering: *History of Bethlehem,* p. 92.

[15] *Pennsylvanische Nachrichten*, p. 144.

[16] *Büdingische Sammlungen*, vol. III, p. 580.

[17] *Pennsylvanische Nachrichten*, pp. 12-13.

ology, and if this doctrine was no longer held in the Lutheran Church, then the Brethren were the only true Lutherans.

The Augsburg Confession, to which the Brethren professed their allegiance, was for Zinzendorf not a systematic statement of their belief. It was a general apologetic statement which set up a wall of division between them and all teachers of false doctrines. It did not particularize but rather set forth the general plan and central ideas of Protestantism. All other confessions, particular confessions confined to certain areas, explanatory of certain truths, were stated in a general way in the Augsburg Confession. Thus, the Augsburg Confession had a universal character in that it characterized Protestantism and might well be accepted by all denominations.

Such a broad view of the Church and its creeds was necessary if the Count wanted to remain consistent with his Trope idea, the Diaspora work in Europe, and the attempt to form a Church of God in the Spirit in Pennsylvania. As William Penn opened the province of Pennsylvania to all who would come, regardless of their beliefs, so Zinzendorf, with his broad conception of the church, could invite representatives of the sects that had collected there to form a Church of God in the Spirit. "He believed that the evangelical churches were essentially one, and that in each of the Christian Churches, even the ultra-montane Roman Catholic and the Gallican, there reposed a peculiar gift for training souls according to its own special method." [18]   The Count believed that "in each religion lies a thought of God which cannot be received through any other religion. . . . Not any religion has the whole; she must take the best out of the other religions to assist her if she wants the whole." [19]   The new unity in Pennsylvania was to be brought about by the One Spirit operating through a diversity of methods in all churches.

This broad view of creeds and the church was shared by the Brethren generally. "We do not believe in exalting minor questions into vital differences. Calvin, Arminius, Luther, Zwingli, and Wesley, might as far as doctrine is concerned,

[18] Hamilton: *History*, p. 121.
[19] Unttendörfer and Schmidt: *Die Brüder*, p. 146.

have all been members of the Moravian Church, if they would have had charity enough to enter into fraternal relations with Christians of diverse views." [20]

The settlement at Herrnhut did not at first interest Zinzendorf as a Bohemian-Moravian Church, but as an ethical and religious pietistic society within the Lutheran Church. Circumstances compelled the Count, however, to cast his lot with the Herrnhuters. The result was that under the leadership of the Count, the Brethren became more organized and gradually took on ecclesiastical distinctiveness, instead of being a small church within the church.

The establishment of missions in foreign parts made Zinzendorf's plan of retaining the Brethren as a pious group within the Lutheran Church impossible. It was only natural for these Moravian missionaries to establish their church order and discipline according to the traditions with which they were acquainted. In 1735, David Nitschmann was consecrated as the bishop of the mission fields. The Brethren now had a bishop over a work which was distinctively Moravian.

Zinzendorf later said: "We were, indeed, made into a church because all the theologians have equally pushed us aside with roasting forks and wanted nothing to do with us. We worked thirteen, fourteen years to remain under the wings of the Lutheran Church, but they did not care to have us." [21]

The relation of the Moravians as an established church to the intended Church of God in the Spirit in Pennsylvania was that they were already an instance of the Invisible Church of which the Church of God in the Spirit was to be another. Nowhere did Zinzendorf say this, being very careful to avoid suspicion. However, previous to his coming to America, he stated his view on the relation which the Brethren have to the "Church of Jesus" at the Synods of Ebersdorf in 1739 and Gotha in 1740. There he set forth that the "Church of Jesus" is a communion of enlightened, living Christians in various churches. The Moravian Church had a peculiar relation to this "Church of Jesus," in that she represented in visible form this Invisible Church of the awakened.

[20] W. H. Romig: *The Moravian Church*, p. 9.
[21] Unttendörfer and Schmidt: *Die Brüder*, p. 147.

With such a view of the peculiar and favored relationship of the Moravians to the visible and invisible Church, Zinzendorf began his American work on the Church of God in the Spirit. The magnitude of the task is seen in a circular letter which Henry Antes sent to all denominations and sects to inaugurate the proposed enterprise.

In the name of Jesus: Amen.

BELOVED FRIEND AND BROTHER:
Inasmuch as frightful evil is wrought in the Church of Christ, among the souls that have been called to the Lamb to follow Christ, mainly through mistrust and suspicion towards each other and that often without reason—whereby every purpose of good is continually thwarted—although we have been commanded to love; it has been under consideration for two years or more, whether it would not be possible to appoint a general assembly, not to wrangle about opinions, but to treat with each other in love on the most important articles of faith, in order to ascertain how closely we can approach each other fundamentally, and, as for the rest bear with one another in love on opinions which do not subvert the ground of salvation; and whether in this way, all judging and criticising might not be diminished and done away with among the aforesaid souls, by which they expose themselves before the world and give occasion to say: those who preach peace and conversion are themselves at variance. Therefore this matter so important has now been under advisement again with many brethren and God-seeking souls, and been weighed before the Lord; and it has been decided to meet on the coming New Year's day at Germantown. Hence you are cordially invited to attend, together with several more of your brethren who have a foundation for their faith and can state it, if the Lord permits. It has been announced to nearly all of the others (persuasions) through letters like this. There will probably be a large gathering, but do not let this deter you; for all will be arranged without great commotion. May the Lord Jesus grant us His blessing.

From your poor and unworthy, but cordial friend and brother,
HENRY ANTES.[22]

Frederick Township
in Philadelphia Co.
Dec. 15 (26. N. S.) 1741.

[22] Found in *Pennsylvanische Nachrichten*, pp. 92, 93. Also *Büdingische Sammlungen*, vol. II, p. 722. The translation in the text by J. M. Levering: *History of Bethlehem, Pa.*, pp. 97, 98.

The object of the first Synod, which met in Germantown, Jan. 1, 1742, was stated by Henry Antes in a resolution: "Whether under the Saviour's blessing, they [23] could not do away with judging and pronouncing sentence, gossiping, injuring and defaming, or to make this so contemptuous in Pennsylvania that every honest person will be ashamed of it, since through it we make ourselves a laughing stock before the world, while at the same time an irrecoverable damage arises to the conversion of souls to their Shepherd." [24]

The sects and denominations represented were the Lutherans, Reformed, Moravians, Quakers, Mennonites, Dunkers, Ephrata monks,[25] Schwenkfelders, Separatists,[26] and the Inspired. "Of all this assemblage, the Ephrata delegation was accorded the place of honor, and it appears that Count Zinzendorf took special pains to ingratiate himself with Prior Onesimus." [27] Why the Ephrata group were afforded the place of honor and why Zinzendorf tried to ingratiate himself with them is difficult to discern. A probable reason is that these Ephrata monks and nuns had much in common with the Brethren in the external organization of the congregation.

[23] This personal pronoun has reference to the assembled representatives at the Synod.

[24] *Authentische Relation*, p. 4.

[25] They belonged to an order of Protestant monks and nuns living at Ephrata in Lancaster County. John Conrad Beissel, the founder, was baptized a Dunker, but soon left the Dunkers, believing that Saturday was the day to be observed as Sabbath. He and his followers were therefore called the German Seventh-day Baptists, or "Siebentäger," and also Sabbatarians. They became increasingly ascetic, living at first as hermits, and later in 1735 built convents for the sisters and in 1738 for the brethren. These convents now unoccupied are still to be seen at Ephrata. The inmates were given monastic names and wore a long white cowl over their clothes. Although Beissel also had married followers, those in the convents, at one time numbering about seventy-five, lived celibate lives. They had many eccentric ideas and ascetic practices. For a full account of them consult the very interesting book, *Chronicon Ephratense*.

[26] These were those who had separated from the church, cutting themselves loose from all ecclesiasticism. Some of these were honest and sincere but others were merely disgruntled and therefore opposed any form of church organization.

[27] Sachse: *German Sectarians, 1708-1742*, pp. 444, 445. Onesimus was his monastic name, his real name being Israel Eckerling.

Where the Moravians had Choirs,[28] the Ephrata settlement had monasteries. Prior Onesimus invited the next Synod to meet at Ephrata. But the reports of this first Synod aroused so much adverse criticism in the Ephrata monastery that Beissel, whose monastic name was Father Friedsam, opposed the gathering of the second Synod at Ephrata.

The matters that were under consideration at the first Synod are set forth in a series of questions and answers.[29] The first question dealt with the basis for such a fellowship as they were seeking. Scriptural proof was brought that the ties between the children of God should be like those between Christ and his Father.

The second question was: "How manifold is the communion of saints?" The unanimous answer was that "the Congregation of God in the Spirit, which is his body throughout the whole world . . . is incalculable, and the members thereof are to be found in places where one would not seek them. Hence all minds that have the same fundamental ideas . . . Paul considered as of one Spirit. . . . They are not obliged to be in one household of faith, since in this diversity is hidden the wisdom of God. And if the many sects are merely divisions of the whole, there is no evil in each having his own affiliations, . . . and no one has the liberty to withdraw from them if they are in need of him. . . . These small groups, divisions, which by reason of place and other considerations bind themselves together, in order that those who have oversight over the souls can give an account, are called by the Saviour the visible church, and by the Holy Ghost the Body. . . . If each such little church grounds herself on Jesus Christ . . . and builds her spiritual house, then diversity is something beautiful." [30]

A further question was: "Does every organization deserve honor and respect?" The unanimous answer was: "Since each properly organized communion was instituted or protected by God, or allowed by him, no Babel could be destroyed un-

[28] The Choirs are discussed in chapter IV.
[29] The minutes and conclusions of the seven Pennsylvania Synods that followed are found in *Authentische Relation*, Beth. Arch.
[30] *Authentische Relation*, pp. 8, 9.

less God himself did it. . . . Hence, God's children have no right to assail established communions, or secretly seek to destroy them. . . ."[31]   Zinzendorf was not interested in erasing denominational lines for the present.   That Pennsylvania was a complete Babel, God and Zinzendorf agreed, but since God allowed it, Zinzendorf and his co-laborers had no right to destroy it.   Zinzendorf's ideal was to make the Church of God in the Spirit so beautiful and lofty a structure that it would overshadow the existing Babel.

The Synod agreed further that all verbal and written quarrels were to come before this body in order to stop all gossip and slander.   And whoever could not await the convening of the Synod should direct his trouble to Henry Antes and John Wüsters.   A written testimonial brought by the representative from his communion was to be sufficient guarantee to make his membership in the Synod valid.

The most important accomplishment at this first Synod was the adoption of a lengthy Confession of faith, defining the main points of doctrine in which they could agree.

The preamble to the Confession contains the words of Scripture: "For God so loved the world, that he gave his only begotten Son, that whosoever believeth on him should not perish, but have eternal life.   For God sent not the Son into the world to judge the world; but that the world should be saved through him.   He that believeth on him is not judged; he that believeth not hath been judged already, because he hath not believed on the name of the only begotten Son of God."[32]

Then follows a statement of their Christology, of which the central ideas are that Jesus alone can save, that he had to die for the world not because he was forced to but of his own accord because of his pity for us.   The Father was willing to surrender his Son.   He is therefore the Saviour of the whole world.   He remains dead in sin whom Christ does not awaken. As soon as the sinner believes in Christ through the power of the Holy Spirit, he is accepted in grace, his sins are absolved, and he has the privilege to sin no more and become holy.

---

[31] *Authentische Relation,* p. 10.
[32] John 3: 16-18.

Christ takes him into his protection against the Devil and the world, and thus he grows daily in sanctification.

The second part deals with Christian practice. When a pardoned sinner translates his belief into practice, he will do everything in the name of Christ. He must abstain from carnal deeds and all such acts as do not issue out of his Christian faith.

The third part explains the method and spirit necessary for the interpretation of Scripture. "Further and finally, for facilitating thorough discussion and transactions at our future corporate gatherings, we have unanimously decided not to allow disputation any longer concerning such passages which sound neither prophetic, mystical nor allegorical, and not only in themselves set forth plainly and clearly for every one but, likewise, in the originals in all editions, and in all common and not obviously absurd translations indicate one and the same meaning. On the contrary, we have determined in such instances fittingly with the sword of the Spirit to set aside adversive teaching and agreed that even though one had not finished presenting his view in that case, he would still in a dignified Christian assembly have no honorable claim to speak further when he has a manifest and clear word of the Holy Scripture against him." [33]

It is at once evident to the student who is familiar with the writings of Zinzendorf that the Count's ideas are recorded in this Confession. The ideas in the various conclusions of the Synod, centering around such words and phrases as the "awakened," the process of "sanctification," and the "privilege of the believer to sin no more," are a reiteration of his views frequently expressed before. The Confession is a mild and orthodox statement to which all could agree, and none of the more radical theological ideas [34] of Zinzendorf are incorporated. The Count was the directing genius of this and the following Synods, and his dominating influence is unmistakable.

The second Synod met in the house of George Hübner in

[33] *Auth. Rel.*, translation by Dr. W. N. Schwarze.
[34] See chapter VI.

Falkner Swamp on Jan. 25-26. At this Synod there were no real Schwenkfelders present. George Hübner was not a strict Schwenkfelder, his father before him having disagreed with them.[35] Christopher Wiegner, who attended, was also not really a Schwenkfelder.[36] After the first Synod the Schwenkfelders were not represented, the reason being that Zinzendorf had offended them when he spoke to them on Epiphany, Jan. 6.[37] It is said that Zinzendorf scolded them on that day, especially their teacher George Weiss, and that he threatened to take their children away from them if they would not change their hearts or within three months have baptism and communion.[38]

Zinzendorf was elected to the office of Syndic. By lot it was determined what subjects were to be discussed. A point of importance arose in regard to the manner in which those German religious groups should be dealt with who were intentionally unrepresented. The conclusion was that with such they had to exercise Christ's patience. No doubt the absence of the Schwenkfelders, for whom the Count was concerned, provoked this discussion.

Toward evening of the first day, the subject of the law and the person of Christ was under consideration. A heated debate, in which a certain person used scathing and severe ex-

[35] Kriebel: *The Schwenkfelders in Pennsylvania*, p. 114.

[36] Wiegner belonged to the Skippack Brethren and was now intimately connected with the Moravians.

[37] "On Epiphany, January 6, Zinzendorf preached the second time at Wiegner's and was listened to by the Schwenkfelders. . . . Zinzendorf questioned them concerning their confession of faith, their organization, their hymns and other points. He said Schwenkfeld taught error, rejected word and outward things of services, that George Weiss led the people around by the nose and taught error, that it was easier to preach to Satan than to them, that he had power over them and was bound to save their souls, that he would not rest until he had destroyed them and torn their children from them, that he would use all his powers to tear souls from them and to save the children from hell." Kriebel: *The Schwenkfelders in Pennsylvania*, pp. 112, 113.

[38] Fresenius: *Bewährte Nachrichten von Herrnhutischen Sachen*, vol. III, p. 178. A letter from Zinzendorf to the Schwenkfelders, having reference to the Epiphany address, and warning them of their heresies, unconverted teachers, and disregard for the sacraments, is to be found in *Büdingische Sammlung*, vol. III, pp. 309-312.

pressions, abruptly terminated the meetings for the day. The following day in the first meeting the materials and the method of presenting them were more carefully considered "under the guidance of the Saviour." [39]

A few of the many questions raised were:

Question 1: Who shall be allowed to come to these conferences in the future?

Answer: (a) The representatives from all beliefs. (b) The teachers of the same, as many as desire to come. (c) Until further instruction, Antes, Stieffel,[40] Wiegner, Conrad Matthai,[41] and John Bartly, as often as they can. (d) The representatives of the first conference and those of the congregations who signed the first Relation are allowed always to be present. (e) Each Communion can allow a few to be present from its district, whom they know well, but they must be people with whom the others will not be offended. (f) We cannot accept those who in view of the above come unauthorized.[42]

Question 4: What is really the purpose of these gatherings?

Answer: The real purpose of the conference of all evangelical religious groups is that a poor inquiring soul, who eagerly wants to know the way of life, be not shown twelve but one way, may he ask whom he will; and if he loves the one who advises him so much that he

[39] *Auth. Rel. Second Synod.*

[40] Stieffel and two others joined Beissel, the founder of the Ephrata ascetics, when the latter built a small hut in the forests of Lancaster County. However, the deprivations of such a life were too severe for Stieffel and he left. When Zinzendorf came to America he had joined the Skippack Brethren. *Chronicon Ephratense,* pp. 13-15.

[41] Matthai was a follower of John Kelpius, who had come from Germany and settled in Germantown. For Kelpius, the thriving community of Germantown hindered his highest spiritual aspirations. He drew around him some kindred spirits and settled in the lower Wissahickon woods, where they built a hermitage. They called themselves the Society of the Woman of the Wilderness and lived in anticipation of the Millennium, which they believed was near at hand, and for the woman clothed with the sun, with the moon under her feet, and the twelve stars on her forehead. After the death of Kelpius, his followers gave up their hermit life, except Matthai, who when he died was buried by a friend beside Kelpius. At the time of these Pennsylvania Synods, the society had broken up and Matthai was living alone. *Chronicon Ephratense,* p. 11. Also see *The Wissahickon,* compiled by P. A. Dale.

[42] *Auth. Rel.,* p. 25.

wants to walk in the same way of life as he, he has the privilege to do so, if as yet he is not connected with any society.[43]

Question 7: What is one to do when Satan wants to help preach, because he cannot oppose?

Answer: When the Dragon begins to speak like a Lamb, then one can introduce a method of speech which he cannot repeat at all, or not correctly, or at least not immediately. It may sound paradoxical, but must not be sarcastic, ambiguous, or careless; and it must be cautiously employed, so that it does not harm, or at least, that the benefit may be greater than the harm.[44]

Question 14: What are the limits of our relationships, and what are our rights one to another?

Answer: We are allowed to admonish each other, to advise sincerely without being suspected; and we must not admonish in answer to admonition, but rather give a reason according to the nature of the case, or confess, or ponder the matter.[45]

Question 16: Will not troubles arise through personal errors?

Answer: Whoever undertakes something in the meeting in good faith, which we consider unprofitable, forward, or out of order, he shall have the privilege to make a public apology immediately, and it shall be as if it had not happened. And whoever takes his grievance home with him and trouble results, he has deceived the whole Conference.[46]

This rule was occasioned by the gossip arising from the first Synod. When the delegates returned home and told of the results of the Conference, favorable and unfavorable opinions were expressed, mostly the latter. As time went on the volume of adverse criticism increased. Christopher Saur, the editor of a German newspaper in Germantown, who was bitterly opposed to Zinzendorf, wrote in his paper: "The Schwenkfelders knew him [Zinzendorf] and had lived with him. Of these none came. Two who lived in Germantown were prevailed upon to attend, but when they saw that they were only wanted in order that it might be heralded abroad that they too had attended, they went home." [47] Similarly, criticism of the first Synod by Beissel fanned the hostility between the Moravians

[43] *Auth. Rel.,* p. 26.
[44] *Ibid.,* p. 27.
[45] *Ibid.,* p. 29.
[46] *Ibid.,* p. 30.
[47] *Pa. Ger. Soc.,* vol. XIII, p. 112.

and the Ephrata people on the questions of marriage and false doctrine.   The former accused the latter of heresy, and the latter blamed the former for emphasizing marriage, making it a carnal necessity.   This issue prompted the following question at the second Synod.

Question 22: Is it true that the Moravian Brethren make too much of marriage, and the Ephrata people too little?

Answer: It has appeared as if the congregation at Ephrata and the Brethren at Bethlehem in the Forks [48] in the matter of matrimony opposed each other.   But when the Brethren publicly explained their position, the former said they had nothing against it. We have, therefore, on the one side acknowledged that the suspicion of carnal necessity, for the sake of which matrimony is extolled, is groundless, until the contrary is seen and found.   And on the other side we declare the congregation at Ephrata in the future to be free from the suspicion of spreading the teaching of the devil.   No one belonging to us is to blame them; and whoever hears such accusations in the future, shall name the person who told him, and not accuse the Congregation. [49]

The personal pronouns "we" and "us" in the above declaration are significant.   The context shows that they probably have reference to the Moravians only, since the controversy was between them and the Ephrata group and did not involve the whole Synod.   This use of the personal pronouns indicates that the Moravians spoke for the whole Synod and were the dominating influence.   The unity sought after was already on crumbling ground, for the Schwenkfelders were absent and the Ephrata group were threatening to corrupt the conferences.

The third Synod met at Oley in the home of John de Türk, a Mennonite, Feb. 21-23.   At this Synod David Nitschmann, a Moravian bishop, assisted by Zinzendorf, ordained Andrew Eschenbach, Christian Henry Rauch, Gottlob Büttner, and J. Christopher Pyrlaeus. [50]

[48] Bethlehem was built between the Forks of the Delaware, which has reference to the land at the confluence of the Delaware and the Lehigh Rivers.

[49] *Auth. Rel.,* p. 32.

[50] Eschenbach was the leader of the Oley Congregation; Rauch was a Moravian missionary among the Indians; Büttner became missionary to

The Ephrata Mystics aroused considerable excitement when they presented a paper on the subject of matrimony. "Here the Zionistic Brotherhood were represented and gave their testimony against the Beast, the Whore and False Prophets, after which a considerable discussion was indulged in regarding the matrimonial state, infant baptism and the Eucharist. The arguments eventually ran so high that the Sabbatarians withdrew before the close of the meeting." [51] "They drew up a paper concerning marriage which they submitted . . . believing that it was only a commendable arrangement of nature, whereupon a furious argument followed. The Ordinary [52] [Zinzendorf] said that he was in no way satisfied with this paper, that he had not thus commenced his marriage, and that his marriage ranked higher than the lonely state in Ephrata." [53] "After that the Ordinary spoke so violently that he had to surrender his office in the Conference, and one from the Scottish Church was put in his place and thus in an angry spirit the session was closed." [54]

The Ephrata representatives continually threatened the harmony of the Synods and gave the Count the greatest concern. After their departure there was such a noticeable spirit of unanimity that all present felt that they really were one Church of God in the Spirit. In order to retain this spiritual union, so suddenly realized, a curious plan was introduced. By lot three trustees, Andrew Frey, a Dunker, Gottfried Haberecht, and Anton Seyffert, Moravians, were chosen. These three were to choose a committee of two in secret, by the approval of lot, whose office was to counteract in a secret way any attempt to break up this union. Should the names of these two be discovered, others were to be chosen in their place by the trustees. Since this committee was unknown to the public and had to work in secret, there is no record of their activities.

the Six Nations; and Pyrlæus became Zinzendorf's assistant in the Lutheran Church in Philadelphia.

[51] Sachse: *German Sectarians, 1708-1742*, p. 447.

[52] "Ordinary" was a title meaning bishop or master, applied to Zinzendorf.

[53] *Chronicon Ephratense*, p. 128.

[54] *Ibid.*

At the later Synods no mention is made of this secret committee. However, the increasing hostilities between the religious groups declare its failure.

Three Indians were baptized at one of the sessions. The method of baptism was decided by lot, to avoid criticism. Then Christian Heinrich Rauch preached a sermon; hymns were sung. The Indians kneeled before the water, and pouring water on each three times, Rauch addressed them, saying: "Abraham, Isaac, and Jacob, I baptize you in the name of the Father and the Son and the Holy Ghost, with Jesus' death." These Indians were converts of Christian Rauch, the Moravian missionary, and their names, Abraham (Shabash), Isaac (Seim), and Jacob (Kiop), symbolized that they were patriarchs of the Indian church. A further reason for naming the Indians after the patriarchs was the belief that the Indians were descendants of the lost tribes of Israel.

The following are some of the conclusions arrived at in this Synod:

"The Brethren from Bethlehem are requested to set forth their view on matrimony as soon as they have organized into a church." [55] Under question 22 of the second Synod the controversy between the Moravians and the Ephrata group had been quieted temporarily. This tolerance of the Ephrata delegates must have been unacceptable to Beissel, their leader, who did not attend any of the Conferences. The paper on marriage which aroused such fury must have been written by Beissel. In the debate which followed, the Moravians could not declare their position on marriage adequately, and even if they had, Beissel was not there to be persuaded. Therefore, they were asked to set forth their views on matrimony as soon as they were organized into a church. The Moravians in America were not as yet organized. For the present they were confining their interests to the Church of God in the Spirit.

(9) "After the Brethren from Bethlehem explained that in the vicinity of Nazareth they expected to form a Congregation of the Lord, the Conference promised to visit them, prove them, and rejoice with them." [56] (A Moravian Congregation

[55] *Auth. Rel.*, p. 50.   [56] *Ibid.*, p. 52.

was formed when the first "Sea Congregation" of fifty-seven members arrived in June of that year, 1742.)

(10) "In order to avoid more religious fanaticism in this land, no new church shall be recognized by us, unless they are poor pardoned sinners, who in order to honor Jesus' death have formed their church. If such a church comes to us, the Congregation of God in the Spirit shall visit and prove her, and after investigation accept her." [57]

(12) "We are of the opinion that certain godly truths and regulations that are neglected, we can establish again from time to time, but not without God's will and a thorough understanding of the times and conditions. . . ." [58]

(13) "Brother Ludwig [Zinzendorf] complained bitterly to us that he missed Europe, because there he noticed in all the baptized a certain sensitivity. And when he preached Jesus there, he found hearts of flesh; but here, with the exception of God's children of whom he met some everywhere, he found almost nothing but enthusiasts, or proud saints, or rude, scornful people, which made the preaching of the gospel very hard for him. . . ." [59]

(14) "Whereas Brother Ludwig [Zinzendorf], as everyone knows, professes to be a servant of God in the Lutheran religion, and has come to this Conference as such, and not only in Skippack, in Fulckner-Schwamm, and Tulpahocken preached the doctrines of this religion openly, but also served the Lutheran Church in.Philadelphia, although he is in the Moravian Church, which is recognized by the church historians of both Protestant religions as a mother; and whereas he preaches in the Reformed Churches, which accept the doctrines of the Synod of Bern; therefore, since some were offended in this, he declared himself as follows: (a) He wondered at and honored Jeremiah, who, when the people against his will and severe warnings went to Egypt, followed his people. The ideas of Moses and Paul concerning their people were also important for him. (b) Who, therefore, will follow Paul in the Separation, will know that he follows his Lord Jesus, and lives and dies in his religion, and until the walls shall have caved in,

[57] *Auth. Rel.*, p. 52.   [58] *Ibid.*   [59] *Ibid.*, p. 53.

which he does not feel himself called to promote, he shall not move out. (c) The Lutheran religion is in practice, perhaps, as bad as but not worse than others like it, but in its teaching more godly than the others, and with his sword he will wage war, as long as there are wars of the Lord for him to fight. (d) Since his Moravian membership protects him against many common usages, which would be against his conscience, he will, therefore, make use of this liberty without judging any servant of the Lord who has not this liberty." [60]

This last declaration is vague and its implications are not at all clear. At least so much is clear, that although he professed to be a Lutheran clergyman, his membership in the Moravian Church granted him liberties which other clergymen of the Lutheran and other churches did not have. Zinzendorf boasted that he was a "free servant of the Lord." In the spaciousness of this freedom he frequently lost himself completely, stumbling on the sensitive feelings of others, and being led into practices repugnant to orthodox circles. His liberty later led the Moravian Church into an era of extravagances, as we shall see.

(17) ". . . We fear nothing but lack of common sense, which causes misunderstanding. . . . But since it cannot be denied that at times people speak about us with unkind feelings, it would be better for them to speak against us openly; . . . but if they do not have the heart to do this, then they should have less heart to speak against us in our absence; they should keep quiet about those matters of which they have no right to speak." [61]

(19) "If the Schwenkfelder have anything against Brother Ludwig, the Conference begs of them to avoid much useless talk and worry by bringing it before the Conference of Evangelical Religions in Germantown, March 10. . . ." [62]

(22) "Those of us who have been at the previous Conferences have noticed an increasingly closer union. The Saviour has been so gracious that although we come from such different and opposing sects, we can now control the evil human trait

[60] *Auth. Rel.*, pp. 53, 54.   [62] *Ibid.*, p. 55.
[61] *Ibid.*, p. 54.

of claiming to be right. We have noticed in this third Conference that the Saviour does with us as he pleases, even if contrary to all expectation. He is near, takes our misery on himself, and carries it away." [63]

It is evident that the Moravians, although not yet an organized church, were the leading spirits of these Synods. The so-called unanimous conclusions of this third Conference are Zinzendorfian in thought and style. The Count was Syndic; he and David Nitschmann, a Moravian bishop, ordained four Moravians at this Conference; and the three Indians were baptized by the Moravian missionary Rauch. These facts indicate that the Brethren had naturally assumed leadership, with the Count as the guiding genius.

The stormy beginning of this Synod, due to the discussion of the subject of marriage introduced by the Ephrata delegates, was indicative of the trend of the remaining Synods. Although such harmony existed among the remaining delegates to the Synod that they thought the Church of God in the Spirit had been realized, the result of these three Conferences was that the Schwenkfelders, the Ephrata group, and the Mennonites withdrew, while the Dunkers held their own annual meetings.

At the close of this Synod Zinzendorf with a few others went to see Beissel. The Count decided by lot whether Beissel was to present himself to him or he to Beissel. The Ephrata leader regarded himself of higher rank and refused to lower his dignity by calling on Zinzendorf. The Count refused to present himself to Beissel, and so left without seeing him. Upon his return to Germantown, Zinzendorf wrote a letter to Beissel, declaring that the Ephrata delegates to the Synod were tools in his hands, that the paper on marriage they presented was written by him, that he considered himself holier than others, and that he should come down to the level of his fellowmen.[64] Following are a few extracts from Beissel's reply.

I hardly know what induces me to issue this mite unto you, without perceiving some inner deep and very secret draughts of love,

[63] *Auth. Rel.*, p. 55.
[64] *Büd. Samm.*, vol. III, pp. 316-326. Also *Chronicon Ephratense*, p. 129.

which urge and challenge me. Should it strike in the spirit, it would be well if in future the heavens would make truth and justice drop down from above and honesty grow upon the earth and the children of man be taught the truth. Then there would be some hope of recovery. . . . It is therefore perceived in a strong degree of light that almost all outward divine worship, as the same appears outwardly, and even what Christ suffered outwardly, was of the Old Testament, and born in the servitude.

Even for this reason there are so few essential Christians. As the Jew with his righteousness is not sufficient and consequently needs a conversion, so the lawless heathen places himself in the gospel, wherefrom such a lawless anti-Christianity is born as we now have at the present day. . . .

For my own part, I have never felt the presence of God so near in sacrifice or in worship as in the mortal life of Jesus, or when I must hang with him upon the cross between the two malefactors.

Even in the same manner have I in him lost my fair features, so that now they are less comely than those of others. This sun of tribulation has already burned into me so strong that its fire can hardly ever be extinguished within me until the day of eternity, when God will wipe away all tears from our eyes.

Ephrata the 9th of
Eleventh Month 1741

This trifle from me, Friedsam, Fr., otherwise called Beissel, at present a stranger and pilgrim in this world.

P.S. This little missive is an outcome of a very secret and intimate epitome of the Spirit. Pray proceed in this so far as practicable, according to the utmost rules of love.[65]

Just before the fourth Synod, Zinzendorf wrote a letter to the Schwenkfelders, stating that the spiritual and temporal care of their people had been entrusted to him and that he was "the appointee of Jesus as Reformer of the Schwenkfelders." [66] But since he had no influence over them, he wanted them to sign a form to release him from his appointed duty by Christ. The form of the release was as follows: "We, the undersigned, release Count Louis von Zinzendorf in the sincerest and most

---

[65] *Büd. Samm.*, vol. III, pp. 64-68. Translation from Sachse: *German Sectarians, 1708-1742*, pp. 449-451.

[66] *Büd. Samm.*, vol. III, pp. 313, 314; also Fresenius, vol. III, pp. 245, 246.

effective manner before God and man from all temporal and spiritual care of the Schwenkfelders in America during the term of our lives." [67]   But the Schwenkfelders were not so easily intimidated as the Count had reckoned. They replied: "We do not believe in that entrusted instruction from Christ against our religion. We decline the demand, we have neither the bestowed nor assumed power or arbitrariness to treat with our people in the manner indicated; it would appear neither formal nor proper, but rather it would appear foolish." [68] This was the Count's last attempt to win the Schwenkfelders.

The fourth Synod met at Germantown, March 21-23, in the house of Mr. Ashmead. At the first meeting the Count expressed deep grief about the insufficiency of some of the delegates and of himself. Although the time had come to transact business, he spent the whole forenoon in supplication before the "Lamb" about his misery and that of others. In the meantime Henry Antes was in charge, and some of the preliminary matters were expedited. The absent churches were to be invited again to come to the next Conference.

At the second meeting of this Synod, some enthusiasm was manifested, some saying, "We have now an open field, we are all brothers." Others said, "We are here as volunteers from the religious groups." Some said, "We are children of God"; and still others said, "A church of God in the Spirit."

Four questions were then put before Christ, which means that they were submitted to the lot. (1) "Do we not have our discharge from these Conferences as yet; must we continue them?" Answer: "We must continue them." (2) "Must we endure what is done to us in them and persevere?" Answer: "We must plague ourselves still more with it." (3) "Must we show ourselves industrious in it, and is it not enough if we let matters go as they please?" Answer: "As yet we dare not allow matters to run their own course; we must be energetic in this work." (4) "Is this necessary with all religious groups?" Answer: "No, only with such as the Saviour will point out." [69]

About thirty questions were handed to the Conference for

[67] *Pa. Ger. Soc.*, vol. XIII, p. 117.   [69] *Auth. Rel.*, p. 64.
[68] *Ibid.*

discussion, but at the suggestion of Antes, they were turned over to a "learned Brother" for private consideration.

At the third meeting of this Conference, five questions were put, which were answered unanimously.

(1) "Shall we continue to work in the Conferences on the basis of mutual trust, or according to the rules of the first Conference?" Answer: "We proceed in the Conferences according to the plan of the first Conference, and that plan is justifying the method, without working any further on trust." [70] According to the plan of the first Synod, the delegates had to bring a written testimonial to prove their membership in the Conferences. But these restrictions became more lax, allowing greater numbers to come, as is seen from question one of the second Synod. As some of the religious groups withdrew their delegates, the membership became less, and they gladly welcomed any who wanted to come, substituting "mutual trust" for the "rules of the first Synod." Some came merely out of curiosity, and the result was much gossip. Under these circumstances they sought to enforce the rule of the first Synod, and the consequence was that the remaining Synods (excepting the last) were poorly attended.

(2) "Since we deal so openly before the Lord, as if we were only a few together, is it necessary to make the rule that those who repeat outside the Conferences what was said within, are to be barred from further attendance?" Answer: "This rule is absolutely necessary."

(3) "Since love, mercy, and patience are not granted us to enforce this rule, how shall we protect the public from deceitful and false information?" Answer: "We must once for all warn against it."

(4) "Since in many places in this land the common rules of nature are set aside, do we help to civilize the people in this, or do we have the permission by all means to lead?" Answer: "We can and must lead."

(5) "What shall be our main purpose?" Answer: "To work for the benefit of the land and the souls, in order that something may be accomplished. Instead of spending effort

[70] *Ibid.,* p. 68.

to create confidence in the minds of people of what is still to come, we will go our way and allow the truth and the evidences thereof to create this confidence among sincere people." [71]

The rest of the subjects for discussion were chosen by lot. The lot, also, determined that the next Conference was to be in Germantown, instead of with the Mennonites. Fortunately for Zinzendorf and the delegates the lot, which they considered as the absolute will of God, had saved them from embarrassment, for even if the lot had decided that the next Synod should be with the Mennonites, they without a doubt would not have allowed it, since they were not present at this or any of the remaining Union Synods. Next, a paper twenty-seven pages in length was read, which had been sent out by Adam Gruber, one of the Skippack Brethren, in 1736, to bring the sectarians of Pennsylvania into closer harmony. [72]

At the next meeting letters from St. Thomas (West Indies) had arrived telling of the death of certain missionaries there. The letters were read, and plans were made to fill the vacancies created by death. Sister Judith Meiningen was considered a good candidate for St. Thomas. She was called before the Conference, and the following questions were asked, which she answered: "Had she not lived long enough for herself?" Answer: "She had lived for herself long enough." "Had she lived long enough for the Church?" Answer: "She did not know." "Had she the courage to die for this?" Answer: "She had the courage and joy to do this." [73] Her husband was not present, and when these same questions were asked of him, he answered that he had not lived enough to himself, and although he would like to go, he was not certain that he was willing to die in the cause. Because of his answers they were not ordained to the work. Zinzendorf's daughter Benigna offered

[71] *Auth. Rel.*, pp. 68, 69.

[72] "Johann Adam Grubers gründliche An-und Aufforderung an die ehmahlig erweckte hier und dar zerstreute Seelen dieses Landes, in oder ausser Partheyen, zur neuen Umfassung, gliedlicher Vereinigung, und Gebets-Gemeinschafft; dargelegt ans dringenden Hertzen eines um Heilung der Brüche Zions ängstlich bekümmerten Gemüths, im Jahr 1736." *Pennsylvanische Nachrichten,* pp. 165-191. Also, *Büd. Samm.,* vol. III, pp. 13-39.

[73] *Auth. Rel.*, p. 71.

herself but was not accepted, since her mother was not there to be asked and had given her permission to go to Pennsylvania only. The tender of Anna Nitschmann was not proposed, since suddenly they were "commanded by the Lord" not to fill the vacancies in St. Thomas for this time, but to visit them, which duty fell to David Nitschmann, the bishop of the mission fields.

When Andrew Eschenbach [74] and his wife asked for aid in Oley, the Syndic (Zinzendorf) held a long discourse on the absurdity of all spiritual undertakings with unbelievers, and of promising things that could not be carried out. The unbelievers to whom Zinzendorf refers were the "New-Born" [75] who had settled at Oley. He entreated the Oley workers to take their time. A discussion of the use of the lot concluded that it was a dangerous matter, since many of the common people looked upon it asquint; and those who were not called to use it, were warned against it.

The important transaction at the fifth gathering of this fourth Synod was a general conclusion drawn up to elucidate further the proceedings of the first Synod. It was submitted to the lot word by word, so that nothing should enter except as the Lord willed. The resolution was: "All the children of God in every religion in Pennsylvania are in duty bound to continue in the Conferences. But when a child of God is at the

[74] Eschenbach had come to America in response to an appeal from George Whitefield to Zinzendorf to send preachers to the Germans in Pennsylvania. *Pennsylvanische Nachrichten*, p. 9.

[75] These New-Born or *Neugeborene*, also called Baumanites after their leader Bauman, were Separatists. The followers of Bauman claimed perfection, that they were free from sin and therefore had no further use for the Bible, except such passages which supported their doctrines. They rejected the sacraments as unnecessary and believed in the celibate state. Bauman claimed to have had revelations and "a call from God to the Unregenerate World." As proof of this, he volunteered to swim the Delaware River. *Chronicon Ephratense*, pp. 13, 14. Before the opening of the third Synod in Oley, Zinzendorf called on Bauman, perhaps with the intent to interest him in the Synods. *Pennsylvanische Nachrichten*, p. 106. After Bauman died most of his followers were absorbed by the Moravians, but a few clung to the doctrines of Bauman and caused much trouble to the other German settlers. See also L. T. Reichel: *The Early History of the Church of the United Brethren*, p. 49.

same time a servant of Christ, he is first of all under obligation to his own religion. And when in the future, a servant of Christ forsakes his own religion without our knowledge, we will not recognize him any longer as Christ's servant. . . . Likewise we declare to every teacher who thinks he is something in himself, and to such as do not eagerly listen to a child of God (this being an unmistakable sign of a pardoned sinner), that they have not yet started in spiritual experience. Therefore, whoever does not love the Lord Jesus Christ, he is Anathema Maranatha." [76]

At the last meeting of this Synod, Zinzendorf declared that, since a Congregation of God in the Spirit has gifts and powers which it can share, he wanted to be the first to receive such gifts to meet his need. Since man is so apt to err, and since in Europe he had been accused of treating the matter of Christ's works and church affairs with much "fire" in such a way that harm came from it, and since he had never been so desirous as this week to lay off this "militant" spirit and be restored to his former natural disposition of friendliness, devotion, and gentleness, he therefore stood in need of two things: grace and forgiveness for the things in which he had failed. For this he had "chosen before the Lord" the gentle brother Joseph Müller to make these needed gifts available for him, in order that in the future he could continue to work in this land with a gentle and patient spirit. After the singing of an appropriate hymn, the Count stepped down to brother Müller, who then spoke to him and laid his hands on him. After Müller had prayed the "Lamb" for his Spirit and grace, they gave each other the kiss of peace. The whole Conference did the same, and they separated with joy in their hearts.

It appears that the Count realized his weaknesses and that he himself was the greatest obstacle in the realization of the Church of God in the Spirit. However, the censorious spirit manifested in the remaining Union Synods indicates that this display of humility and gentleness was probably made with other motives as well. The "fiery" and "militant" spirit of Zinzendorf had been the chief source of offense, as is clearly

[76] *Auth. Rel.*, pp. 74, 75.

evident in his relations with the Schwenkfelders and the Ephrata Mystics. Since this demonstration of humility occurred at the very close of this fourth Synod, he may have hoped to make a favorable impression on the Conference and others who would hear of it before the convening of the fifth Synod.

There was a constant decline of interest in these Union Synods, so that this fourth Synod spent much time in devising plans to re-enlist co-operation. With the withdrawal of several sects, the meetings became more Moravian-centered, as is evidenced by the time used in such matters as the reading of the letters from the Moravian missionaries in St. Thomas and devising plans to fill the vacancies there.

The interesting item of this Synod was the Count's declaration of his preference for the Lutheran Church. There was much uncertainty in people's minds because of the indistinctness of Zinzendorf's position. This was used against him to prejudice many, and so he reiterated the claim, which he made when he first came to Pennsylvania, that he had undertaken this work in the capacity of a Lutheran clergyman. He declared further that the Lutheran Church was rightly the most blessed one, being preferable even to the Ancient Unitas Fratrum, and that he greatly doubted whether a servant of God who had separated himself from the Lutheran Church had gained anything by joining another.

The fifth Synod was held in a German Reformed Church in Germantown, April 17-20. On the first day no one but the Moravians and some persons from the town came. The second day an enlarged catechism, containing the twelve main articles of the Synod of Bern, was read and approved, and immediately delivered to the printer.[77]

---

[77] This catechism, compiled by Zinzendorf and Bechtel, the minister of the German Reformed Church in Germantown, was based on the twelve articles adopted by the Synod of Bern in 1532. The manuscript was read at this fifth Synod and approved. After Christopher Saur, the editor of the Germantown newspaper, refused to print it on account of his antagonism toward Zinzendorf and the Synods, it was printed by B. Franklin. The title page was: *"Kurtzer Catechismus Vor etliche Gemeinen Jesu aus den Reformirten Religionen in Pennsylvania. Die sich*

On the third day the lack of manual laborers for Bethlehem and Nazareth was deplored.   Zinzendorf answered that the land might better remain untilled for another year, since the sowing of the seeds of the souls took precedence in this land. It was reported that James Logan, Brother Ludwig (Zinzendorf) and Sister Anna (Nitschmann) had written to the general meeting of the Quakers, and that such correspondence had been accepted with love.

On the last day of the fifth Synod, the following business was transacted:

(1) "The Congregations were advised to pursue a more stringent course than before and to spare their patience until they had something worthy of it, in order that these evil and deceitful workers on whom patience has been exercised may not in time become dragons who use their tails to pull down the stars. . . .

(2) "The Saviour was asked: 'In what respect shall there be a difference in this matter in Pennsylvania?'   The lot declared: 'The above rule should be observed more strictly in Pennsylvania than in Europe. . . .'   This brought us to the fundamental question: How, then, does the Saviour look upon Pennsylvania?   This we examined at length before the Lord, until at last the following was considered an adequate expression of it. . . .

(3) "Pennsylvania is a complete Babel, out of which the moaning prisoners must be saved first. In this we cannot observe ordinary rules, since one must carry everything through with apostolic power.

(4) "In each congregation, no matter how small, vice-elders shall be appointed from among the elders, since on this holy and godly office the opponents may immediately be crushed as on a stone, as soon as they want to remove it.

(5) "Before the elders shall become vice-elders, they must have the attestation of all and of the truth.   After that they shall not be accused, except such accusation comes from two

zum alten Berner Synoden halten; herausgegeben von Johannes Bechtel Diener des Wortes Gottes.   Phil. Gedruckt by B. Franklin, 1742."

or three witnesses. The people at Oley are recommended to read Rom. 16:17 and 1 Cor. 16:15, 16." [78]

These two Scripture references speak of those "that are causing the divisions and occasions of stumbling," and of being in subjection to those who "have set themselves to minister unto the saints." The sect of the "New-Born" created much trouble and division in the Oley congregation. Andrew Eschenbach, the pastor, seems to have lost his influence, and therefore Zinzendorf advised that he should be replaced by Henry Antes. [79]

(6) "Public teachers shall not become elders if they attend to instruction only and have no colleagues.

(7) "Congregations are chosen by grace, and there is no danger of a member remaining outside who belongs to it.

"Then certain individuals and the things entrusted to them were discussed. Brother Ludwig [Zinzendorf], however, could not say much to this, since the Saviour had forbidden him to expose this man. . . ." [80] The person referred to here was Christopher Saur, who used his paper to cast aspersions upon the Moravians and Zinzendorf in particular. [81]

(8) "Since the Saviour is present in the church buildings as well as in the barns, He commands us not to look down upon these church buildings which He himself has cleansed. His witnesses should not be ashamed of them, since in this land He loves churchmen [*Religions-Leute*] more than the sectarians, and the sectarians more than the Separatists. . . ." [82] This has reference to those sects and Separatists who worshiped in barns or out-of-doors in preference to church buildings. This practice arose out of fear lest there should be a return to institutionalized religion as in the Catholic Church, the rudiments of which some detected even in the Protestant churches.

(9) "To love Jesus Christ and His reconciliation and then

[78] *Auth. Rel.*, p. 98.
[79] *Büd. Samm.*, vol. III, pp. 314, 315.
[80] *Auth. Rel.*, pp. 98, 99.
[81] "This meeting was chiefly conspicuous for the quarrel between Count Zinzendorf and Christopher Saur." Sachse: *German Sectarians, 1708-1742*, p. 451.　　　　[82] *Auth. Rel.*, p. 100.

to hold it in abeyance until His coming is like starting to build a tower from the top. If one should speak to such an one of the foundation, he would answer that he will think of that when he comes to it." [83]

The Synods became increasingly occupied with the problems that threatened their discontinuance. Zinzendorf, the leading spirit, was greatly concerned about the Synods for their own sake. What these meetings were to accomplish was lost sight of under the pressure of increased opposition. Instead of the spirit whereby such a Church of God in the Spirit was to be achieved, as originally intended, they now dealt with the mechanics. But the system employed broke down at every stage, due to the inadequacy of the machine and incompetency of the engineer.

The sixth Synod met in Germantown, May 16-18. It was the least important of all in respect of attendance and results. Some of the delegates who had attended hitherto were absent. A proposal was made to invite all parents in the four counties of Pennsylvania to send one man from each township to a conference in Bethlehem to discuss the establishment of a general boarding school. Zinzendorf wanted to establish general boarding schools for all the Germans. The proposal was found impractical, and the deliberations led to no results.[84] Zinzendorf had made an earlier attempt to establish such a school.[85]

This sixth Synod accomplished no more than the preceding ones. Its resolutions grew out of a process of rationalization in view of the conviction that defeat was imminent. Although the attempt to establish a Church of God in the Spirit was frustrated, it was concluded that the Synods were a work of the Lord in opposition to Satan. Then to protect and justify the Lord it was decided that the opposition of Satan in Pennsylvania was necessary. Neither the Lord nor the faithful in the Conferences were to be blamed; the fact was that they were caught in a vicious circle of opposition by Satan. Thus

[83] *Auth. Rel.*, pp. 100, 101.

[84] Beginning with the year 1743, the Moravians established and maintained schools at Muddy Creek, Lancaster, Oley, Mübach, Warwick, Heidelberg, Maguntsche, and Walpack.

[85] Fresenius, vol. III, pp. 176, 177.

EXTRACT

AUS DES

CONFERENZ-SCHREIBERS

JOHANN JACOB MÜLLERS

REGISTRATUR

VON DER

Sechſten **VERSAMMLUNG**

DER

EVANGELISCHEN ARBEITER

In PENNSYLVANIA,

UND

DER GEMEINE GOTTES im GEIST

SIEBENDER

GENERAL-SYNODUS

Zu *Philadelphia* am 2. und 3ᵗᵉⁿ Junii 1742. ſt. v.

Daſelbſt gedruckt und zu haben bey B. FRANKLIN.

EXTRACTS FROM THE MINUTES OF THE SEVENTH GENERAL SYNOD,
PRINTED BY BENJAMIN FRANKLIN

they eased their minds, and as evidence that they were willing to go more than half way in these wars of the Lord, they called another Synod.

The seventh and last of the Union Synods convened in Philadelphia, June 13-14. It was better attended, but largely by the Moravians. Hitherto the Moravians had not been represented at these Synods as an established church in America. On June 7, fifty-seven Moravians, who constituted the first "Sea Congregation," arrived in Philadelphia in time to be present at the seventh Synod, and their request to be a member of the Church of God in the Spirit was granted.

At the official opening of the Synod, the Count spoke briefly about the coming of the "Sea Congregation" and the necessity of investigating their circumstances, since now the Moravian Brethren were in a position to go to Bethlehem as a Congregation. George Piesch, John Brandmüller, Peter Böhler, and Adolph Meyer, the leaders of the newly arrived pilgrims, spoke about their journey. The names of those who were to comprise the *Orts-Gemeine* in Bethlehem, were read, one hundred and twenty in number.

The chief work of this Conference was the formulation of unanimous conclusions concerning the religious groups in Pennsylvania. A study of the conclusions reveals that what were called unanimous conclusions were Zinzendorfian conclusions.

(1) "The dominant religion of the Quakers has not received enough respect. It is the only Separatist Church that deserves the name. . . ."

(2) "The Moravian Brethren submit themselves here, as in Europe, to the Invisible Church of the Lord, who honors the Martyr Jesus, and rules through its head, and deals with those religions as it pleases him. And as long as the Moravian Brethren remain in this position, so long will they remain a house in this Church of the Lord and carry this sectarian name without shame for the truth.

(3) "The Lutheran German ministers at Philadelphia and Tulpehocken let it be known in Pennsylvania that they are heartily satisfied with the institutions erected in their territory to teach 'on whom I have believed,' and are humbly bowed

before the grace of the Saviour, as small as the beginning may appear. They declare openly that they will have nothing to do with Casper Stiever [86] and that man who baptized Philip Beyer's children on the Manhatawny as well as all illegally called, self-arisen, or improperly ordained mercenaries, so long as they identify themselves with the business of taking in money and not with true faithfulness to souls and their salvation. They recognize in part the difficulty of helping the matter, and therefore are not so particular as in Europe. However, they can not and will not leave unchanged the shameful misuse, known deceit, and open offences leading to the prostitution of the whole religion, but they will depose Stiever from his appropriated office. They will bring the present state to the attention of that Lutheran University to which the American land has been accustomed to address itself, and propose to them that this land be assisted with worthy ministers soundly indoctrinated with the Augsburg Confession. Also, the future collegiate churches in Philadelphia, with the council of the Swedish, will hear those who are concerned about organization, who can have their faithful advice and whatever they do for them without cost and trouble.

> Von Thürnstein, Theol. Tubingensis.
> Joh. Christoph Pyrlæus, Theol. Lipsiensis.
> Paul Dan. Pricelius, V.D.M. Upsaliensis.
> Gottlob Büttner, V.D.M. in Tulpehocken.

[86] Casper Stiever, who was not ordained, preached among the German Lutherans and formed them into congregations. At Tulpehocken, where Stiever had preached frequently, they applied to Casper Leutbecker from Skippack, who had been ordained in London, to secure for them an ordained minister from Germany. When it was learned that the expected minister had died at sea, they called Leutbecker as their pastor. When Leutbecker refused to baptize a child whose father was intoxicated, the latter had the child baptized by Stiever. This gained a following for Stiever in Tulpehocken, and the congregation was divided. Finally Leutbecker had to flee. When Zinzendorf came to America he placed Büttner, later a Moravian missionary, there to preach to the followers of Leutbecker. The division continued, and at the sixth Synod, Zinzendorf and three others resolved themselves into a consistory of the Lutheran Church in Pennsylvania and deposed Stiever from the ministry. *"Die Confusion von Tulpehocken,"* Ms. Beth. Arch. Also see *Büd. Samm.*, vol. III, pp. 76-79, and vol. II, p. 830.

(4) "The doctrines of predestination of the first-fruit out of all people, and the disciples of the Lamb, and the certain recompense for the suffering of the martyr in body and soul, are the most precious godly truths.   But since those teachers, coming from the Classis of Holland for conscience' sake, are bound to teach that God does not want to save all people, therefore the whole Reformed religion in Pennsylvania is herewith warned.   We want to show before their whole assembly that whoever does not take this doctrine to America, and does not practise it, will not be recognized as a true teacher; but whoever practises it, is compelled to oppose the prophets and the apostles.   Since we can now call upon the testimony of our fellow-countrymen that in Germany we never believed this strange doctrine, therefore each must decide whether he shall teach it here, or in the Classis of Amsterdam and New York, where they imagine it is taught in Germany.   Those who are enlightened by the twelve known Articles of the Synod of Bern will make confession to it openly, and allow the holy office of the ministry to be organized and directed accordingly.   Their well-known, faithful Bechtel, who has now preached the Gospel to them for fifteen years, Henry Antes, Peter Müller, and John Brandmüller, who was a book dealer in Basel, ask to be maternally accepted by all sincere Reformed souls, without in the least being in the way of other servants of Christ, who unite with them in this purpose.   As soon as we know the opinion of a few concerning this, we will call a general conference to formulate a Christian church organization.

(5) "On the Mennonite Church we have no judgment to pass.   It is known in the country of Holland that the blessing of the Lord has come among them there, many of them being united in this and true helpers of the Invisible Church.   But those of this land, from the beginning, are more against us than for us. . . . But also, it is a small religion for itself with boundaries and gates.   Therefore it is rightly treated according to the rules of the first Conference and is left in the hands of the Lord.   Only we must guard ourselves, since we have not been commissioned to improve and preserve what is theirs, nor can this be expected of us.

(6) "The so-called Schwenkfelder find themselves in lamentable circumstances. A system of their own they do not possess. In Germany they have their children baptized, and here not. Those who have offered to help have wronged them, and Brother von Thürnstein . . . was received in such a manner that caused him to be severe with them, which they truly deserved. . . . He has turned away from their teachers, but he remains unchanged in his tenderest love for the members of this sect. He begged for an agreement from them, that they set him free from his obligation to them as long as they live, which they returned unsigned. But he received a strong assurance from a sufficient number of them that they were not in need of him, nor cared to deal with him. He spread both their letters of 1734 [87] and 1742 immediately before the Lord, since almost the same names were signed to both, and the Lord assured him that as soon as the time had come to awaken a Saviour amongst this little forsaken group, he would unite them to the visible church. This he believes he sees, and he considers his tears of twenty years as wiped away. (Thürnstein.)

(7) "The Baptist Church has not proved its origin, but they have sufficiently shown that they have nothing in common with the Anabaptists, against whom the Augsburg Confession strove. They are a gathering of God-fearing people, acting according to their conscience without light and earnest, and for that reason an amiable people. We thought it to be natural for them to unite with the Mennonites, if they could agree on the manner of baptism, there being then one sect less in the country. So long as children of God are willing to live amongst them and show loyalty to them, they are happy; and we want to think that through them Christ only is preached.

(8) "The gathering in Connestogoe, whom we unjustly call Seventh-day Adventists (*Siebentäger* or Ephrata Mystics), since the seventh day is no mockery, withdrew at the fourth [88]

---

[87] This was the year in which the Schwenkfelders emigrated to Pennsylvania instead of Georgia as the Count had planned. The latter was highly displeased with them on that account.

[88] They withdrew at the third Synod and not the fourth.

Conference, partly because of the necessary private reminders to their teachers, and partly because of their disapproval of our conduct, but especially because of the rule we decided upon, requiring much discretion and forbearance. Since all our efforts with their teachers were in vain, and the mistakes of others against them have been recognized and put away, and since they do not want to profit by their private differences, the Church of the Lord declares, without having received word from them, that the instituted sect in Connestogoe with its two cloisters is a mere faction of those Baptists from whom they sought to steal their baptism and vocation. And after they had done so and had alienated the most sincere souls of those Baptists little by little with many pretenses, they were finally formed into an apparent organization. But it was indeed founded only by the devil to hinder the approaching Kingdom of Jesus Christ from the start, to introduce the Separatists strongly against everything that has unity, to lead the people of the religious groups through awful heresies into a mistrust and fear against the future dispensation of grace, and finally that those souls who really want to escape might be bewitched into a false doctrine and communion, so that when the Gospel came, there would be no one there to hunger for it. We have nothing to prescribe for these people, since we do not know how they came under this influence, whether because they rejected God's wrath or because in his everlasting wisdom He did it for their own good. To deal with this matter we consider ourselves incapable, but each one who in his fellowship with them shall come to trouble will prove this for himself, especially those captured cloister-maidens at Kedar. May the Lamb shortly trample this Satan underfoot.

(9) "The Separatists, who are united with no one and also not with us according to the Conference rules, but who joined with us only for the sake of appearances, are of the most unusual sort in Pennsylvania. Their heads and hearts are bad. Their main book against us is 'der Gross,' [89] and ours

---

[89] This has reference to a book written in 1730 by Andrew Gross, a Separatist in Frankfurt, Germany, condemning the Moravians, which was read by many in Pennsylvania.

against them is the Bible. They fled the Conference because they were not able to give reasons. To print libels was deemed the most advisable by them, and when they were questioned about it, they answered: 'One can do that here unpunished,' and moreover we can call no one to account, because as disciples of the Lord we must suffer everything. Those who still have an honest spark in them are sorry, and those who for thirty years have seen Separatists, marvel at this. We have agreed to suffer their scoldings, and in the future we will not answer their personal attacks. And in regard to the historical information that Christoph Saur wants to send into this country, which is contrary to truth, we want to appeal to him who is at the helm of truth. And as often as is necessary we will make a catalog for the sake of righteous souls in this country, so that each one can judge for himself whom he considers the most worthy of belief. They would rather have cut the child asunder than allow the right mother to have it. Theirs and our controversy will be settled by Him, who is greater than Solomon." [90]

The decision of importance for the future at this Synod was a resolution to call a quarterly ministerial conference "to be attended by all those who had remained faithful to the decisions of the first Conference, and open to all servants of Christ who acknowledged His divinity, did not believe in the doctrine of reprobation, and promised not to abuse the confidence of the Synod."

On the evening of the last day of the Conference, a service was held in the Lutheran Church. The Count spoke about the Congregation of God in the Spirit, the method of converting souls, and the election by the Lamb of a visible church, which sets forth the invisible body in one pattern. The purpose, success, and conclusion of the Synods were spoken of, and the fact that they were to be continued in the form of a worker's conference every quarter year.

The accomplishments of this last Union Synod are a series of judgments on the fellow-sectarians, which vibrate with the personal grievances of the Moravians and of the Count in par-

[90] *Auth. Rel.,* pp. 113-118.

ticular. Zinzendorf realized the failure of his ideal, and seeing the "handwriting on the wall," he could not forego a last opportunity to sit on the judge's bench. A diametrically opposite result from that originally intended was obtained. Instead of stopping the slanderers and gossipers the Synods had greatly increased their numbers, among whom Zinzendorf was chief, as is evident by the resolutions of this last Conference. The so-called Church of God in the Spirit, which had as its aim the harmonizing of discordant voices, added still greater confusion to the existing Babel.

The seven Synods were held within a half-year's time. The seventh Synod was the last one in which Zinzendorf participated personally. After the seven Synods he made extensive journeys among the Indians and then sailed for Europe in January 1743. Only some Lutherans, Reformed, and the Moravians were present at the last three Conferences. Although the ideal of a Church of God in the Spirit was worthy of admiration, the Synods that were instituted to promote this ideal, instead, intensified sectarian and denominational differences. The quarterly meetings decided upon at the last Union Synod were continued by the Moravians for six years.

At the Conferences following the seven Pennsylvania Synods, Lutherans, Reformed, and members of some of the sects continued to attend, but they were mostly those who had come into the membership of the Moravians, while still being considered as belonging to their former churches. Such an arrangement was possible by the Trope plan, which Zinzendorf introduced, to which we have already referred. For instance, Henry Antes and John Bechtel were still considered as belonging to the Reformed Trope, and Laurence Nyberg and Christopher Pyrlæus as belonging to the Lutheran Trope, although they had now joined the Moravians. Thus, these quarterly Synods were not so union in character as at first appears, although they were called General Synods. In the Synod of March 1745, the Lutherans, Reformed, Anglicans, Scotch, Moravians, Baptists, and Separatists were present, but the names of these delegates show that they were mostly those who belonged to the Moravians. The twelve persons who attested the correctness of the synodal minutes, although belonging to various Tropes, had joined the Moravians [91] at a Synod in November 1746. Of the one hundred and twenty-four who were present at this Synod, nineteen were considered as belonging to the Reformed, nine to the Lutherans, three to the Mennonites, and the rest to the Moravian Trope. Judging by the twenty-two places from which these delegates came, which were all Moravian settlements and preaching stations, they must have been almost if not exclusively Moravians.[92]

The spirit of the quarterly Synods was in accord with the idea peculiar to the Moravians of being witnesses in the whole world and among all sects and persuasions. In the Synod of March 1745, they were still devising ways and means to be of assistance to the Reformed, Lutheran, Dunkers, and even the Ephrata Mystics. At the Synod in September 1747, the Babel in Pennsylvania was again the topic under discussion. Of the Separatists it was said that they are bent on tearing down; of the Lutherans that they exclude the "salt," the very best, from their communion; and that none can be good Reformed or Lutherans if they do not have the "experience of the Lamb and his wounds." [93]

The Conferences in 1747 were entirely Moravian in character, as is evident by the subject-matter under discussion, the time spent in formulating methods of procedure in the settlements, preaching stations, Moravian schools, and missions among the Indians and Negroes.[94] In the minutes of the quarterly Synods of 1747, we see the first signs in America of a strange mystical and symbolical language which the Moravians employed in speaking about the profundities of the Atonement. Because of this the Moravians became the object of much ridicule and slander by the other religious groups, and there-

[91] *"Kurze Relation von dem General Synodo gehalten in Friedericks-Town den 10-11 Marti st. N. 1745."* Ms. Beth. Arch.

[92] *"Verzeichnisz dererjenigen Geschwister und Freunden welche auf dem Synodo in Creuz-Creek in Namen Jesu bisammen waren von 29 Oct.-2 Nov. 1746."* Ms. Beth. Arch.

[93] *"Conclusa oder Verlasz der vom 3/14-8/19 Sept. 1747 in Bethlehem gehaltenen Synodi der Brüder."* Ms. Beth. Arch.

[94] *Ibid.*

fore the Synods were necessarily Moravian; otherwise the extravagant language could not have continued. In 1745 these Conferences were still called General Synods; in 1746 and 1747, *"Synodi der Brüder"* (Moravians); and in 1748 they were already called Provincial Synods, as they are today.

The beautiful ideal of Zinzendorf and the Skippack Brethren, most of whom had been absorbed by the Moravians, failed of its realization, and after 1748 the quarterly meetings changed into Synods of the Moravian Church. In his last address in America the Count said that it seemed to him that in Pennsylvania many people, except the Quakers, retained their religion in order to plague other people.[95]

A first reason for the failure of the proposed Church of God in the Spirit is the fact that the sectarians of Pennsylvania never understood what Zinzendorf meant by a Church in the Spirit or the "Church of Jesus." It was understood by them, and even by some students of today, that the Count wanted to effect an organic union in which denominational lines were to disappear, or that it was to be a mere league of sects, held by external ties, to bring about a more cordial fellowship and understanding. Some said of Zinzendorf "he sought to bring them all under one hat, that is, his own hat."[96] Or that the purpose of the Synods was "to unite all the various parties into one large church body, which would have gladdened all the saints, if only the builders themselves had been different from the Babel."[97] A Christian union in the modern acceptation of the term was not intended. What Zinzendorf had in mind by the Church in the Spirit, as the Invisible Church embodied, was not the conception held by the rest. Much less could the majority of the people, who were uneducated, comprehend the meaning of his ideal. Due to the fact that Zinzendorf and the Germans in Pennsylvania never reached a common ground of understanding, the sectarian lines were intensified and the religious warfare increased.

Another reason for its failure was Zinzendorf's connection

[95] *Büd. Samm.*, vol. III, p. 210.   [97] *Chronicon Ephratense*, p. 125.
[96] *Pa. Ger. Soc.*, vol. X, p. 115.

with the Moravians. Students of Moravian history hold that Zinzendorf never intended to use the Church of the Spirit to spread Moravianism, that he actually opposed Moravian expansion. We can speak of his intention only in the light of his conception of the Brethren in relation to other denominations. In the light of our present conception of what a denomination is and how it should be extended, and in the light of the exclusive community which the Moravians later established, Zinzendorf did actually hinder the progress of the Brethren. But for him the Moravians were not merely one church among many, they were the visible representatives of the great Invisible Church, composed of the "awakened" in many communions. Moravianism in that sense, Zinzendorf sought to increase. At the Synods the Moravian spirit prevailed. The Count himself was the life of the Conferences and his genius was the directing influence. Moravian hymns were sung and their "daily texts" were used; and even the Moravian custom of the use of the lot was frequently resorted to. The other sectarians naturally suspected Moravian denominational propaganda.

Furthermore, Zinzendorf must have had in mind to establish the Church of God in the Spirit through the agency of the Moravians. His idea of the Tropes is evidence for this conclusion. The Germans in Pennsylvania saw that the Trope theory, which was the principle underlying this movement for unity, could aid only Moravianism, since that was the principle already in use in the Moravian Church and the means by which she had gained her recruits. The first Sea Congregation was declared to be a "true Church of Jesus." Here then was the nucleus of the Church of God in the Spirit.

But how was this true church to grow? Exiles from other countries now were forbidden to settle on Zinzendorf's estate in Saxony, shutting off a possible source of growth. If this "Church of Jesus" was to grow, it must get its recruits from the "awakened" in the Lutheran and Reformed Churches. This forced upon him the idea of Tropes. "This adroit plan for making the members of the three denominations feel at home in the Unity of the Brethren worked admirably, and laid the foundations for future harmony. Its influence appears in the old Catalogs of the Congregations in Wachovia, where one column always stated the 'trope' to which the member belonged. The connection retained by members with their ancestral denominations was only theoretical, for they became full communicant members of the Unity, giving their time and effort to the Church of their adoption." [98]   That such would be the case was already anticipated by the various sectarians at the time of the Union Synods.

A more obvious reason why this enterprise did not succeed was the wide-spread opposition to the Moravians and to the Count in particular. Rumours of the Count's troubles with the Saxon Court, the suspicions cast on the Herrnhuters as a Separatist movement, the governmental commissions sent to investigate affairs, and finally the Count's exile in 1736, all prepared the way for a general mistrust in America as well as in Europe. Knowing this, Zinzendorf laid down his title as Count, resigned as bishop of the Moravians, and wanted to be known as a Lutheran clergyman by the name of de Thürnstein. However, he never succeeded in hiding his identity; it only amused his opponents. The Count was suspected from the very first among his own fellow-countrymen in Pennsylvania. Some of the controversial literature had come into their hands, as well as rumours to their ears. They believed the worst of the peculiar customs of the Moravians and called them "papists." Also the Schwenkfelders, whom the Count had sheltered for a while on his estate in Saxony, were hostile. Christopher Saur carried on controversial correspondence with Zinzendorf, accusing him of deceit and injustice,[99] and used his newspaper to slander the Moravians. The monastic society at Ephrata, which at first was congenial with the Moravians, soon rose in open opposition against them on the question of marriage.

Speaking of his coming to Pennsylvania the Count said: "At my arrival I was somewhat discouraged. I had expected love and trust, but instead found much opposition and mis-

[98] *Publication of the North Carolina Historical Commission,* vol. III, p. 993.

[99] Fresenius, pp. 534-540.

trust against me. . . . This made me at first sad; and the lukewarmness of my fellow-countrymen in Philadelphia disheartened me; but I thought: I will keep silence and not open my mouth; He will make all things well." [100]

This opposition extended beyond the boundaries of Pennsylvania. The students of Yale who came on board the ship of the first Sea Congregation, which had stopped at New London, presented the Brethren a statement of twenty-two doctrinal errors [101] of the Count, who was conducting the Pennsylvania Synods at the time. The Brethren in a letter to the Bishop of London wrote: "Words can scarcely express the exceedingly hostile fury with which we are persecuted by the so-called presbyters of New York on the one hand, and on the other by the ambulatory teachers of New England, of Pennsylvania, and of the Raritan [New Jersey] district, distinguished by the name of Methodists, Tennent, Finley, Whitefield and the rest." [102] In New York the Assembly passed laws against the Brethren " 'that no vagrant preacher, Moravian or disguised Papists, shall preach or teach either in public or private without first taking oath (of allegiance and abjuration) appointed by this act, and obtaining a license from the Governor, or Commander-in-chief for the time being; and every vagrant preacher, Moravian or disguised Papist, that shall preach without taking such oaths, or obtaining such license as aforesaid, shall forfeit the sum of forty pounds, with six months imprisonment without bail or mainprize, and for the second offence shall be obliged to leave the colony, etc.' " [103] "What rendered this act still more objectionable to the Brethren was, that it included in the proviso, that 'nothing in this act contained shall be construed to oblige the ministers of the Dutch and French Protestant Reformed Churches, the Presbyterian Ministers, Ministers of the Kirk of Scotland, the Lutherans, the Congregational Ministers, the Quakers, and the Anabaptists, to obtain

[100] *Pennsylvanische Nachrichten,* p. 11.

[101] "John Philip Meurer letter to his uncle and aunt wrote at sea between Long and Plock Island twenty miles from New London in America, May 21, 1742, on board the ship *Irene* or *Peace.*" Ms. Beth. Arch

[102] Benham: *Memoirs of James Hutton,* p. 164.

[103] *Ibid.,* pp. 169, 170.

certificates for their several places of public worship already erected, or that shall be hereafter erected within this colony, anything in this Act to the contrary notwithstanding.' " [104]

Gilbert Tennent preached vehemently against the Moravians. Three of his sermons preached in New York City were published in a volume called *The Necessity of Holding Fast the Truth*. These sermons were approved by the New England ministers, six of them endorsing them in the preface of this volume. Tennent speaks of the Brethren as "a pernicious new Sect of people, called Moravian Brethren, or Hezenhouters,[105] who have lately come from Germany into this country. . . . I cannot stand as an unconcerned spectator, to behold the Moravian tragedy; my heart bleeds within me to see the precious truths of Christ opposed, slighted and trodden under foot by our new reformers; and that under a pretext of extraordinary sanctity, love and meekness." [106]

Tennent asserts that, in a conference with Zinzendorf in New Brunswick, N. J., he noticed many errors in his theology, a few of which he mentions in a summary statement: "What are the Count's sermons but a bundle of contradictions and nonsense, damnable errors and heresies, interspersed with passages of truth and sense? In them a preparatory work by law of God is denied, repentance excluded, perfection asserted eighteen times and denied twice; a new purgatory invented, as well as a new election of faith and justification are dreadfully corrupted; historical faith is asserted to be saving; and all persons are said to be justified from the time of Christ's death; the active obedience of Christ is excluded from bearing any part in our justification and salvation! In them enthusiasm is asserted and recommended in diverse instances, as well as all use of means with sinners; to instruct and alarm, denied! In them all manner of wickedness is encouraged, as the most direct way to conversion; all virtue and religious duty unhinged and discouraged: according to them, no means must be used by poor sinners to obtain conversion! In them sin

---

[104] *Ibid.*, p. 170.
[105] Herrnhuters.
[106] *The Necessity of Holding Fast the Truth*, pp. 1, 2.

is represented as a mere trifle, unworthy of our fear or grief!
In them the happiness of heaven is destroyed, by making the
saints to be poor and needy there!   In them the faithful ministers of Christ are condemned for using means with poor
sinners, to convince them of their misery, and bring them to
Jesus! . . . preaching of terror to the unregenerate is denied
. . . propitiation for sinners in eternity is asserted! . . . universal redemption and universal salvation are asserted, as well
as inspiration after the apostolical times! . . . our Lord is
represented as paying a ransom after his death for persons
under conviction! . . . the detestable Arminian doctrines of
Free Will, and the final apostacy of the saints are inculcated
. . . the Count urges the universal necessity of assurance on
pain of death eternal! . . . the doctrine of original sin imputed
is denied, and the popish doctrine of the sacraments asserted
. . . a good thought at death is represented as sufficient to
obtain happiness! . . . sin is asserted to be something material. . . . God's holy law is condemned as the cause of sin.
. . . The Moravian notion about the law is a mystery of detestable iniquity!   And indeed this seems to me to be the main
spring of their unreasonable anti-evangelical and licentious
religion! . . . But I have not time at present to mention all
the other abominations of the Count's sermons!" [107]

A letter to Benjamin Franklin contains the following comment on the Moravian-Tennent controversy: "The Count says
in very serious terms that he never was in conference with Mr.
Gilbert.   He remembers, that Mr. Gilbert Tennent gave him
a visit at New Brunswick; but besides that the Count could
not understand Mr. Gilbert, because he spoke in such Latin as
was very strange for a German, and that the Count himself
could not find expressions which were plain enough for Mr.
Gilbert; he had not a mind to confer with that gentleman in
such a matter, being convinced by long experience, that he
must not discourse with any Presbyterian Reprobant, except
in a company of different Principles." [108]

An influential defender of the Brethren was William Living-

[107] *The Necessity of Holding Fast the Truth*, pp. 100-103.
[108] *Büd. Samm.*, vol. III, pp. 308, 309.

ston, the editor of *The Independent Reflector,* an important liberal periodical of the province of New York. His editorials in behalf of the Brethren, no doubt, were an answer to Tennent and others. He writes: "The pulpit scold is the most despicable scold in the world. He is a cowardly scold that gives his antagonist no opportunity of scolding back. . . . They [Moravians] are a plain, open, honest, inoffensive people . . . their whole conduct evidences their belief, that 'the Kingdom of Christ is not of this world.' . . . In regard to their religious principles, it must be owned, they have their peculiar sentiments, which distinguish them from others. But that is saying no more, than that they think for themselves, or at least, that they think not like others, and Rome is just as far from Geneva, as Geneva from Rome. . . . Every man is orthodox to himself, and heretical to all the world besides; but that he should therefore be calumniated or butchered, the Scripture saith not. . . . The religion of the Moravians is as orthodox as any religion in the realm, except only with this difference, that it promises nothing but peace of mind; while some others are decorated with places and preferments, greater revenues and better wages. . . . Instead of giving them the right hand of fellowship, nothing is more common than to see a parson mount the pulpit, and like a dragon, worry and hector the most peaceable people in the world, for believing in Christ, without worshipping the clergy." [109]

Among the opponents of the Brethren must be mentioned George Whitefield, and John and Charles Wesley. Whitefield employed a group of Moravians on his Pennsylvania estate in building a school, but he soon engaged in a dispute with them about doctrine, especially about predestination, ordered the Brethren to stop work at once, and turned them out as soon as provisions were made for them. When Zinzendorf arrived in America he said: "I had hoped for a permanent result from my brother George Whitefield's work, but I heard him boast more than was pleasing to me; and I did not see enough of what he did that was commendable." [110] In London the Count

[109] *The Independent Reflector,* Jan. 4, 1753.
[110] *Pennsylvanische Nachrichten,* p. 11.

said to Whitefield: "You must first formally recant, and preach openly free grace in the blood of the Lamb, and an election of grace as taught in the Scriptures, which is quite different from the doctrine of predestination which you teach, and if not, our church must necessarily be opposed to you." [111]

The Wesleys, who worked hand in hand with the Brethren in the Fetter Lane Society in London, claimed to have been brought into a clearer religious light through the friendship of Peter Böhler.[112] In 1736, the Wesley brothers came to Georgia in the company of twenty Brethren. In Savannah John Wesley was on intimate terms with the Brethren, and it seemed as if he wanted to cast his lot with them. Upon their return to London the Wesleys, although they gave Böhler the credit for their conversion,[113] accused the Brethren of "Universal Salvation, Antinomianism, and a kind of a new-reformed Pietism." [114] And the Wesleys were accused by the Brethren of holding to sinless perfection. The controversy heightened and drove them apart.

Zinzendorf finally made a public declaration against the Wesleys, saying: "I find myself at this time under an obligation of withholding no longer my declaration that in my opinion the Rev. Mr. John Wesley and Mr. Charles his brother, though very learned and gifted men, are both in the plain way of false teaching and deceiving souls. I have no other view in

[111] Benham: *Memoirs*, p. 112.

[112] Böhler was a graduate of Jena University. In 1737, he joined the Moravians in Herrnhut and was commissioned to go to Georgia, where the first colony of Moravians had settled. He was asked to go to England first to speak to the Oxford students. This led to the introduction of Moravianism into England and his acquaintance with the Wesleys, who had just returned from Georgia. A recent Methodist historian writes: "If it had not been for Böhler, Wesley might never have come out from the cloud of depression that he had been under ever since, in defeat he turned away from Georgia." *Luccock & Hutchinson: The Story of Methodism*, p. 63.

[113] John Wesley wrote in his *Journal:* "I found my brother [Charles] at Oxford recovering from pleurisy, and with him Peter Böhler, by whom in the hand of God, I was on Saturday the 5th clearly convinced of unbelief of the want of faith whereby alone we are saved." *The Journal of the Rev. John Wesley,* Everyman's Library, vol. I, p. 84.

[114] *Ibid.,* p. 334.

this my declaration than to preserve the little flock of sinners, who love their Saviour, from being confounded with pretenders to such perfection, of whom I cannot but be suspicious that while they preach perfection, they are wilful servants of sin, and whom, I fear, I shall see, sooner or later, running with their heads against the wall for a punishment of their high spirits, which (for want of public and seasonable disavowing them) would involve all the servants of Christ in the same scandal." [115]

What caused still more prejudice among the American Churches, as well as among those of Europe, was a "pastoral letter" (*Hirtenbrief*),[116] issued by the Amsterdam Classis, declaring that the followers of Zinzendorf were not descended from the ancient Bohemian-Moravian Brethren, but were merely a sect of mystics, neither good Lutherans nor good Reformed. This document was written by several ministers of Amsterdam against Zinzendorf and was published in America by John Philip Böhn, an ordained German Reformed minister.[117]

Further opposition to the work of Zinzendorf arose through the arrival of Henry Melchior Mühlenberg, sent from Halle at the request of Francke to take charge of Lutheran interests in America. We cannot say with certainty that Francke, who was hostile to the Brethren, sent Mühlenberg at this juncture in order to counteract Zinzendorf's undertaking to form a Church of God in the Spirit as a Lutheran clergyman, but Mühlenberg's arrival certainly had this effect. The *Church Miscellany* of March 1850, a Moravian publication, quotes from the *Evangelical Review:* "As soon as the Reverend Mr. Mühlenberg arrived in this country (1742) the proposal was made that the two churches of Sweden and Germany should unite. Several Conferences were held upon this subject in Philadelphia, but the plan was for the time frustrated by the

---

[115] *Büd. Samm.*, vol. III, p. 852.

[116] *"Väterlicher Hirten-Brieff an die blühende Reformirte Gemeine in Amsterdam, zur Entdeckung von, und Warnung gegen die gefährliche Irrthümer von denen Leuten welche unter dem Nahmen der Herrnhuter bekannt sind. Gechrieben durch die Prediger und Ältesten des Kirchen-Raths von Amsterdam, 1738."* *Büd. Samm.*, vol. II, pp. 289-339.

[117] *Ibid.*, p. 888.

Crypto-Moravian Nyberg, who was then at Lancaster, and who was no doubt, much chagrined that Count Zinzendorf's crooked, though, it may be well meant plans were frustrated by the arrival of Mühlenberg in Philadelphia, and the consequent adherence of the Germans there to him." Christopher Saur delighted in broadcasting the controversies between the Moravians and Mühlenberg in his paper, *Pennsylvanische Berichte*. In the issue of May 16, 1746, four of Mühlenberg's opponents blamed him for the trouble. The next month, June 16, there was a Lutheran answer signed by six, saying that Nyberg was a hypocrite and a Moravian, and that they did not want him in their church, although he claimed to be a Lutheran belonging to the Moravians. And the Brethren were accused of trying to proselyte the Lutherans, under the pretense that they also were Lutherans.[118]

A Swedish Lutheran minister named Bricelius, ordained by the Brethren and belonging to them, and serving at Penn's Neck and Racoon on the Delaware, became involved in considerable trouble with a newly-arrived Lutheran minister by the name of Naesman, who attacked his orthodoxy. Finally Bricelius had to leave, the church being locked against him and he being forcefully expelled.[119]

Zinzendorf accused Mühlenberg of having lent his name to the charge that the Brethren allowed in their theology no Saviour, no merits of Christ, no baptism and Lord's Supper; while Mühlenberg accused the Brethren of lies, deceit, and leading the people astray.[120] Mühlenberg soon became the leader of the Lutherans in America and the organizer of their Church. The greater part of Zinzendorf's congregation in

[118] *Pennsylvanische Berichte*. In the library of the Pa. Historical Society.

[119] Of this incident L. T. Reichel wrote: "How far pastor Mühlenberg was connected with the strange proceedings of Mgr. Naesman, as related above, we are not able to say, and would willingly believe that he knew nothing about them, if his behaviour at a conference of several ministers, held at Philadelphia in May 1744, did not plainly show, that he was still under the influence of early prejudices imbibed at Halle among those divines, who for a time denounced Zinzendorf and the Moravian Brethren almost as heretics." *Church Miscellany*, March 1850.

[120] *Naturella Reflexiones*, pp. 208-209.

Philadelphia joined Mühlenberg, only a few remaining in connection with the Brethren.   Hence, even the Lutheran con-
stituency on whom the Count had depended so strongly failed
him at the critical moment.

The final organization of the Lutheran and Reformed
Churches in America brought to a close any further attempt
to form a Church of God in the Spirit.   During the six years
after the seven Pennsylvania Union Synods, while the Quarterly Union Synods were still convened, ordained Lutheran and
Reformed ministers arrived on the field.   In 1748 the Lutherans organized under Mühlenberg, while the Reformed Churches
under Michael Schlatter's direction joined the Classis of Amsterdam.   The Lutheran and Reformed members among the
Moravians now had to decide which ecclesiastical affiliation
they preferred; some preferred the Lutheran, others the Reformed, and some chose the Moravian.

Finally, the Count's own personality stood in the way of
the realization of his ideal.   He had a natural disposition to
make enemies.   His outstanding characteristic was his dom-
ineering spirit.   This insistence on his authority was due to
his training and life in the Court.   A certain pride in his
nobility made him unwilling to share authority.   His office in
the Saxon Court and the position of authority that he assumed
after his return to Europe from America clearly illustrate
this.   His instability exposed him to constant misunderstanding.   He had a temperamental nature and a restless spirit.
The least provocation tempted him to discard one plan and
start another.   Although he was a talented man, he followed
his imagination and feelings rather than reason.   His deep
feelings overbalanced his judgment.   Since for him the heart
convinced the head, he was inconsistent in his thinking.   His
enthusiasm prompted him to say and do things that he would
not have done in his saner moments.   His imaginative mind
carried him away into mystic symbolism, in which others could
not follow him.

Such practical obstacles to a Church of God in the Spirit
proved to be insurmountable.   At bottom the Moravians and
the Count were obstacles to each other.

CHAPTER III

THE GENERAL ECONOMY

THE Saxon governmental commission in 1733 forbade any more exiles to settle on Count Zinzendorf's estate. Not only was this privilege denied to newcomers, but even those who had already settled there were in danger of being ordered to leave. Consequently in the year 1734 a movement was inaugurated to spread Moravianism to the far ends of the earth. A new center for missions was begun in Greenland; a reinforcement of Moravians was sent to the West Indies; a Christian colony was begun at Disco Bay; and John Sargent began his labors among the Stockbridge Indians. This was also the year in which large groups of the Brethren started their trek to America.

The first company of Moravians, consisting of Spangenberg, David Nitschmann, John Töltschig, Antony Seifferth, Godfrey Haberecht, Gotthard Demuth, Peter Rose, Michael Haberland, Frederick Seidel, and George Waschke, arrived in the spring of 1734. This group was joined by a larger group in 1736 under Bishop Nitschmann. (Governor Oglethorpe and John and Charles Wesley came over on the same boat.) They settled on a piece of land along the Savannah River in Georgia offered to Count Zinzendorf by the English trustees through the negotiations of Bishop Spangenberg, who was in London at the time.

These peaceful Brethren were soon disturbed by the Spanish, who made war against the English colony. The Moravians refused to join the militia, because, like the Quakers, they were non-combatants. Consequently they were molested by their neighbors, both English and Spanish.[1] The situation became

[1] The Brethren were recognized in 1749 by Parliament as an ancient Episcopal Church, and granted the right to worship as they pleased. They were also relieved from taking arms in England or her American colonies, and were permitted to affirm instead of taking the oath.

so strained that they abandoned Georgia, and in 1739 some began to arrive in Pennsylvania. A group of them came north with George Whitefield in his sloop, arriving in Philadelphia in April 1740. At the invitation of Whitefield, these Brethren, who were now without shelter and means of livelihood, started for the Forks of the Delaware to build a school for Negro children on his tract of 5,000 acres in what is now upper Nazareth township in Northhampton County. But owing to doctrinal disputes between them and Whitefield, they were ordered to leave his land at once.

At this time Bishop David Nitschmann, who had conducted the second group to Georgia, was in Europe. He hastened to return to America to establish a settlement for these Moravians in their straitened circumstances. He purchased a piece of land on the Lehigh River, ten miles south of Whitefield's land. Work was begun immediately to provide shelter. When Zinzendorf came to America, he gave this place the name Bethlehem, which it still bears. The Count came shortly before Christmas and was with the Brethren in their log house, with only a wall between them and the animals. On Christmas Eve Zinzendorf conducted the Lord's Supper.[2] "Above them shone the keen, cold stars, God's messengers of peace; around them ranged the babel of strife; and the Count remembering how the Prince of Peace had been born in a humble wayside lodging, named the future settlement Bethlehem."[3]

When Whitefield's business manager, William Seward, suddenly died, the former found that his finances would not allow him to proceed with his plans for the Negro school or even to retain the land. When in 1741 the Moravian authorities in Europe heard of this, they purchased the estate for the Brethren in America and named it Nazareth. Upon this extensive tract of land exclusive settlements patterned after Herrnhut

[2] "*Beylage zum Monat Junius 1787 des Bethlehemishen Diarii, kurze historische Nachricht vom ersten Anfang des Gemein Orts Bethlehem und erster Einrichtung der Brüder Gemeine daselbst aus archive Nachrichten zusammen gezogen.*" Ms. Beth. Arch.

[3] Hutton: *History*, p. 371.

were begun, and around them numerous Moravian preaching stations arose.[4]

Since the Moravian Brethren in this country were transplanted from Moravian settlements in Europe, it was only natural that the community life in America should be largely an inheritance of European culture, especially from the birthplace of the Renewed Church, Herrnhut. Their social and religious customs were not washed overboard on the sea. They cherished a heritage of beliefs and customs that separated them from their neighbors, and their isolation made them cling all the more to the traditions of their fathers.

The social plan, called the General Economy, had Bethlehem as its center, including the settlements at Nazareth. The entire membership of the Brethren in America in 1748 was 812; [5] in 1753, 896; [6] in 1756, 980; [7] in 1758, 1,091; [8] in 1759, 1,100; [9] and in 1761, 1,140.[10] The Brethren grew in number through the various Sea Congregations and other immigrations. The immigrations of Moravians to America for a period of twenty years, as reviewed by Bishop Spangenberg, were as follows: [11]

1734—George Bönisch with Schwenkfelders in Sept.

1735—March—10 men.

1736—Feb. 16—3 married couples, 14 single men, 4 single women.

1740—July 21—Christian H. Rauch.

1741—Oct. 26—3 men.

1741—Dec. 2—Zinzendorf and daughter, 1 married couple, 3 single men and Nitschmann's wife.

1742—July 7—First Sea Congregation, 16 married couples, 23 single men.

1742—Sept.—4 married couples, 2 single women, 1 single man, 1 child.

---

[4] *"Orte in America wo unsere brüder gepredigt und noch predigen, arbeiten oder die uns doch besonders anliegen, Jan. 1747."* Ms. Beth. Arch.

[5] Levering: *History of Bethlehem*, p. 220.

[6] *Catalogus der Geschwister (1753)*. Ms. Beth. Arch.

[7] *Pa. Arch.*, vol. III, p. 69.

[8] *Catalogus der Geschwister (1758)*. Ms. Beth. Arch.

[9] H. Erbe: *Bethlehem, Pa.*, p. 88.

[10] Levering: *History of Bethlehem*, p. 378.

[11] *Pa. Mag. of Hist. and Biog.*, vol. XXXIII, p. 228.

1743—Sept. 17—33 married couples from Herrnhut; 9 married couples, 5 single men, 1 single woman, from England; 7 married couples.

1744—Oct. 25—3 married couples, 3 single men.

1745—Sept.—1 married couple, 1 widow, 1 single man.

1746—Dec. 28—4 couples, 3 single men, 1 widow.

1748—June—15 single men.

1748—Sept.—1 couple, 5 single women.

1749—May 12—John Nitschmann Colony, 10 couples, 2 widowers, 1 widow, 40 single men, 3 Greenlanders, 48 single women.

1749—Summer—4 single men from England.

1749—Oct. 15—70 single men, 10 single men from Zeyst, 3 single women, 1 Negro.

1751—Sept. 26—2 couples, 3 single men.

1751—May 17—2 couples, 1 widower, 1 widow, 1 single man, 1 single woman.

1751—June 17—1 married couple, 2 ministers, 2 single men, 1 single woman.

1752—July 6—18 single women, 1 widow, 2 single men.

1753—Apr. 5—3 married couples, 2 children, 24 single men.

1754—Apr. 15—5 married men, 7 married couples, 12 children, 9 single men, 3 single women.

1754—Nov. 16—50 single men.

1756—June 2—14 single men.

1756—Dec. 12—5 single men.

1761—Oct. 19—3 couples, 26 single men, 9 single women, 3 widowers, 2 widows.

1763—Nov. 4—2 single men, 8 single women.[12]

In addition to this growth from abroad, there were converted Indians, of whom 82 lived in the Bethlehem Economy in 1756, besides those young Indian women who lived in the Choir House with the Single Sisters.[13] In 1757, the number of Indians was 214.[14] Then there were some converts among the colonists. For example, most of the Skippack Brethren joined the Moravians. Among other individuals who after a few years were attracted to them were Josiah Pricket and Samuel

[12] A similar list of immigrations until 1747 is found in *"Beylagen zum Bethlehemisches Diario 2/13 Dec. 1747."* Ms. Beth. Arch.

[13] *Pa. Arch.*, vol. III, pp. 69, 70.

[14] *Catalogus der Geschwister (1758).* Ms. Beth. Arch.

Green, Jr., of New Jersey; Captain Garrison and Timothy Horsfield of Long Island.

The family of the Brethren grew steadily. The motto of their one household was: *"In commune oramus, in commune laboramus, in commune patimus, in commune gaudimus."* (We pray together, we labor together, we suffer together, we rejoice together.) [15]

The General Economy, though it turned out to be a typical American experiment in religious communism, had its beginnings in the Herrnhut community and came to birth in the first Sea Congregation, which arrived in 1742. It consisted of fifty-six members, including, besides Piesch, their conductor, Moravians from Herrnhut, Herrnhaag, and Marienborn, and sixteen from England. They settled at Bethlehem and Nazareth, and, together with the Brethren already there, formed the first Moravian congregation in America.

There were manifestations of religious communism in the organization of this first Sea Congregation. In 1742 the European Moravian authorities secured full control of a transport ship by charter. The company of sixteen married couples and twenty-three single men, who were to reinforce the Brethren in America, was organized into a Sea Congregation, divided according to the Choir divisions.

Before sailing Peter Böhler was made Chaplain, having two assistants among the married people, another for the single men, and his wife for the single women. Officers and elders were chosen, and committees selected, making an organization patterned in every respect after the Herrnhut congregation.[16] For this reason this company and two others like it, one in 1743 and the other in 1749, were properly called Sea Congregations. On board ship daily texts were read and meditated upon at their morning and evening devotions; the Night Watch or Hourly Intercession was observed; one whole day was set

<hr/>

[15] Reichel: *Early History,* pp. 165, 166.

[16] "John Philip Meurer letter to his uncle and aunt wrote at Sea between Long and Plock Island twenty miles from New London in America, May 21, 1742, on board the ship *Irene* or *Peace.*" Ms. Beth. Arch., in both German and English, 33 pages.

aside as a day of prayer and thanksgiving; Love Feasts were frequently observed. One such feast was in honor of the cook, Wahnert, on his birthday, because he had not been seasick and had therefore been able to attend to his culinary duties every day. Another was in commemoration of the eleventh anniversary of the conversion of Peter Böhler. They said they "went to America at the Lord's command," that the "Saviour had helped them through many difficulties," and that they "gave themselves over to the Saviour with a childlike believing heart," all of which were sufficient reasons for the frequent Love Feasts.[17]

Regular times were set apart in these floating congregations for worship, and regularity and promptness were meticulously observed. At six o'clock in the morning came the call to arise, wash, and dress; at seven was the morning blessing; at eight, breakfast; from nine to twelve, the English Brethren studied the German language and the Germans the English; at twelve, the noon meal; the afternoon was spent in some useful occupation, as spinning, sewing, mess duties, and making hammocks; at six, the evening meal; at seven, song services, one in German and another in English; at nine, a conference of the officers, class-leaders, and supervisors; and at ten the night watch began, continuing until 6 A.M. These night watchmen, working in pairs and hourly shifts, spent their time in prayer and vigil.[18]

A system covering minutest details was carried out to provide cleanliness, proper decorum, and discipline. Before the sailing of the second Sea Congregation, Spangenberg, who was in Europe at the time, divided it into six groups, three of men and three of women. The women, both married and unmarried, lived on one side of the ship, and all the men on the other. Each person was assigned definite duties: one struck the hour on a bell; some were teachers, others exhorters; a health committee was appointed, consisting of a doctor and assistants; some were chosen as nurses; other committees were the cook

[17] *Ibid.*
[18] *"Der Reisenden Geschwister Nach Pennsylvanien Diarii 1743."* **Ms.** Beth. Arch.

and his assistants, the steward and his assistants, those who had to wait on the tables, and finally the ship crew, all Moravians, working under Captain Garrison.[19] The third Sea Congregation was similarly organized.[20]

If ever an enterprise bound together a group of adventurers this did. They felt that they must forget all differences and individual pursuits in an undertaking, the success of which depended upon their co-operation and the contribution of each to the common cause. So with the sailing of the ship, they pooled their time and labor for the sake of the group. Further than this they had no definite scheme of social organization when they landed in America. The new social scheme was not definitely planned, but grew upon them gradually, and really did not receive clear and explicit formulation until Bishop Spangenberg returned from Europe and became the general supervisor of the Economy in 1744.

The formative period of the Moravian colony lasted from the founding of the settlement at Bethlehem in 1741 until 1744, with no definite plan for its development and growth as such. Whatever plans Zinzendorf may have had for the Brethren in America concerned the intended Church of God in the Spirit in Pennsylvania. From December 1741 to January 1743, the Count, with all his enthusiasm, tried to effect some sort of union among the many sectarians. The rôle which the Brethren played in the enterprise has been sufficiently described in the previous chapter. The entire attempt was an absolute failure. The Count himself must have been persuaded of this fact by the time he left for Europe.

The Brethren now had to lay their plans anew. Two possible courses were open to them. They had already established some preaching places. Others could be started and developed into Moravian churches by proselyting from other denomina-

---

[19] "*Der Reisenden Geschwister Nach Pennsylvanien Diarii 1743.*" Ms. Beth. Arch.

[20] "*Verzeichnis der lieben See Gemeine on Bord Deal.*" Ms. Beth. Arch. See also "*Catalogus der Geschwister des See Gemeinleins auf dem Schiff Irene,*" and "*Dritte See Gemeine,* Snow-Irene, Captain Garrison arrived in June in eleventh week in New York in May 1749." Ms. Beth. Arch.

tions. The other way was to keep the American Brethren within the European organization, making all the Brethren of both continents subject to the same rules and plans, controlled by one government, and amenable to a central board.

Of the two courses they chose the latter, the former presenting too many obstacles. Lutheran and Reformed clergymen were now in the field organizing their churches, with which most of the Germans interested in any church affiliated themselves. The minor sects were deeply entrenched in their fanatic customs and traditions. In addition, the Brethren in America were ridiculed and even persecuted. The burden of reproach which they had born in Europe weighed heavily upon them here. They had their friends, but the number of their enemies was astounding. All this was added proof that their work was not to win other churches, but rather to preach the gospel among the heathen in the utmost ends of the earth, that is, in America among the Indians and the Negroes. To insure the efficiency of this enterprise they formed little groups of Pilgrims, separated from the world and even from the rest of the Christian Churches. Their aim was to form a holy brotherhood for the practice of personal piety. The European plan, with all its exclusivism, was thus introduced into America, and to it was added the communism of the Sea Congregations. In 1744 there were only three large buildings, one in Nazareth and two in Bethlehem, and some small buildings such as barns and granaries. One of the large buildings was occupied by the married members of the group, the men and women having separate quarters. The single women were in Nazareth, living in the large stone building that Whitefield had intended for a school, and the single men in the other building in Bethlehem. The patriarchal form of government was in force, an elder being the executive and pastoral head, with subsidiary elders over the various divisions. The women were made eldresses over the members of their own sex. Executive conferences of the elders and eldresses were held at stated intervals. Such regulations were especially necessary, since they were quartered in a few overcrowded buildings.

The General Economy proper began at the close of 1744,

when Spangenberg assumed the duties of general superintendent, and terminated, as we shall see, in 1762. This régime was definitely conceived in the minds of those in authority as a form of social structure adapted to all the Moravian communities in America, although it was never carried out in practice except in Bethlehem. Spangenberg returned from Europe with sixteen definite rules, which he, no doubt, worked out with the assistance of Zinzendorf. These were the rules of procedure, known as the "General Plan": [21]

(1) "An itinerant congregation and a local church settlement (*Pilgergemeine, Ortsgemeine*) are to be established and small congregations are to be formed wherever needful and possible." This rule was carefully carried out. The Brethren believed it was their special mission to "go unto the ends of the earth." In order to carry out this mission as effectively and efficiently as possible, those capable of spiritual labor resided in Bethlehem and were called the Church of the Pilgrims (*Pilgergemeine*), or a school of the prophets, from which all America was to be supplied with workers for God. There were two local church settlements (*Ortsgemeine*), one at Nazareth and the other at Bethlehem, who were to support the itinerant congregation in the Lord's work, the former with their farming, and the latter, who were mostly artisans, with their trades and business.

(2) "The itinerants are to have their rendezvous ordinarily at Bethlehem, but are to move about 'as a cloud before the wind of the Lord to fructify all places.'" Bethlehem was the abode of the local preachers, itinerant workers, and missionaries on furlough, all of whom when not otherwise engaged assisted on the farms, especially in the busy harvest season.

(3) "There shall be a central household (*Hausgemeine*) at Bethlehem to have charge of the general establishment, support the itineracy, and abide at the place while the pilgrims are in the field." This rule briefly states the very essence and the whole aim of the social and religious organization of the

[21] "General Plan." Ms. Beth. Arch. These rules in substance are translated by J. M. Levering: *History of Bethlehem, Pa., 1741-1892*, pp. 178, 179.

General Economy, as distinguished from any private economies. It had its headquarters at Bethlehem, but it embraced all the trades and industries as well as the entire personnel of the Brethren at Bethlehem and Nazareth. The large household was governed on a representative basis. The representatives from each division of labor met in regular sessions to consider the problems and promote the work of the various departments. Their plans in turn had to be submitted for execution to the highest central board working with Spangenberg. In addition to this, there were numerous committees such as those on buildings, education, supplies, food, clothing, and sanitation, and numerous secretaries and bookkeepers.

(4) "A house for the single women, and one for the single men, and the organization of the older boys and girls into Choir divisions are to be held in view." This was elaborately carried out to the minutest details. Economic reasons made such a plan necessary. There were not enough houses nor land for each to pursue his private interests and have private family life; hence the introduction of the Choir system into America, whereby the settlers were divided according to age and sex.

(5) "The centralizing of large numbers of single persons, remaining single, in such establishments is not advisable in America, where there is less difficulty connected with instituting married relations than in the European settlements, and married persons are more serviceable." This rule, prompted by the experiences of the European Choirs, anticipated trouble that was bound to come. Therefore, since "married persons were more serviceable," thirty young couples of the second Sea Congregation were married [22] at one time at Marienborn shortly before their sailing, and thirty-one couples of the third Sea Congregation upon their arrival at Bethlehem in May 1749.[23] Married men and women proved to be more patient and contented in this Moravian experiment than single adults, who began to chafe under the rigidity of the monastic Choir system, and at various times threatened to free them-

[22] Levering: *History of Bethlehem,* p. 166.
[23] *"Dritte See Gemeine."* Ms. Beth. Arch. Also Levering: *History of Bethlehem,* p. 234.

selves from it. Especially was this true of the Single Brethren.

(6) "Six farms are to be opened on the Nazareth land, on which groups of people are to be located and organized as a Patriarchal Economy." The practical farmers tilled the soil of the Nazareth farms to support the itinerant congregation; therefore they were called the Patriarchal Economy. In the same year that Spangenberg arrived, preparations were made to develop these farms, and large barns, stables, and granaries were built. Four such farming centers, at Nazareth, Gnadenthal, Christiansbrunn, and Friedenthal, were developed, but two others which were to be called Gnadenhöh and Gnadenstadt were never realized.[24]

(7) "The large house, the Whitefield house at Nazareth, is then to become an institution for children." At first the Single Sisters lived in the Whitefield house, but on Jan. 7, 1749, the nursery was transferred from Bethlehem to it, and it was used thus until 1764. The building still standing is now a museum and the headquarters of the Moravian Historical Society.

(8) "The Brethren in America should not call themselves Protestant or Lutheran or Moravian, but simply Evangelical Brethren and a Brethren's Church." The uncertain position of the Brethren had already provoked much gossip and misunderstanding. Because of their monastic system of Choirs some called them "papists." Zinzendorf on the other hand insisted that he was a Lutheran clergyman, though he was the leader of the Moravians. The new name, Evangelical Brethren, was adopted as less distasteful to their opponents, and less liable to misunderstanding.

(9) "It shall not be the purpose to make everything Moravian (in carrying on the general evangelistic work); but if a church settlement (*Ortsgemeine*) comes into existence at Nazareth, it could be formed as a Moravian congregation, *'ceteris paribus.'* " Under the system of exclusive settlements it was impossible to "make everything Moravian," for church membership implied membership in the social order of these Moravian communities. Financial circumstances did not allow

24.Levering: *History of Bethlehem,* p. 271.

further growth under the existing social order, even were it desirable.

(10) "The work among the Indians is to be prosecuted on apostolic principles (without regard to denominationalism), but Indians who have been baptized under other religions are to be associated with them, unless first spiritually awakened through the ministrations of the Brethren."

(11) "Wyoming must not be lost sight of, for the Ordinarius (Zinzendorf) had the firm conviction that a congregation from among the heathen would arise there." Zinzendorf, himself, had undertaken three journeys among the Indians, the last one being the most extensive. On it he was away from Sept. 21 to Nov. 8, 1742, and went into territory where few white men had dared to venture in upper Susquehanna and into the Wyoming Valley.[25]

(12) "The Synod shall remain a general one, open to all servants of Christ who desire benefit from it for their denominations or for the salvation of their fellowmen. It shall be regarded as a Church of God in the Spirit with a general direction extending among people of all denominations." These so-called General Synods were continued until 1748 and were in the nature of workers' conferences rather than synods. After the seven Union Synods, they were in reality Moravian synods as we have indicated in chapter II.

(13) "The fundamental principles adopted in the first seven Conferences of Religions are to be undeviatingly adhered to."

(14) "The testament of the Ordinarius (at the house of Benezet), made before his departure from Pennsylvania, elucidates those conferences and is not to be ignored." Before Zinzendorf left America, he gathered those who had been loyal to him in the Synods in the house of Benezet and read to them a document of about seventy pages, which he called his will or testament. It contains the main ideas which he desired to leave with the faithful. At great length he instructs them in the method and procedure among the religious groups, the basis of their future harmony, the relation of the Moravians to

[25] Loskiel: *History of the Missions Among the Indians,* vol. II, pp. 24 f.

others, the erection of schools and the education of the children, and the substance of the gospel to be preached.[26]

(15) "In money matters, drafts are to be avoided; and if the issue of a draft becomes necessary (*i.e.*, on Europe), notice must be given long in advance in order not to embarrass the treasury."

(16) "The appointment of general overseers and matrons of the children (*Kinder-Eltern*) is to be had in mind and suitable persons are to be sought."

While these rules related in a loose and general way to the whole Economy, Zinzendorf prescribed very definitely the course of procedure for Spangenberg in another set of rules, called the "Special Plan." [27] The substance of it was that Spangenberg was to discharge the office of Bishop over all denominations, that he was to receive orders from Zinzendorf only, that the latter would receive no communication from America if not signed by him, that his signature must also be attached to any correspondence to the Moravian Synods in Europe, that Spangenberg and his wife were to be in absolute control in America and were to be known as the House-father and House-mother, that he had the power to ordain others when and where necessary, that he was not to call himself Lutheran, Protestant or Moravian, but a free servant of Christ who serves the Moravian Church and is debtor to all.

Such, then, were the simple rules for the members of the General Economy and for Spangenberg, the superintendent, drawn up without legal contracts or formal agreements. Upon this basis they proceeded for ten years until 1754, when changed circumstances and conditions compelled them to draw up what was known as the Brotherly Agreement [28] and also a

[26] *"Bruder Ludwig's Rede zum Abschied und Verlasz mit den einländ-ischen und Europäischen in Pennsylvanian zurückgelassenen Arbeitern, gehalten in Herrn Stephan Bennezet's House in Philadelphia am 29 Dec. 1742/3."* Ms. Beth. Arch.
9 Jan.
[27] *"Special Plan vor Spangenberg mit welchem or anno 1744 nach America abgegangen."* Ms. Beth. Arch.
[28] *"Einige zur Bethlehemschen und Nazarethschen Gemeinschaftlichen Brüder Oeconomie gehörige Momenta."* Ms. Beth. Arch. See Appendix A.

legal contract [29] which everyone had to sign who wanted to be a member of the General Economy.

The only ties that bound them together were their promises, their good will, and the sense of a mission that was peculiarly theirs. Thus with nothing more than a verbal contract it was understood that the members had to donate their time and labor in exchange for no other compensation than food, clothing, and shelter for themselves and their children, and were to receive no other reward than the joy of seeing the gospel preached and the salvation of their souls in return for their willing sacrifices upon the altar. Material reward in the form of wages in such a spiritual enterprise as theirs was for them much beneath the holiness and dignity of their work. They belonged to no man and therefore would accept no man's wages; for, as they themselves said in the Brotherly Agreement of 1754: "We all belong to the Saviour, as IIe is our Lord, and what we have, that all belongs to Him, and He shall dispose of it as pleases Him." [30] They had joined the General Economy not as its servants but as servants of the Lord; therefore they declared: "We do not, accordingly, regard ourselves as men-servants or maid-servants, who serve some man for the sake of wage, and who have for this reason joined the aforesaid Economy in order that they might demand hire or pay for their labor; but we are here as brethren and sisters, who owe themselves to the Saviour, and for whom it is, indeed, a token of grace that they may do all for His sake. We declare, therefore, not only in general, but also in particular each one for himself, that we do not for this time nor for the future pretend to any wage or have reason to pretend to any. We were received into the said Economy with no idea of having, taking, or seeking wage, the Economy having dedicated itself to the service of the Saviour, and with no promise that wage or pay should be given; we, on the contrary, regard it a mark of grace that we are here and may labor according to the above-stated intention." [31]

The private possessions of the members were not surren-

[29] *"Copia des an Gemein—Rath den 12 Nov. sub. Signo a. No. 10 mentionirten Reverses."* Ms. Beth. Arch. See Appendix B.
[30] See Appendix A.   [31] *Ibid.*

dered. Since they were newly arrived immigrants they had no property except that which belonged to the whole Unity of the Brethren. Those who had money deposited it in the treasury of the General Economy without interest. For this sum the depositor received credit in the ledger, but no further security. The depositor could withdraw any desired amount, or all of it, if he so desired.[32]   The land, consisting of more than 12,000 acres, the buildings that were erected on it, and the numerous industries of these thrifty Moravians were not the property of individuals nor of the General Economy, but of the entire Unity of the Brethren in all lands.   The American property was held for the whole Unity in the names of three proprietors, David Nitschmann, Henry Antes, and Spangenberg.[33]   Membership in this society implied a complete surrender of one's time and labor to the service of the Church, or the General Economy, which to the Moravians were one and the same. While the members pledged such submission to the Economy, the latter in turn pledged itself to provide them the necessities of life, now and in their old age.   It was really religious feudalism.[34]

It is obvious from the above account that this Economy was not founded on a purely theoretical basis nor merely as an experiment.   It was the practical result of exigencies in the new situation; the Brethren bound themselves together for purposes of mutual support, protection against the Indians, missionary endeavors, the preservation of the customs of their Fatherland, and the continuance of their religious practices. Nevertheless there was a definite theological idea behind both the European and the American Moravian communities.   After the renewal of the Church, they thought of themselves as a small theocratic republic.   This theocratic idea, and the idea of being God's peculiarly chosen people, was gradually in-

---

[32] Erbe: *Bethlehem, Pa.*, p. 48.

[33] *"Die Gemein Orte oder Settlements der Brüder in Pennsylvanien, Bethlehem, Nazareth und Lititz."*   Ms. Beth. Arch.

[34] *"Beylage zum Monat Junius 1787 der Bethlehemischen Diarii, kurze historische Nachricht vom ersten Anfang des Gemein-Orts Bethlehem, und erster Einrichtung der Brüder Gemeine, daselbst aus archive Nachrichten zusammen gezogen."*   Ms. Beth. Arch.

stilled in their minds by many persecutions. Overwhelmed with troubles they embraced the consoling philosophy that theirs was the lot of God's people, and Scriptural proof was not wanting to confirm this. Such ways of God with his people were past finding out. But for better or for worse, they saw the hand of God directing the individual and community life in its smallest details. As Samuel of old insisted upon a theocratic form of government against the will of Israel and failed, so the Brethren many years later insisted upon a theocratic republic and succeeded as far as was possible in the midst of a world governed by monarchs and over-lords. Such a theocratic community did not allow extensive intermingling with outsiders. The community was a family of which Christ was the head, and their whole system of worship was built about this theocratic idea. It implied that the community life had to be exclusive.

The Bethlehem colony not only had to maintain itself but had to expand and develop its resources and make provision for an increase of its numbers. After the land was secured for the Brethren, they could not look for any further support from Europe; on the contrary, the Brethren abroad soon found themselves in financial stress, and the Brethren in America had to help liquidate their debt.[35] To meet this financial crisis all the members of the Unity of the Brethren had to pay a fixed annual sum into what was known as the *"Mitleidenheit und Tilgung's Fund."* [36]

It was Spangenberg's aim that the General Economy should be self-supporting and completely independent of others. Their own land was to yield the timber and stone for building, produce grain, vegetables, and fruit, flax for clothing, and feed for the stock. Enough stock was to be kept to provide meat, milk, butter, eggs, leather, and wool. Their own mills were to saw the wood, grind the flour, and produce the oil. And all this was to be done by the voluntary labor of the Brethren.[37]

[35] Hutton: *History*, p. 391.
[36] Letter from Spangenberg to Gambold, pastor in Sechem, N. Y. Ms. Beth. Arch.
[37] G. Reichel: *August Gottlieb Spangenberg*, p. 135.

At the head of this organization stood a central board, of which Spangenberg was the chief administrator. There was a general supervisor of the external affairs of the Economy, who was the chairman of a board consisting of the supervisors of the four departments of the Economy—farming, trades, business, and construction. In addition to conferences of the supervisors of these four branches with the general supervisor, who was a member of the central board with Spangenberg, each branch had its own conferences, at which the foremen of the further divisions of labor were represented.

Every trade, business, and industry had to keep accurate accounts, which, in turn, were compiled in a general account book. This was carried out to the very minutest details. In the many account books in the Bethlehem Archives, every pound of butter, every egg, every pound of pork, beef, and mutton, the bushels of various grains, the tons of hay, the number of horses, hogs, cattle, and sheep are recorded on balance sheets.[38]

In 1748, 675 acres of the forest had been cleared and put under cultivation; in 1756, 1,800 acres; and in 1759, 2,454 acres.[39] The amount of grain grown on all the farms in the year from June 1756 to June 1757 was: wheat, 5,034 bushels; rye, 2,436½; barley, 1,031¼; oats, 6,521; buckwheat, 456¼; and millet, 33. Some of the other crops were: hemp, 10½ bushels; flax 421⅛; beans, 45; and peas, 3.[40]

Of live-stock in the same year (1756-1757) they had on hand: cattle 568, born 227, bought 289, total 1,084; sheep 242, born 81, bought 32, total 355; horses 71, born 7, total 78; hogs (by the pound) 1,870 pounds, raised on the farms 6,744, bought 2,221, total 10,835.[41]

As the colony increased, there were not enough products raised on the farms to meet the demand of the Brethren. In the above-mentioned year they bought 1,925⅝ bushels of

[38] In the Bethlehem Archives are to be found over one thousand volumes of these account books.
[39] Erbe: *Bethlehem, Pa.,* p. 58.
[40] "General Account of the year June 1756-1757." Ms. Beth. Arch.
[41] *Ibid.*

wheat, while they sold 713⅜; bought 1,065%₁₆ bushels of rye
and sold 389½; bought 37,440 pounds of beef and sold 5,343;
bought 2,221 pounds of pork and sold 463.[42] In 1747 the
Bethlehem-Nazareth Economy consumed 3,318 bushels of
wheat and 20,578 pounds of meat; [43] in the year 1756-1757 the
consumption was 5,427¼ bushels of wheat and 65,739¾
pounds of beef, 8,377 pounds of pork, and 72 head of sheep.[44]

Thus over a period of ten years the consumption of wheat
was less than doubled, while that of meat was quadrupled.
This indicates the increasing meat ration per capita. In 1747,
when the Brethren were not so well established, they were
wholly dependent on the fertility of the land and made their
manner of living very frugal, adding meat only twice a week to
their diet of soups, baked goods, and vegetables.[45] However,
a decade later their farming industry enabled them to sell
food, and their handicrafts likewise opened up external trade.
They could enjoy a few luxuries and a more generous bill of
fare.

To the cost of providing food for this large family must be
added the expense of clothing for 1,140 [46] persons in 1761, of
the schools within and without the Economy, of the itinerant
preachers and the missionaries and their traveling expenses by
sea. To all this must be added the cost incurred by the extensive building program, consisting in 1759 of 17 congregational and Choir houses, 5 schools, 20 buildings in which the
trades were carried on, 5 mills, 2 inns, and 48 farm buildings,
making a total of 97 buildings.[47]

To meet the expenses of the General Economy, the Brethren
had as a source of income, besides the farms, the various trades,
of which there were thirty-two in 1747 [48] and forty in 1752.[49]
The Brethren in Bethlehem, where most of the trades were

[42] *Ibid.*
[43] Reichel: *Early History*, p. 166.
[44] "General Account of the year June 1756-1757." Ms. Beth. Arch.
[45] Erbe: *Bethlehem, Pa.*, p. 61.
[46] Levering: *History of Bethlehem*, p. 378.
[47] Erbe: *Bethlehem, Pa.*, pp. 78, 79.
[48] Reichel: *Early History*, pp. 169, 170.
[49] Erbe: *Bethlehem, Pa.*, pp. 65, 66.

located, were divided into the following trades and occupations in the year 1759:[50]

Potters	4	Tin-smiths	2
Tanners	6	Nail-smiths	4
Curriers	3	Gunstock-maker	1
Saddlers	3	Turners	3
Purse-makers	3	Cart-wrights	3
Locksmiths	3	Joiners	3
Silversmith	1	Carpenters	4
Farriers	3	Coopers	3
Masons	2	Cooks	3
Mason's helper	1	Keeper of the Cellar	1
Clothmakers	5	Launderers	5
Linen weavers	10	Caretakers of horses	15
Stocking weavers	3	Caretakers of cattle	4
Lace-maker	1	Shepherd	1
Hatters	2	Harvesters	12
Dyers	2	Beer carrier	1
Fullers	2	Congregation store-keeper	1
Tailors	7	Waiter	1
Shoe-makers	13	Choir and house supervisors	2
Book-binder	1	Nurses	2
Physicians	5	Attendant upon strangers	1
Glazier	1	With the Indians	1
Soap-makers	2	Watchman	1
Bakers	4	Night-watchman	1
Millers	2	Bookkeepers	2
Oil millers	2	Secretaries	6
Wood workers	3	Teachers	22
Gardeners	2	Silk manufacturer	1
Arborator	1	Tobacco manufacturer	1
Butcher	1	Warder	1
Store-keepers	3	Remaining Brethren	17
Inn-keepers	3	Total	227

The Brethren on the Nazareth lands at Nazareth, Gnaden-thal, Christiansbrunn, and Friedensthal were distributed in a similar way according to their abilities. At Christiansbrunn,

[50] "*Vertheilung der Brüder in Bethlehem in ihre verschiedene Hand-werke und andern Arbeiten.*" Ms. Beth. Arch.

where a colony of 88 single men located and organized in 1749, the division of labor was as follows: [51]

Farmers	3	Baker	1
Caretakers of the oxen	2	Caretaker	2
Stable attendants	3	Caretaker of cattle	6
Shoe-makers	3	Shepherd	1
Cook	1	Hackel-smith	1
Brewers	2	Threshers	16
Carpenter	1	Secretaries	2
Joiners	3	Wood-choppers	9
Mason	1	Distillers	2
Smiths	2	Malt manufacturer	1
Saw-miller	1	Steward	1
Butcher	1	Lector	1
Shirt-mender	1	Overseer	1
Gardener	1	Warder	1
Tailors	3	Choir supervisor	1
Launderers	2	Nurse	1
Night-watchman	1	Musicians	11

Total 88

Each of the trades had its masters and apprentices. There were stated conferences of the masters, the purpose of which was to see that a high quality of product was maintained, to regulate prices, to meet outside competition, and to provide proper training for those in apprenticeship. When outsiders came to buy wares, there was to be no bickering about prices; on the contrary the prices set at the tradesmen's conferences were to be strictly observed.[52]

Thus the General Economy had become a bee-hive of activity. The Brethren were clothed with fabrics their own hands and machinery had woven, among which were to be found eleven qualities of linen. Their large pottery, the products of which were in great demand by outsiders, became famous. The brewery in Christiansbrunn supplied not only the Breth-

[51] *"Vertheilung der Brüder in Christiansbrunn in ihre verschiedene Handwerke und andern Arbeiten."* Ms. Beth. Arch.

[52] Spangenberg's *"Gedanken die Gemeinen und Pilgersache in Pennsylvania betreffend."* Ms. Beth. Arch.

ren but also their neighbors with beer. The large forge of
those days has developed into the present Bethlehem Steel
Corporation, and three large saw-mills converted the rough-
hewn timbers into building materials.[53]   Spangenberg's wife
organized and supervised the industries among the women.
They were employed in work suited to their abilities, such as
baking, weaving, spinning, dyeing, and tailoring.   Since the
Economy was one large family, the united strength of the
group was exerted where the need was the greatest.   In the
busy seasons on the farms, some of the tradesmen left their
shops to help in the harvest fields;[54] and when members of
the Pilgrim Congregation were not engaged, or were at home
on furlough, they had to work wherever they could be of assistance.[55]

The baker, the butcher, the potter, the weaver, the smith,
the farmer, and others engaged in secular pursuits had agreed
to make the whole *Unitas Fratrum* the direct recipient of the
benefits derived from the consolidation of their time and labor.
We are making distinctions that did not exist if we separate
the community and the Church.   The various settlements of
the Economy were communal families, all laboring for the
same Church.

[53] Erbe: *Bethlehem, Pa.*, pp. 69-71.
[54] *Ibid.*, p. 67.
[55] Spangenberg's *"Gedanken die Gemeine und Pilgersache in Pennsylvanien betreffend—Die Öconomie in Beth."*   Ms. Beth. Arch.

CHAPTER IV

A HOLY BROTHERHOOD

THE Brethren, under the guidance of the Count, and in accordance with their own ideals of a holy brotherhood, erected a social structure that was peculiarly Moravian. As the small group at Herrnhut grew in numbers, their problems became proportionately complex. In 1727 there were about three hundred on the Count's estate. While many went as missionaries, there had to be a strong enough force at the home base to support them. There was a constant danger of losing young men and women, unless provisions were made to give them employment and housing. These needs were met in the Choir arrangement, which at first was used only with respect to the single men and single women, but later applied to all classes. Large houses were erected for them in Herrnhut, where the young men and the young women lived, segregated and under strict supervision. Each house had sleeping quarters, a place for worship, a kitchen, and a dining-room. In connection with these institutions there were workshops, where the men, who were mostly mechanics, carried on their trades, and the women their weaving and needle-work. Each retained his earnings (except in the years of the General Economy in America) and paid for his room and board. The exclusive village system of Herrnhut and the pioneer conditions in America compelled them to adopt some such arrangement. This was the beginning of the Choir system, which was soon elaborated and applied to all the Brethren. The devout Brethren saw in all events, especially in the origin of the Choirs, a religious significance. The establishment of these houses for the single men and women was considered as a special covenant of grace, whereby the inmates pledged themselves to growth in piety and spiritual knowledge.

93

In 1727 Zinzendorf had established an orphanage as a boarding school for boys and girls, very similar to the famous orphanage at Halle. After his return from America in 1743, he abandoned the Halle tradition of admitting children from any and all parents, and also of grouping the children on the basis of conversion and religious experience. A similar orphanage was established at Herrnhaag. The children were now divided according to age and sex, and instruction was provided according to the Choir divisions. The children, including those of pre-school age, the young people, and parents were all considered as belonging to the congregation. The settlement was the Church, and the Church was the settlement. In this holy brotherhood distinctions between the secular and the sacred in their community life did not exist. The Choirs, which served the community in an economic and educational way, were made to serve religious purposes also.

The Brethren were interested in a settlement the chief aim of which was to praise God and serve Him. They were interested in things of this world only in so far as they furthered this end. As a result they were willing to forego luxuries and undergo privations. The community was arranged so that physical needs made the least possible demand on their time and money, which were the Lord's. The economic advantages of an efficient economy were regarded as secondary. But the fact remained that both their religion and their physical environment demanded an efficient community organization. The Choir arrangement adequately served this end. Under this system food and clothing could be bought in large quantities; and one roof over many heads simplified the lodging problem.

Although the houses of the Single Brethren and Single Sisters were erected in Herrnhut before the exile of the Count in 1736, this new arrangement was not applied to all ages until after his exile. It was the formation of the Pilgrim Congregation, which traveled from place to place with the Count in his exile, that made a division according to age and sex not only practical but economically necessary. The Count's exile forced him to take the executive officers of the Brethren with him. Instead of naming this traveling group the administrative

RECEPTION INTO THE BRETHREN'S CHURCH

(A) The Pastor reading the Liturgy. (BB) Deacons receiving new Brethren with the Holy Kiss. (CC) Deaconesses receiving new Sisters in the same manner. (DD) Brethren and Sisters of the Congregation.

board, they called it a Pilgrim Congregation. Thus the officers with their families went from place to place. Under such circumstances the luxury of family life had to be sacrificed as economically unsound. This traveling of the Pilgrim Congregation proved so costly that after a few years it was abandoned, and they settled permanently in the Wetterau.

The activities of the Pilgrim Congregation are described in the following quotation: "In the beginning of March, therefore, his [Zinzendorf's] household in Geneva was complete and consisted in all of from forty to fifty persons. The Count himself with the Countess and children, with those whom he wished to have near him resided in the 'Plein Palais'; the rest were divided into other houses, according to their several choirs. The Count's residence, therefore, constituted a little church in Geneva, with all its different choirs. Each choir held first its own matins. The whole church then came together, and the Count generally gave them an address. At eight o'clock in the evening they again assembled, and edified each other with singing; on which a Bible lesson followed with some of the learned brethren, at which others were also present. Afterwards the brethren and sisters assembled, who divided the hours with each other from four in the morning till midnight for intercession and converse with the Lord. At the same time there was an evening service for those who were not of that company; and from twelve till four oclock, there was a night-watch for prayer, which was held by the brethren in turns. Besides this, the members of this domestic assembly were divided into little companies according to their sex, and the choirs to which they belonged, for the purpose of promoting their love to each other, and their advancement in the divine life." [1]

This description not only affirms the view that the group considered itself a holy brotherhood, but also shows that the Choir system was applied to all ages in this Pilgrim Congregation. What Spangenberg writes from America also supports the statement that the elaborate Choir plan was conceived in these travels. "Our married people are living as if they were

[1] Spangenberg: *Life of Count Zinzendorf*, pp. 282, 283.

still traveling, the husbands and the wives and the children each for themselves." [2] These Choirs were obviously not intended to destroy family life but were adopted as a temporary expedient necessitated by the conditions of travel and poverty. However, they were believed to be as practical in the settlements as in the Pilgrim Congregation, and therefore took hold at Herrnhut and in the Wetterau.

This plan eventually proved to be a great educational device far in advance of its time. The division of the congregation according to age and sex enlarged the problem of providing instruction, for now more instructors and helpers were required and subject-matter and methods had to be accommodated to the capacities of the different groups. In the year 1755 Spangenberg wrote that in America there were about three hundred children in the institutions, and that the teachers and the helpers, who sew, cook, and wash, numbered about eighty.[3] Modern educators have credited the Count with being an educator almost two hundred years ahead of his time, but, as we have seen, his system developed out of a social and economic necessity; his educational policy was an after-thought, suggested by the system itself. At this distance the effect is easily mistaken for the cause.

Similarly theologians have found the reason for the elaborate Choir system in the Count's theological convictions. A Moravian theologian writes: "The subordination of the family life to the 'choir' regulations took place only after Zinzendorf had developed the theological conceptions which he deduced from the truth that the perfect life of Christ as well as His sufferings and death avail for man's salvation." [4] But these meritorious effects of the life of Christ were not stressed by Zinzendorf until 1741, when he had been in Wetterau for some time; the Choir system in the Pilgrim Congregation was in operation before that. After the system had been put into effect, the theory grew that since Christ passed through all the stages corresponding to the various Choirs, from infancy to manhood, his mer-

[2] Unttendörfer and Schmidt: *Die Brüder,* p. 107.
[3] Letter to J. P. Weiss, Feb. 23, 1755. Ms. Beth. Arch.
[4] Hamilton: *History,* p. 42. Also Hutton: *History,* p. 221.

itorious life is immediately applicable to each division. Jesus was a perfect example for all classes and conditions of men from the cradle to the grave. This new theological concept was the effect and not the cause of the Choirs. And what could have been more natural? Zinzendorf often spoke to the various Choirs, and most likely chose his topics from those years of Christ's life which corresponded to the age of the Choir he was addressing.

The Choir system of Europe was carried out even more extensively in America. The reasons of economy for which it was instituted in Europe were even stronger in America. The first few years in America, the members of the Choirs lived in different rooms of the same building; but as their numbers increased and new buildings were erected, they occupied separate houses. In 1748 the Single Brethren built a house for themselves (which is now part of the Women's Seminary), and the building vacated by them became the living quarters of the Single Sisters. The older girls were then in Bethlehem, and the younger girls in Nazareth, while the small boys were on Henry Antes' farm. The married men and the married women lived separately in two buildings a short distance north of where the Church in Bethlehem now stands. Even the children of pre-school age were taken charge of by the Church. When children became eighteen months of age, they were placed in nurseries.[5] As soon as provisions could be made, the widows and widowers also were given their separate living quarters. The married people, the widowers, the widows, the unmarried men, the unmarried women, the older boys, the older girls, the little boys, and the little girls constituted the various Choirs.

The garb of these Brethren was distinctive and simple. A cap called a *"Schnepfen Haube"* because it was in the shape of a snipe's bill was worn by the women and girls. It fitted tightly over the head and was held in place by a broad band of lace tied around the forehead. It was fastened by a ribbon under the chin. The color of these ribbons identified the Choir to which the wearer belonged. Married women wore a light

[5] Reichel: *Early History,* p. 164.

blue, widows white, Single Sisters pink, girls crimson, and the little children scarlet. The men wore a straight, unlapelled, dark coat, a broad-brimmed, low-crowned hat, knee-buckled trousers, and a broad round-toed shoe. The uniformity in dress, with its cloister flavor, immediately branded them as belonging to some religious order. Indeed, the Brethren were almost monastically organized. It was a holy brotherhood.

The emphasis in these Choirs became increasingly religious. The Brethren lived to glorify God. In the Choirs the faith of the fathers was carefully nurtured and the supply of missionaries replenished. And the fathers of the Church, by strict discipline and supervision and a constant dwelling on religious themes in song and speech, sought to make their religious experience the experience of their children also. At the head of each Choir was a supervisor with a number of helpers, who were responsible for the spiritual welfare of their wards. Each Choir attended public services in a body, and in addition had services of its own. To afford opportunity for all the members to participate, each Choir was divided into "bands," which met for prayer, song, and testimony. The married Choir, for example, was divided into five groups: the newly married, those married several years, the elderly couples, the nursing mothers, and the pregnant.[6]

The training and education of the young was entirely in the hands of the Church. Distinctions between secular and religious education did not exist for these Brethren. The only kind of wisdom they were striving after was that which began with "the fear of the Lord." From the earliest years children were taught that they belonged more to the Church than to their parents. They became the property of the Church, and it was expected that when they grew up they should serve the institution which had nurtured and cared for them in their childhood and adolescence. The basis for the wide-spread mission work of the Moravians is found chiefly in their firm belief that the Church had first claim on their lives. None could be compelled to work for the Church, but all had to be either within or without its walls. Those who were within

[6] Erbe: *Bethlehem, Pa.,* p. 42.

were the servants of the Church, and any who objected had
to move beyond its bounds. Such rebels automatically ostra-
cised themselves from Moravian society. But most of the
young Moravians knew no other world than the one they
lived in, which the fathers of the Church had carefully walled
in. Their ideals of purity and piety in religion could best be
realized by keeping themselves "unspotted from the world,"
by retreating safely within the Choir walls.

The claims of the Church upon the individual completely
broke up the family circle. The training of the children by the
Church and for the Church meant that they were taken from
their parents at a tender age and put under the strict religious
discipline of the institutionalized Choir houses, which in many
respects resembled military academies more than homes.
When later they were called upon to go into distant mission
fields, their past training made it easier for them, since they
had very few parental and home ties to break.

In connection with each of the Choirs there was a celebration once a year, commemorating some outstanding event in
the history of the Church. There was also an annual festival
of the combined Choirs. Before members of the Choirs could
enter upon these festivities, they had to have personal interviews with their respective superintendents to receive admonition and make inquiries about their souls. These interviews,
called "Speakings" (*Sprechen*), were held monthly and also
previous to the Communion services.[7] They were not like the
Roman Catholic Confession, although they were so regarded
by outsiders.

The appointed festival days for the various Choirs were:
April 30, for the widows; May 4, for the Single Sisters; June
4, for the older girls; July 9, for the older boys; August 17,
for the children; August 29, for the Single Brethren; August
31, for the widowers; September 7, for the married couples.
The service of worship at these festivals consisted of hymns,
prayer, Choir litanies, and a Love Feast. Vocal and instru-

---

[7] On Dec. 3, 1751, Seidel was the spiritual advisor at these interviews
of the Single Brethren in Christiansbrunn. *"Das Chor Gemein Diarium
in Christiansbrunn."* Ms. Beth. Arch.

mental music was always given a prominent part in these festivals. The Choir litanies of these festivals emphasize the merits which Christ can bestow upon the members of each particular Choir, since he passed through all the stages of life.[8] In these litanies the doctrines of the Trinity and the Atonement through Christ's blood were set forth, and the claim of the Brethren that they preach nothing but the crucified Christ is amply corroborated. The children as well as the adults were deeply impressed by the orderliness of these services, the sounds of the instruments, and the rhythm of the antiphonal singing. Their emotions were aroused and their imaginations stimulated, and the Brethren interpreted their feelings as unmistakable signs of the presence of the Holy Spirit. "He revealed to babes what he kept hidden from the wise."

The emphasis in these Choir litanies on the merits of the various stages in the life of Christ is illustrated in the following hymn:

> Lamb of God my Saviour!
> Explain before me
> Thy matchless love, and by thy grace procure me
> A mind like thine.
>
> Thy humiliation
> In leaving heaven,
> In being poor, and to a stable driven,
> Teach me to stoop.
>
> Thy birth of a virgin,
> Make me live chastely,
> Unspotted from the world, and manifestly
> Sealed for the Lord.
>
> Thy flight into Egypt
> In such great danger,
> Teach me to be a pilgrim here and stranger
> In every place!
>
> Thine innocent Childhood
> And meek behaviour,

[8] A litany for each Choir is to be found in *The Litany Book,* London, 1759.

Teach me to be a little child for ever
Before thy face.

Thy wond'rous obedience
And true subjection
Unto thy parents, melt to like affection
My stubborn heart.

Thy carpenter's labour,
Thy work and travel;
Daily preserve my handiwork from evil,
And bless my toil.

Thy good will to all men
By thee created,
Teach me to honour all, and tender hearted
Behave to all.

Thy forty days fasting,
Thy self denial,
Thy being sorely tried in every trial
Deliver me.[9]

In connection with the Choir festivals there were Love Feasts. This custom was revived by the Moravian Church after the memorable celebration of the Lord's Supper on August 13, 1727, when they experienced a new spirit of brotherly love and God's Spirit among them. These Love Feasts were a revival of the "*agape*" of the early Christians, a common meal of which the learned and the illiterate, freemen and bondsmen, rich and poor, partook. The Love Feasts, which disregarded rank and position, impressed the Brethren with their brotherhood.

There were four kinds of Love Feasts: those for the entire congregation, including old and young; the Choir Love Feasts; workers' Love Feasts; and those preceding the Holy Communion for communicant members only. At first, these Love Feasts were held in connection with many occasions, many small festivals and social gatherings: at weddings, funerals, conferences, on days of commemoration, anniversaries, at meet-

[9] *Collection of Hymns* (1754), part II, no. 148.

ing and departure of friends; and all the birthdays were observed with little home Love Feasts. In the beginning, enough
food was served at these Love Feasts to satisfy hunger.

The workers' Love Feasts were numerous. With the opening of the harvest season the reapers held an early morning
Love Feast. In addition to the common meal, they had a short
devotional service and a discourse on the rules of diet. After
that the sickles were handed out, and the whole band set off
for the harvest field to the accompaniment of music. When
the Single Brethren went to the forest for several days to fell
trees, they had a Love Feast before they started and another
when they returned. When the carpenters had completed the
oil-mill, they observed the occasion with a Love Feast. The
spinners had a Love Feast once a week.[10] "The joiners, the
weavers, the cartwrights, the smiths, the hewers of wood, the
milkers of cows, the knitters, the sewers, the cooks, the washer-
women—all had their special lovefeasts."[11] All this tended
to impress the laborers with the religious character of their
work.

As they made no distinction between secular and religious
education, so they did not distinguish between secular and religious work. All work was religious. A religious spirit was
put into the most menial tasks. Milking, spinning, washing,
knitting, and all the other occupations of the Brethren were
services unto God, because the purpose of them was not to
accumulate wealth but to support the itinerant preachers,
teachers, and missionaries. As the apostle Paul worked with
his hands that he might preach the gospel without cost to
others, so the Brethren of the stationed congregations (*Ortsgemeine*) were diligent in their tasks as the chief servants of
the Pilgrim Congregation.[12] The caretaker of the stable was
on a mission for the Lord as well as the missionary among the
savage Indians.

"At Bethlehem the Brethren accounted it an honour to chop
wood for the Master's sake; and the fireman, said Spangen-

10 Gerhard Reichel: *August Gottlieb Spangenberg*, p. 139.
11 Hutton: *History*, p. 375.
12 Erbe: *Bethlehem, Pa.*, p. 89.

berg, felt his post as important 'as if he were guarding the Ark of the Covenant.' " [13]   "They mix the Saviour and his blood into their harrowing, mowing, washing, spinning, in short, into everything.   The cattle yard becomes a temple of grace which is conducted in a priestly manner." [14]   Therefore Spangenberg could write: "In our Economy the spiritual and the physical are as closely united as a man's body and soul, and each has a strong influence upon the other.   As soon as all is not well with a brother's heart, so soon we notice it in his work. But when he is happy in Jesus' wounds, and his love to the Lamb is tender, then one notices that also immediately in his outward conduct." [15]

Their work was part of their devotions.   For each occupation special hymns were composed and sung.   Some of these were composed by Spangenberg but most of them by the workers themselves.   There were hymns for the shepherds, ploughers, threshers, reapers, spinners, knitters, washers, and tailors. At a Love Feast of the attendants of the barn in Bethlehem on December 31, 1753, the workers sang:

> *Gelobet seyst du Jesu Christ*
> *Du unser lieber Herr,*
> *Dasz du ein Mensch geboren bist*
> *Du Haupt vom Vater her,*
> *Im Stalle lagst zu Bethlehem*
> *Nicht nur vor jenem lieben Sem;*
> *Nein, auch vor den verfluchten Cham;*
> *Als auch vor Japhets Stamm.*[16]

Spangenberg composed a hymn for the spinners:

> Know ye sisters, in this way
> Is your work a blessing,
> If for Jesus' sake you spin,
> Toiling without ceasing.

---

[13] *Ibid.*, p. 374.
[14] Unttendörfer and Schmidt: *Die Brüder,* p. 106.
[15] *Ibid.*
[16] *"Auf ein Liebes Mahl der Stall—Brüder in Bethlehem, Dec. 31, 1753."*   Ms. Beth. Arch.

> Spin and weave; compelled by love;
> Sew and wash with fervor,
> And the Saviour's grace and love
> Make you glad for ever.[17]

All work was holy because everything was the Lord's, and the milkers, the washers, and those who winnowed the grain needed to be consecrated.

> *Du Süsster Herzbezwinger,*
> *Die Melker, Wäscher, Schwinger,*
> *Die sehen jetzt auf Dich;*
> *Und warten mit verlangen,*
> *Um Segen zu empfangen*
> *Aus Deinem blut'gen Seitenstich.*
>
> *Du bist bei allen Dingen*
> *Beim Melken, Waschen, Schwingen,*
> *Das einz'ge Augenmerk,*
> *Dir leben wir auf Erden,*
> *Bis wir Dich sehen werden,*
> *Dir thut man jedes Tagewerk.*[18]

An accompaniment of instrumental music during their labors aroused their ambition and kindled their imagination. In the Single Brethren Choir alone at Christiansbrunn in the year 1759, there were eleven musicians.[19] With the sound of music they proceeded to the harvest field. Preceded by trumpeters the tired Single Brethren went to work on their Choir House every evening, after they had spent the day in the fields or elsewhere; and when they had finished these quarters, to the tune of triumphant music they took possession.[20]

When the Love Feast had gradually become limited to Church festivals and strictly religious services, it ceased to be a common meal and assumed a symbolical meaning, which lay in the ceremony of breaking and eating bread together. The general congregational Love Feasts were joyous occasions. The

---

[17] Reichel: *Early History,* p. 174.
[18] *Ibid.,* p. 175.
[19] *"Vertheilung der Brüder in Christiansbrunn, 1759."* Ms. Beth. Arch.
[20] Levering: *History of Bethlehem, Pa.,* pp. 198, 199.

Brethren, old and young, assembled in the church on Sunday afternoons. Half of the church was occupied by the women and girls, seated according to their Choir membership, indicated by the color of the ribbons in their caps. The men and boys occupied the other half of the church. All co-operated to make the service orderly and dignified. Even the young were aware of the seriousness of defiling the holiness of the Lord's temple. The organ, accompanied by violins and trumpets, played softly, while some of the men and women distributed fresh buns or cakes to the whole congregation. Then coffee was carried in on large trays and distributed.

Under this system no one could avoid being influenced in some way by the elders or leaders. The Church reached deep into the life of everyone. Those who were without the desired religious experience were carefully nurtured and always remembered in prayer. So zealous were the Brethren that they hardly allowed time for natural religious growth. Many were stimulated into a religious experience and were "spoon-fed" upon the bread which the fathers generously provided. Only now and then did someone rebel against this democratic religious autocracy. Most of the Brethren either had a religious experience, or pretended to have it. In the latter case they had the choice of being hypocrites or of forfeiting the privileges which the system afforded. Many of those who chose the former did so unconsciously, for under the existing conditions religion became more and more an external conformity: a repetition of litanies that became increasingly meaningless, and the singing of hymns that were foreign to their experience. But on the whole the Moravian litanies and feasts have remained to this day a genuine expression of a common devotion and an inspiring participation in the life of a single family.

CHAPTER V

DEVOTIONS

IT is said that one day while Zinzendorf was burning papers, a piece fell to the ground untouched by the fire. When the Count saw these words on it:

> Oh, let us in Thy nail-prints see,
> Our calling and election free,

he, and those to whom he told the incident, looked upon it as a call from above.

The sense of Christ's immediate presence in the daily routine of individual and congregational life dominated their devotions and made them extremely vivid. In a description of the rite (on Nov. 13, 1756) commemorating the Chief Eldership of Jesus, a participant says: "The Redeemer's presence was so perceptibly felt as to stop words, prayer, singing and everything. Such a perception of Thy nearness! O my God! Almost every eye was in tears while we lay prostrate on the ground. About twenty-four persons were present; I cannot, I will not describe it. It was something like the Lord's celebration of his Last Supper, or as if He had come to fetch us home; but we are all as yet in the body, though not without feeling and foretaste of what will be experienced when He shall come to close the day and make an end of all trials." [1]

The idea of a God detailed to oversee the physical, material, and external conditions of his people, gave them almost a sense perception of God. The presence of Christ became actual and physical to them, as is seen in all their early hymns. The vivid imagery of the body, the corpse, the blood, the wounds, and sweat was a natural expression of their sensual conceptions. His providential guidance and physical presence was made a

[1] Benham: *Memoirs*, p. 321.

106

Das anbeten vor dem HERREN.   Prosternation devant le Seigneur.

PROSTRATION BEFORE THE LORD

compelling reality to them, not by reason, nor even by faith, but by vivid symbolism and sensual imagery. This was done in the most childlike simplicity, without restraint, sham, or erudition. Their religious exercises were characterized by their own term, *Einfalt*. Concerning the first Sea Congregation, Spangenberg wrote: "They are certainly little children, who suck the breasts of divine grace, and know of no danger nor misfortunes, nor even think of any. They are protected under the wings of the Lord with tender care, like chickens under the wings of a hen. They know of nothing else, but this one thing: Our Saviour loves us poor sinners, for he died for us. We feel his love, and need not fear his wrath, for he has shed his blood for us. We love each other, and our fellowship is blessed." [2]

This childlike simplicity in their devotions was natural to them because their faith was equally simple. One of their hymns says:

> By various maxims, forms, and rules,
> That passed for wisdom in the schools,
> I strove my passion to restrain;
> But all my efforts proved in vain.
>
> But since my Saviour I have known,
> My rules are all reduced to one;
> To keep my Lord by faith in view,
> This strength supplies, and motives too.

Such a simple faith in God's redeeming love stimulated an extravagant gratitude for it, which manifested itself in devotional observances and religious living, rather than in formulated creeds. The belief in the approachableness of God, because he can be felt physically, explains the peculiar quality of Moravian worship.

To the childlike minds of these Moravians, these sensual symbols were a means of approach to concrete reality; they served as the medium between the feebleness of their understanding, to which they gave frequent expression, and the pro-

[2] Ledderhose: *Life of A. G. Spangenberg,* p. 49.

fundity of the atonement in Christ. The direct perception of
the agony of Christ transformed the sense of their own hardships into the ecstatic joy of communion with the Redeemer.
For example, when Spangenberg was dismissed from the University of Halle, because of differences with the faculty, he
wrote to Leonard Dober: "The people of Halle received me as
an angel of God, and loaded me with honours and praise; this
made me fear and tremble. I cried unto the Lord to preserve
me from the snare of worldly grandeur, and to keep me a fool
in Christ. The Lord heard my prayer and delivered me from
my troubles. My want of prudence and my stubborn conduct
were overruled for the furtherance of his gracious designs.
Blessed be his holy name." [3]

The religious life of the Brethren of the Renewed Church
centered in their hymns, for the "hymn-sermon" was their
distinctive invention. It was peculiarly adapted to their need
of giving vivid, sensual form to their ideas. In the preface to
the 1754 English edition, the editor says: "Hymns surely
ought to be supposed a faithful, if not the faithfulest, picture
and conveyance of the heart."

The use of hymn verses was combined with the use of the
Loosungen or Daily Scripture Texts. After 1731 texts from
the Bible for each day in the year were collected in book form
and printed in German, English, French, Danish, Swedish, and
every other language in which the Brethren labored. These
books were put in possession of all the congregations and mission stations at the beginning of each year. The fact that the
Brethren in many parts of the world were meditating upon
identical texts, served to maintain a unity of thought as well as
a unity in organization. And since these Daily Texts were used
in both personal and group devotions and at congregational and
public meetings, the sense of the power of their united prayers
was very real.

These Texts were considered as God's comment on whatever
difficulties or joys the particular day might have in store for
them. Through these, God spoke to them. On June 2, 1736,
when the Herrnhuters held a conference to discuss the matter

[3] Ledderhose: *Life of A. G. Spangenberg,* pp. 20, 21.

of leaving the place because of persecution, the text was: "It is not necessary that you leave, give them to eat." [4]   On May 22, 1728, when they heard that two of their brethren, Nitschmann and Schmidt, had been arrested, the text for the day was: "How great shall be my joy, if I remain true to thee." [5]   For them, nothing occurred by chance; everything was providential, and God led them with his own hand.

A knowledge of the hymnal as well as of the Bible was required for inspiration and instruction.   Instead of singing all the stanzas of a hymn or several stanzas of the same hymn, they sang selected stanzas from many hymns, successively or interspersed by prayer, testimony or address, according to the nature of the service.   The result of these "hymn-sermons" was the composite authorship of many of the hymns, and also the preparation of hymn books in which verses from many hymns were arranged according to subject-matter.   Thus a new and endless combination of verses could be made according to the subject under discussion.   "It is supposed that not less than 70,000 hymns are in existence, under the various forms of composition in which they have appeared from time to time." [6]

In the introduction of the *Christliches Gesang-Buch* (1735) we read: "Most of the hymns that you see here are used in our church, though not as they stand here, but after our method of singing, in which materials are repeated in song.   We do not sing entire hymns of ten or twenty stanzas, but as many half and whole stanzas of many hymns as the unity of the subject requires.   Most of the members of the Congregation are accustomed . . . to sing along at once in such a hymn-sermon without a book, since God gives them the grace to hold easily in heart and memory whatever with us serves a purpose.   From the nature of the case it is evident that the hymns are mixed in innumerable ways, and on that account it becomes impossible to edit a truly *Herrnhuterisch* hymn-book."   In an introduction to the *Zugaben* we read: "The *Anhänge* and *Zugaben*

[4] Unttendörfer and Schmidt: *Die Brüder*, p. 221.
[5] *Ibid.*, p. 218.
[6] James Henry: *Sketches*, p. 141.

have for some years no longer been hymn-books, but merely collections of *Elegantien, Cantaten, Carminibus* and some hymns. Whoever has visited our song services knows that we do not use books, that the so-called *Herrnhutisches Gesangbuch* is known to few of us, and that our singing is always a sequence of thoughts and changes every day according to the subjects."

The hymnals now in use in the Moravian congregations are abridgments of the older hymnals. The *Christliches Gesang-Buch der Evangelischen Brüder Gemeinen* (1735) was the first hymnal of the Brethren as a reorganized Church. It was a revised edition of an earlier hymnal, *Sammlung geistlicher und lieblicher Lieder*, by Zinzendorf, the first edition of which appeared in 1725. The revised edition of 1735 contains a collection of 972 hymns, which are "translations and adaptations from the Primitive Church, classic hymns from the Latin Church, hymns of the Reformation, hymns from the Ancient *Unitas Fratrum*, and hymns contributed by Zinzendorf and his contemporaries in the Renewed Moravian Church."

After this, sixteen supplements appeared, the first twelve of which are called *Anhänge* (1737-1745), and the last four, *Zugaben* (1749). These are the products of the Brethren of the Renewed Church, a total of 2,357 hymns. The *Zugaben* contain the hymns written during the emotional Wetteravian period.

In 1754 a hymn-book for the English Churches was edited, called *A Collection of Hymns of the Children of God in all ages, from the beginning till now.* It was "designed chiefly for the use of the congregations in union with the Brethren's Church." It is divided into two parts, the first "containing hymns of the Church of God in preceding times," and the second "hymns of the present congregation of the Brethren." The first part has 695 hymns, of which, by reason of their source, the majority are translations. The second part, containing the hymns of the renewed Brethren's Church, has 460 hymns, to which are added twenty-six pages of "single verses" and the Church Litany. The hymns of the second part are both translations from the German and those written in the English language. The English translations cannot do justice to the thought expressed in the German original. Much of it seems crude, due especially to the fact that the translators sought to preserve the rhythm and the number of syllables to fit the tunes.

"The tunes principally used were collected and published by the Rev. C. Gregor, in Germany, entitled, *Choral Buch, enthaltend alle zu dem Gesangbuch der Evangelischen Brüdergemeinen vom Jahr 1778, Gehörige Melodien:* Leipzig, 1784. These tunes were set in the tenor clef and written in semibreves, and figured for thorough bass. They are productions of the best masters, and are religious emanations from the very soul of the science of music. They were not named but numbered, and 9, 10, 15, 22, 26, or any other number in the tune book, was as familiar to the organist as Meer, Hotham, or any other cognomen to modern productions. But they were also set to particular hymns, and the first line of almost any one of them was sufficient indication of the melody to follow." [7] The organist was required to know about 400 church tunes, since the minister generally commenced the singing of the hymn without announcing the words. The organist and the congregation joined in as soon as they recognized the hymn.

In addition to the organ the trombone was a favorite instrument. Although trombones were used in the State Churches of Europe, in America these instruments were so exclusively used by the Brethren that it became a distinctive feature of their church. The "trombone choir" played at all solemn religious festivities. This instrument came to be so peculiarly associated with church use that nothing but hymn tunes and other compositions of a dignified character were played on it. From the belfry of the church, at an early hour, the trombonists announced the great church festivals. Although their services were required at most of the major church devotionals, their most frequent function was to announce the death of a member from the belfry of the church. The first and last tunes used in this announcement were the same for all members; the middle tune indicated the Choir to which the deceased belonged.

[7] Ritter: *Church in Philadelphia*, p. 149.

What has been said affords a picture of the characteristic congregational participation in the Brethren's worship, which continued as long as Moravianism remained primarily a lay movement. The religion of the exiles in Herrnhut was not imposed by an ecclesiastical system, but was a spontaneous expression of the group. Although the introduction of the elaborate Choir and "band" system by Zinzendorf later proved to be the beginning of a rigid ecclesiasticism, these very Choirs and "bands" for many years kept Moravianism a lay movement and threw the responsibility of their religion upon the congregations instead of on the clergy. The division of the congregation into Choirs according to age, sex, and condition of life, and the division of these larger groups into "bands" or "little societies" according to temperaments, inclinations, and preferences, all tended to keep the whole Moravian movement close to the people. Spangenberg said: "We must not forget the little societies, otherwise we shall come into the way of the religions where everything depends upon the preacher, and what is not done by him, remains undone." [8]

The chief doctrine of Zinzendorf, which was the vicarious suffering of Christ, found continual expression in the imagery of his blood, wounds, agony, and pain. The emphasis in the separate Choir meetings was on the doctrine that the merits of Christ's whole life from his birth to his death can be appropriated by man, and that his merits and virtues have particular benefits for each stage of life from the cradle to the grave. What the peculiar benefits for each group were we find in the hymns and litanies composed or arranged for the different Choirs.

Every Sunday afternoon there was a meeting of the small children's Choir. A hymn that Zinzendorf wrote for the children contains the following:

> My Saviour, hear; thou for my good
> Wert pleased a child to be,
> And thou didst shed thy precious blood
> Upon the cross for me.

[8] Unttendörfer and Schmidt: *Die Brüder,* p. 159.

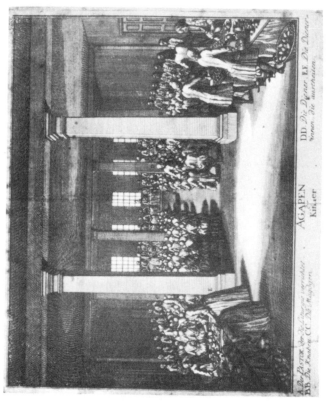

THE CHILDREN'S LOVE FEAST

(A) The Pastor reading the Liturgy. (BB) The boys. (CC) The girls. (DD) Men serving. (EE) Women serving.

I think, since I so often hear
That thou dost want my heart
As thy reward and purchase dear,
That thou in earnest art.

Come then, and take this heart of mine,
Come take me as I am,
I know that I by right am thine,
Thou loving, gracious Lamb.[9]

Selected stanzas from another children's hymn:

Us too he can lowly render,
Burn up all the baits of pleasure,
Us from all self-interest hinder,
Sanctify us unto work.

Or, are we puffed up already;
Swayed by avarice so speedy;
Or by lusts and passions giddy;
Or else sloth and laziness.

O then he can lower sink us,
Bid of his poor life bethink us,
Fleshly motions curb within us,
His sweat industry inspire.

Father! for thy dear Child's honour,
Be thou purger still and pruner
Of his branches, till in tenor
They be truly like their vine.[10]

Another children's hymn:

Thou children's congregation,
Who with the illumination
Of the nail-prints art pleased,
And by the Lamb embraced;

Ye flocks, who lust's vile passion,
Which is the heart's desolation,
With all your heart have hated,
To covenant-grace translated.

[9] *A Collection of Hymns*, London, 1754, part II, no. 253.
[10] *The Litany Book*, London, 1759, p. 176.

To the heart's joy of your parents,
And all the Lamb's adherents,
The pilgrims, and all others
Who cared for you as Mothers!

Are you't a grace esteeming,
In the wounds both to be swimming?
Then may God farther lead you,
And with his body feed you! [11]

In the hymns and litanies for the Choir of older boys, the brotherhood of Jesus was stressed, and his circumcision was spoken of as the covenant wound that symbolized his oneness with them. With his "first wound" (circumcision), which occasioned his first suffering, Christ made a covenant with God; and on the strength of this and his own youth, he hallows every boy's life who appropriates the blessings thereof.

Spirit! the imperial glory
Hath none but the Son of Mary,
He alone is "Fons Salutis"
He is "princeps juventutis."

Be our boys' sanctification,
In their doubtful situation;
For that one boy's sake, forever
All our boys with blessing cover!

Therefore let all our boys classes,
In remembrance of dear Jesus,
And through his boy's—age's merit,
His first wound's full bliss inherit.[12]

If all boys did think each minute,
Open Pleura, mine thou art!
If their souls and Limbs were in it;
They would sleep away that smart,
Where we else do find it,
That in youth yet blinded,
Motions in the flesh are raised, that thro' blast
Of wild fire they grow unchaste.

[11] *The Litany Book*, London, 1759, p. 178. [12] *Ibid.*, p. 180.

Let that blest boy be regarded,
Who was, Anno Christi twelve,
So forgot, so little guarded,
That he was left by himself.
'Twas then not the fashion
T' have Choir-regulations;
Yet Jesus was such a mild and good child,
That he all with wonder filled.

But to those hearts dear and precious
Of the choir-boys fellowship,
Who close to the corpse of Jesus
And his bitter passion keep,
Shows the first wound's power
In the Covenant hour,
How their limbs obtain by this, corpse-likeness,
And their mind is made like his.[13]

The hymns and litanies of the older girls' Choir emphasized Christ's love for them and the fact that he did not despise "his poor handmaids of low estate." He was called the "Beloved," with whom they could spend their days in familiarity. By virtue of the fact that the Virgin Mary's heart was warmed by Christ's coming into the world through her, the girls could hope for grace by which to gain the same "virgin's crown."

A great girl,[14] O dearest Saviour!
Can't boast that she gave yet ever
Many proofs, which could be named
Real, and must stand ashamed.

For remember, that thou'st warmed
A girl's heart, and in her formed
God in human flesh revealed,
Let our virgin grace be sealed.

For remember of God's mother,
And her child our dearest brother,
Let us all be found possessing
Lasting virgin crowns and blessing.[15]

[13] *Ibid.*, pp. 181-183. [15] *The Litany Book,* London, 1759, pp. 178-180. [14] *Grosses Mädchen.*

This picture is that corpse of his,
His grave-cloths are the skirt; with this
To each poor Maiden he draws nigh
When her heart after him does cry

Ev'n as that highly blessed maid,
In her inspired hymn, hath said,
That her Lord never does forget
His poor handmaids of low estate.[16]

In the Single Sisters' Choir, Jesus was glorified as the "spouse" and "bridegroom" of the virgins. They besought him to become their guest and make their hearts his "bridal palace." As his betrothed they sought his protection from harm. The fact that he was conceived in a virgin's womb made their virgin state especially blessed and made Mary the pattern after which they were to model themselves. The temptations of Christ in the body were an assurance to them that they also could maintain their virginity because of the blessing Christ promised to be to them.

This in the virgins' hearts take place,
Make them his bridal palaces.
Take soul and body in thy arm,
And O preserve them from all harm.

O thou the only Virgin-man!
Each of thy maidens look upon;
Thou sinful human souls we be,
Void of angelic purity.[17]

Thou the Virgins soul's creator,
Of their vessel the wise potter,
Of their rule first thought and Center,
Of their frame through out inventor.[18]

Rest, redeemed members! like to you were those,
Which, as flesh he entered, he to bear him chose:
Should your breast lusts noisome to profane get leave,
When yet Mary's bosom suck to Jesus gave?

[16] *The Litany Book*, London, 1759, appendix.   [18] *Ibid.*, p. 189.
[17] *Ibid.*

No: for to prevent it, our Lamb, God and Spouse,
Hung on the cross extended; even the curse so close
He of lusts unholy killed by his flesh then.
Who believed this fully, would be ever clean.

Dear Choir-flock, his portion! on his breast sleep warm,
Dream of Jesus' person in the Mother's arm;
On his smart be feeding; view the hands and feet,
And the Pleura bleeding; then your sleep is sweet.[19]

In the Single Brethren's Choir, the unreproachful single state of the man Jesus as an example to them, and the merits of his perfect life in the flesh for their sanctification, were described.

His chaste young man's state
Is the garland of the single choirs.
His holy celibacy till death,
Transforms his Choir-companions
Into virgins.
His precious sweat when at work
Makes all labour sweet to us.
His sweat in his agony
Bedews our souls and bodies.
The points of the thorny crown
Mark us on our foreheads.
His meritorious cross
Comforts and blesses us.[20]

Ye single Brethren, lend an ear!
As we see young and hearty
Unmarried Brethren among us here
Of twenty years or thirty;
So was the everlasting God,
So he felt alteration,
So he drew breath, so moved his blood,
So was his perspiration.[21]

In the married Choir, the merits of Jesus as the husband of the soul was emphasized. Since all souls were female, Christ was the husband of the men as well as of the women. Christ was able to sanctify and bless the married state, since he him-

[19] *Ibid.*, p. 190. [20] *Ibid.*, appendix. [21] *Ibid.*, p. 185.

self was Man.   But while yet in the flesh, they looked for the
day when they as creatures should marry the Creator.

> Thou of the Catholic Church High-priest great,
> Bless the holy married state.
> Yea may thy pierced hands consecrate
> The holy married state,
> With priestly power and grace,
> And everlasting peace.[22]

> The virgins have devoted
> Body and soul unspotted
> A thousand times to him,
> Who with the bride's attire
> Decks them, and does desire
> Soon as they're ripe, to marry them.

> O God, O Chaste Lamb, Jesus!
> Blow up thy clean flame in us;
> Our marriage stands in need
> Of thy blood's overspreading,
> The interim proxy-wedding
> Was done in Jesus' name indeed.[23]

> May faith in the marriage of the Lamb
> Be the girdle of our reins!
> Call our chamberlains thy espoused ones!
> This will be a girdle to our loins.
> Purify our souls, through the Spirit,
> In obeying the truth,
> Unto unfeigned love of our Brethren.
> Preside at the solemn seasons of the matrimonial state.

> Till Christess shall to Christ be fled,
> And creature shall creator wed,
> And Abba blessing speak thereon,
> The heart cleaves to its flesh and bone.[24]

Although Jesus was the husband of all souls, in the Choir
of the widows he was exalted as the bridegroom of the widows

[22] *The Litany Book*. London, 1759, p. 196.   [24] *Ibid.*, appendix.
[23] *Ibid.*, p. 192.

in a special sense. The widows were, therefore, peculiarly favored. It was adultery for a widow to marry, and adultery for a man to marry her, unless she received Christ's permission.

> To this, that the Bridegroom avows,
> That he will be the widows spouse,
> Add Paul's tremendous thunderbolt,
> Of widows who against Christ revolt.
>
> Therefore among us it is allowed,
> That widows, in the church of God,
> (For which Him humbly they may thank)
> Have of all stations the first rank.
>
> And a true widow does not wed,
> Unless commands be on her laid,
> To the Church-sense agreeably,
> Or by his hand immediately.
>
> Suppose the bridegroom Jesus Christ
> On such a step does not insist,
> But is content a widow pass
> Her time as yet in loneliness:
>
> Then would a person certainly
> Be guilty of adultery
> With Jesus' bride, if he should dare
> With such a view to look at her.[25]

In the hymns and litanies of the widowers' Choir it was emphasized that the widowers could find comfort in the thought that their departed wives, "doves," were now safely in Christ's side. Christ himself was a widower who died for his "dove" who had strayed away from him.

> O holy Father God,
> Of the God of Sabaoth,
> (Who is all the world's God),
> And his dear Christians', God!
>
> Here hast thou a society,
> Which thy dear son brought up for thee,

[25] *Ibid.*, p. 197.

And whom the Spirit ministering
Doth teach, the Abba right to sing.

We weep, being of a dove bereft,
Which is gone safe to the Rock-cleft,
That universal rendezvous
Of doves, since the Side was pierced through.

But he wept, 'cause his dove did stray,
Decoyed and torn from him away;
The cruel hawk had her, and die
Must he or she infallibly.

His tears so meritorious,
Dear Lord and God, now comfort us!
The soul of Christ thee sanctify,
Make me one spirit with him to be.[26]

O Father! dwell with the widowers;
Mother! give incense for their prayers.
Thou, who on widows kind doth look,
Put them to thy Side, there to suck! [27]

We pass now from the personal pietism of the Choirs to the
more public and general themes of worship.   The extensive
devotional observances in America were an inheritance from
the Brethren in Europe.   In Herrnhut there were three meetings for the whole congregation each day, the first of them at
five o'clock in the morning.   In addition each band had its
special meetings; and a group of men and women made arrangements whereby someone was praying at each hour of the
twenty-four, so that the Brethren were continually brought
before the Lord's presence, day and night.   The night watchman would sing a hymn at the stroke of the clock instead of
the usual announcement that all was well.   Or he would sing
a verse of a rhyme composed for the occasion by Zinzendorf:

The clock is eight! to Herrnhut all is told
How Noah and his seven were saved of old.

[26] *The Litany Book,* London, 1759, appendix.
[27] *Ibid.,* p. 197.

Hear Brethren hear! the hour of nine is come;
Keep pure each heart and chasten every home.

Hear Brethren, hear!   Now ten the hour-hand shows;
They only rest, who long for night's repose.

The clock's eleven! and ye have heard it all
How in that hour the mighty God did call.

It's midnight now! and at that hour ye know
With lamps to meet the bridegroom we must go.

The hour is one! through darkness steals the day;
Shines in your hearts the morning star's first ray?

The clock is two! who comes to meet the day,
And to the Lord of days his homage pay?

The clock is three! the Three in One above
Let body, soul, and spirit truly love.

The clock is four! where'er on earth are three,
The Lord has promised he the fourth will be.

The clock is five! while five away were sent,
Five other virgins to the marriage went.

The clock is six! and from the watch I'm free,
And everyone may his own watchman be.

Sundays were entirely taken up with devotionals. There was a "morning blessing" at five, a meeting for the Choirs at six, a children's meeting at ten, a public service at eleven, at which hymns were sung and a sermon preached, a meeting for the old and feeble in the afternoon, also Choir festivals, and at five a meeting of those attending the Lord's Supper, a public service with a sermon in the evening, followed by song services and the "evening blessings" in the various groups.

Much of the preaching was of an impromptu nature, consisting of a simple narration of the story of salvation as they knew it. Of necessity it could not be otherwise, since most of the Brethren who went out as preachers and missionaries never had a higher education, this advantage being afforded only to such of their leaders as Zinzendorf, Spangenberg, and Peter Böhler.

The average Moravian preacher did not attempt a systematic exposition in the pulpit. In fact, even Zinzendorf and Spangenberg [28] would not have devoted time and energy to making systematic declarations of their faith, had they not been forced by circumstances to do so in self-defense. The Brethren in the main considered academic theology not conducive to edification; it was considered really dangerous and an entanglement which they did well to avoid. Their simple preaching was consistent with their simple faith, and the singing of hymns was more stimulating for the kind of religious experience which they sought.

The program of their weekly devotionals shows that hymns and litanies were their chief liturgical materials. Some of the litanies were: The Great Church Litany; The *Trisagion;* The *Te Abba;* The Prayer to the Father; The *Te Matrem;* The Prayer to the Holy Ghost; The *Te Logos;* The *Te Agnum;* The Prayer to our Head and Lord; The Litany concerning his Life, Sufferings and Death; Hymns of the Wounds of Jesus; The Pleurody; The Testament of the Lord; The Bride's Song; and the great Easter Morning Litany. There were also Sunday litanies, used before and after the congregational meetings. Other liturgies for special services and festivals were: The Good-Friday Liturgy; The Agape; The *Pedilavium;* The Holy Sacrament; The Kiss of Peace; The Baptism Liturgy; Hymns and Litanies for the various Choirs; liturgies for the reception of members into the congregation and for burial.

In 1733 the Brethren in Europe received permission from the Evangelical Lutheran University of Tübingen to use the Lutheran liturgy.[29] So the first liturgy of the Renewed Church was Luther's, who in his compilation had before him the ancient productions. As the Herrnhut congregation became better established, a liturgy more expressive of their temperament, religious views, and customs was developed. Zinzendorf's highly organized congregation needed an elaborate and extensive liturgy. The Lutheran liturgy was too circumscribed to take account adequately of the many customs and church

[28] See his *Idea Fidei Fratrum.*
[29] *Auth. Rel., Anmerkungen,* pp. 11, 12.

festivals of the Brethren. Most of these traditions were so peculiarly Moravian that they demanded a distinctive liturgy. Their litanies were not new compositions but symphonies of lines and verses collected from their hymns. In 1754 such a collection was arranged in a publication called the *Litaneyen Büchlein*. The liturgy book of 1755-57 shows that much of it had been written under the influence of the fanatic Herrn-haagian theology. In a later revision by Spangenberg many of the objectionable themes were removed. Thus in the Brethren's liturgy, we find the forms of Luther, Zinzendorf, and Spangenberg all interwoven.

On Sunday, at an early hour, The Great Church Litany was chanted responsively by the pastor and the congregation. The following extracts will give its general style and thought: [30]

Kyrie	*Eleison!*
Christe	*Eleison!*
Kyrie	*Eleison!*
Christ	*Hear us!*

Liturgist: Lord God, our Father, who art in Heaven!
Hallowed be thy name, thy kingdom come, etc.

Chorus: For thine is the Kingdom, and the power, and the glory, for ever and ever. *Amen!*

Liturgist: O *Immanuel,* Thou Saviour of the World!
Confess thyself our own!

Chorus: O my Lord most faithful,
Give me what Thou'st merited,
And I'm rich and thankful.

Liturgist: Lord God Holy Ghost,
Abide with us for ever!

Chorus: God Holy Ghost, sweet Comforter,
Give thy folk one mind everywhere.

Liturgist: Our Lord Jesus Christ,
Be gracious unto us!

[30] From *The Litany Book,* London, 1759. The responses of the con-gregation are in italics.

Liturgist:	Thou only God of the Church, *Love us!*
Liturgist:	Thou only Mother, *Maintain thy temple in honour!*
Chorus:	Most Holy blessed Trinity! We praise Thee to Eternity.[31]

Then follow petitions for protection from sin and evil:

Liturgist:
From all loss of our glory in Christ,
From all coldness to his merit and death,
From all error,
From unhappily becoming great,
From untimely projects,
From needless perplexity,
From confusions,
From light-minded or dark enthusiasm,
From the murdering spirit and devices of *Belial*
From tumult and sedition,
From the wicked world,
From misunderstanding and hypocrisy,
From the deceitfulness of sin,
From sins unto death.
From all sin

Preserve us our dear Lord and God!

Liturgist:
Prevent or destroy all designs and schemes of SATAN
Fight our battles against him, and defend us
against his accusation;
Let us find with men that peace, which we have
with Thee, and with the rest of thy creatures;
As for our slanderers and persecutors, lay not that
sin to their charge;
Hinder all schisms and scandals,
Put far from thy people all seducers,
Bring back all that have been seduced;
Grant love and Unity to all our Congregations!

Congregation: In Jesus' love and peace,
Who our heart's pleasure is,

[31] This line first sung by the men, then by the women, and the third time by the choir, in which the congregation may join.

Dwell our congregations:
You too beyond the seas,
Feel our heart's salutations!

Blessings are asked upon the missionaries, the Church, the
government, their enemies, their voyages, the work of their
hands, the sick and distressed, their matrimony and their youth.
For example:

Liturgist: Let our Marriage be honorable among all men,
And our bed undefiled;
Make the wife subject unto the man, as unto the Lord,
And teach the husband to be benevolent to
the wife, as unto the Church; . . .
Let our pregnant sisters reap the blessing of
thy having lain under a human heart,
And let those who give suck, enjoy the blessing
of thy having sucked the breasts of a Mother, etc.

Liturgist: Through the merits of thy Covenant-Wound
circumcise the hearts of our boys;
And thy becoming man in a virgin's body,
Make the girls Chaste.

The praises of the blood and wounds of Christ are sung.

Chorus: Thy blood, that precious gore,
Is of such strength and power,
One drop, how small soever,
Can the whole world deliver
From all claim of the Devil
And wash away all evil.

Liturgist: Keep us in everlasting fellowship with
the whole Church triumphant,
And let us once rest together in thy
Wounds from all our Labour.
HEAR US, O DEAR LORD AND GOD!

Congregation: When my mouth shall grow pallid
In Jesus' Lap and Arms,
The Corpse's Myrrh so valid,
Which in his heart's-blood swarms,

Embalm my body dying;
No other salve at all!
Myself to Salem flying,
Shall once that flesh recall.

The Great Church Litany closes thus:

Liturgist: Unto that Man, who purchased our Souls for himself;

Congregation: Unto that Friend who loved us! and washed us from our sins in his own blood;

Liturgist: Who died for us,

Congregation: That we might die unto sin once;

Liturgist: Who rose for us,

Congregation: That we also might rise

Liturgist: Who ascended for us into heaven,

Congregation: To prepare a place for us;

Chorus: And to whom are subjected the angels and powers and dominions:

Liturgist: To him be glory at all times,

Congregation: In that Church which waits for him, and in that which is about him;

Chorus: From everlasting to everlasting.

Congregation: Amen!

Liturgist: Little Children abide in him!

Chorus: That you be not confounded before him on the day of his appearing.

Liturgist: The Lord bless thee, and keep thee! The Lord make his face to shine upon thee, and be gracious unto thee! The Lord lift up his Countenance upon thee, and give thee peace!

Congregation: Amen.

Early Moravianism is characteristically expressed in the communion service. In it the Moravian attitude of mind, their childlike simplicity, their sensual devotion, and their simple theology are manifested. At these services discourses were avoided, and no attempt was made to explain whether the words "this is my body" were to be taken symbolically or literally. The general theme was that Jesus, the husband and redeemer of souls, comes down to "embrace" and "kiss" them, revealing both his love and his agony. The hymns thus combined the imagery of the *Song of Songs* with the imagery of "bathing in the blood of the Lamb."

According to the liturgy in *The Litany Book* (1759) the communion service progressed in six distinct stages, from which selected lines follow.

(1) Confession and Absolution.

> Among the list of all those things
> Which soul and body grieve,
> So formidable smart none brings,
> As that sins to us cleave.

> In a moment stands before us
> The prince with his open side,
> And one feels he's most desirous
> Our poor souls therein to hide.

> I wipe my eye from weeping sore,
> That sinful red appears no more;
> Yet the aspect of that God who bled,
> Does keep my eye still wet and red.

> All thy smart and sweat-drops bloody,
> All the wounds in thy dear body,
> Thy distress and agony,
> O Lord Jesu, comfort me!

> Thy precious sweat when at work, make
> all labour sweet to us!

(2) Entrance into the Holiest. Adoration and praise of the corpse of Jesus was sung. In the sacrament, Jesus the Lover was again incarnated, so that his people could embrace and kiss him, live in his side and feed their souls on his body and blood.

Blessed spirits, you may covet
The Side's cleft to pry into:
But this cave, you can't disprove it,
Was for sinner hearts pierced through.

This holy corpse to death a prey
Was given, that we might live thereby;
No greater love could he show us,
Shall we to think on him refuse?

Thy blood-sweat, dear Saviour!
Rain on us like water;
For, all the world over,
Nought can bless us better:
O sweat's dear flood! O holy blood!

Thy hand, with its print of the nail,
We kiss with heart's affection,
That hand so stiff and so death-pale,
Stretched out by Crucifixion.

Thy holy testaments,
Thy sweet nearness,
Thy embodying in the sacrament,
Bless us, O dear Lord and God!

My soul feeds on roses sweet,
When she smells wounds-flavour,
And reviews her safe retreat
In thy grave, my Saviour.

Draw us to thee, and we will come
Into thy wounds deep places,
Where hidden is the honey-comb
Of thy sweet love's embraces.

My dear bleeding Saviour,
O let me embrace thee,
While thousand drops cover,
Hang on thee and grace thee,
And catch the juice thy wounds produce.

O Meal! I can't thy sweetness be expressing,
Because thou art all thoughts and words surpassing.

Now strikes my hour, now runs my spring,
The blood stream now does roll,
Its rushing sound to sleep does sing
My body and my soul.

(3) Partaking of the Lord's Corpus. His body enters into the true members of his Church, who are the "particles of the Church dough," in which the martyred corpus works as a leaven.

Lord Jesus, through affection
And eternal election,
Would mankind's bridegroom be:
With this view did he make them,
In his arms for to take them;
All souls proprietor is he.

According to his testament
We keep the holy sacrament:
Ye particles of the Church-dough,
The martyred Corpse's leaven go
Quite through you now!

That in these days our beloved
To ask for each by name be moved,
And with his pierced Side may cover
The poor love-sick child all over.

Pale lips, kiss us upon the heart!
Open arms, take us!
Yea thou holy martyred corpse, do as Elijah did!
We will be the child.

O church, rejoice now tremblingly!
The Lamb's death now pervadeth thee.
In the sacrament does he my Saviour,
Stretched in death's form, my whole body cover.

This moment does all senses captivate!
The Lord goes in, the spirit locks the gate,
And lets me have my private conversation;
Then I sing praise with humble exultation.

Jesus, thee to the hen I liken,
Me to the chicken;

Grace's wings are spread, I see,
Over me.

Might I thy corpse expanded
Here on my lap enfold!

(4) Echo after the Holy Corpus.   The echo is the memory
of the last embrace of the Lover and the beloved.

Silent tears let us be shedding,
And in Jesus' grave be hiding,
Nor come forth out of those places
Till the time of next embraces.

We honor thee, thou heavenly commander!
Only lock up thy bridal hearts so tender,
O shut the door of thy dear wounds and Side-Hole,
Over the bride-soul!

And what a look thy last look was,
When thou, for us acquiring
Eternal life and happiness,
Wert on the cross expiring.

O how inwardly
Do I think on thee,
Thou blest place in my Lamb's body,
Which the Son's sign wide and bloody
Ever will abide, cleft made in the side!

O yes, I will observe with care
Each wound and bloody spot,
And all the beauties, which appear
In him from head to foot.

Ave, thou dearest spouse,
Who borest the curse for us!
Ave, for thy toil great,
Ave, for thy blood-sweat,
Ave, for limbs ice-set,
Ave, thou cheeks cold dew,
Ave, thou ghastly view!
Ave, thou skin so sore,
Ave, forehead cut all over,
Pleura, Ave evermore!

Till I kiss thee,
O dear Side-hole, keep my soul.

(5) At the Blessed Cup. The blood is adored as the means
of salvation. They rejoice that his Side is still bleeding and
pray that his wound may continue to bleed on them to quicken
their souls.

Thou death-sweat mixed with blood,
Which the Lamb's body covered,
When pale his face was viewed,
His soul by a thread hovered,
His heart together pressed,
His eye in tears was drowned,
And ice cold dew full fast
Over all his hair was found!

We are certified
That the bleeding Side
Stands opened wide
For all sealed members of the Lamb's dear bride.

Therefore the church, the feeling bride,
Sings: Glory to the holy Side,
Glory be to the holy Side!

Awake, O Church, from thy deep rest,
Arise, and sit down at the breast
Of thy beloved, which was pierced,
From when did blood and water burst,
There quench thy thirst!

Take, drink the blood so richly spilt
For thine and every sinner's guilt.
And thou, soul's bridegroom, it among us divide;
Thy congregation's mouth is opened wide.

I pray thee, give unto my heart thy blessing,
And let thy blood rain on it without ceasing.

O that thy head, which thorns were rending,
Were all its blood down to us sending!
Thy brows sweat make us a nice
Clean and lovely paradise!

Let thy open wounds sweet juice
Verdure in my heart produce.

A thousand times be then adored,
Thou blood of Jesus Christ my Lord
From every wound's incision!
Thou bloody death-sweat in the wine,
Which he for Covenant did ordain;
Sweat in the garden-passion!
Bloody body!
Skin so furrowed, thorn-crowned forehead,
Hands, feet bored!
Side's rent!   God reward him for it.

And thy poor sinner's heart keep wet,
With blood let it be filled,
Till once thy drops of deathly sweat
On my corpse will be smelt.

(6)   After the Sacrament.   After the sacramental embrace,
the bride beholds the bridegroom in his glory and awaits the
great wedding day.

Unto the Rock-cleft lift your eye,
And in that cleft the pit's hole spy,
Whence, chosen people! every one
Of you have been dug out and hewn.

God's dear Lamb, in purple dyed,
In his figure bloody,
Midst us walks, and shows his Side
To the Church his body.

Christ's wife, till she to Christ is gone
Cleaves fast to him her flesh and bone:
His coming in the flesh so blest,
Preserves her soul and body chaste.

I feel, my heart does burn for Love;
I am thy dust, my maker!

My heart's concern is properly,
That every day more sensibly
In private he would me embrace,
That over his Love might blush my face.

> Let now, until the wedding day,
> Repeat the passion story
> All what I sing or say.

The custom of foot-washing (*pedelavium*), in imitation of the example of Christ in John 13, was performed at first in single instances and small groups. But the practice became more general, and the rite was observed at Choir festivals, and by the congregation, before the Lord's Supper. On Maundy Thursday not only the elders but all communicant members washed each other's feet. "This was a solemn rite, and solemnly performed, and was a corresponding influence calculated to chasten the moral turpitude of the natural man, else uprising to the prejudice and waste of the beauty of holiness." [32] While the rite was being performed by the members (only for others of the same sex), the leader sang appropriate hymns of cleansing and washing from sin by the blood of Christ.

> What did he do, that matchless heart,
> The soul full of desire,
> The body with death pangs and smart
> Pervaded as with fire?
> He did fetch water, and did gird
> A towel round his body,
> And then to lave their feet desired,
> Which he to wash was ready.
>
> Now you, who know my word (which once
> Shall judge each tribe and nation),
> You've seen, that on you these my hands
> Performed this operation;
> My last will is, that I think meet
> You should wash one another,
> As I, your Lord, have washed your feet,
> So each shall wash his brother.[33]

In their attempt to make their church as apostolic as possible, they also introduced the "kiss of peace." This ceremony, too, was practised only among members of the same sex. The men

[32] Ritter: *Moravian Church in Phil.*, p. 104.
[33] *The Litany Book*, London, 1759.

and women being separated in their sittings, it was free from abuse. This ceremony symbolized the kiss of the bridegroom Christ and was also interpreted as a greeting from the saints who had passed on, the ancient races, the Lutherans, the Reformed, the heathen in distant lands, the Ancient *Unitas Fratrum*, etc. In the "kiss of peace" they symbolized the command: "Thou shalt love the Lord thy God, and thy neighbor as thyself." It was used in the communion service and some of the liturgies, whenever the words of the hymn suggested love, peace, and fellowship.

> Now then a kiss received,
> With all that peace can give;
> Dearest heart, receive it
> From our dear husband's love,
> Whose heart once sorely grieved
> Broke for me and thee
> In death's agony,
> When he bought us free.
>
> Receive also a kiss
> And greetings of sweet peace
> In the name so precious
> Of all the saints in bliss, etc.
>
> From such as Kibboda,
> Mammukka, Tochtanoh,
> Kajarnak and Sarah,
> Johannes, Simeon,[34]
> Hewn from the savage quarry,
> Whom the Lamb hath wooed,
> With his blood bedewed,
> And thus quite renewed.[35]

One of the most significant and symbolically beautiful rites of the Brethren was the manner in which Easter was celebrated. This custom had been handed down to the Brethren from the early days of the Church at Herrnhut. The Easter morning service was announced by the trombonists from the

[34] That is, "Hottentots, Mingrelians, Canadians, Greenlanders, Malabarians, Arawacks."

[35] *The Litany Book,* London, 1759.

Der heilige Kuß des Friedens | Saint Baiser de Paix

THE HOLY KISS OF PEACE

church steeple at a very early hour. These musicians then passed through the streets of the town to awaken the members with the hymn:

> Christ is risen from the dead,
> Thou shalt rise too, saith my Saviour,
> Of what should I be afraid?
> I with him shall live forever,
> Can the dead forsake his limb,
> And not draw me unto him?

The service in the church began about five in the morning with the Easter Morning Litany, which opens with a magnificent confession of faith. As the people left the church, the musicians met them with appropriate hymns and led them in solemn procession to the cemetery. The program was so scheduled that these early worshippers reached the burial ground (*Gottes Acker*) just as the sun rose, symbolic of Jesus' resurrection. A square was formed around the graves, the services were continued, and the Litany finished. Selections from the Easter Morning Litany follow.[36]

Liturgist: I believe in the one only God, Father, Son and Holy Ghost; who created all things by Jesus Christ, and was in Christ reconciling the World unto himself.

Chorus: I thank thee, O Father, Lord of heaven and Earth! That thou hast hid these things from the wise and prudent, and hast revealed them unto babes. Even so, Father, for so it seemed good in thy sight.

Liturgist: Father, glorify thy name!

Congregation: Our Father which art in heaven, . . .

Liturgist: I believe in the name of the only begotten Son, . . .

Chorus: The spirit and the bride say: Come!

Liturgist: And let him that heareth say: Come!

Congregation: Amen, come, Lord Jesus! do not long tarry, With longing hearts we are waiting for thee. [Sisters] Come! [Brethren] Come! [All] O come!

[36] *Ibid.*

Liturgist: The Lord will descend from heaven with a shout, with the voice of the archangel, and with the trump of God.

Chorus: To judge both the quick and the dead, who shall 'fore him be gathered.

Liturgist: This is my Lord who redeemed me, . . .

Congregation: This is certainly true.

Liturgist: I believe in the Holy Ghost, who proceedeth from the Father, and whom our Lord Jesus Christ sent us, . . .

Liturgist: I believe, that our Brethren —— [37] and our sisters —— are gone to the Church above, and entered into the joy of their Lord; the body was buried here. . . .

Congregation: We poor sinners pray thee to hear us, O dear Lord and God!

Liturgist: And to keep us in everlasting fellowship with the Church triumphant; especially also with those servants and handmaids of the whole church, whom thou hast called home within this year, as ——, and to let us once rest with them at thy wounds.

Congregation: Amen!

Chorus: His eyes, his mouth, his Side, His body crucified,

Congregation: Whereon we lean unshaken, To see we shall be taken, And pay our thankful kisses To the hands and feet of Jesus.

Liturgist: Glory to the resurrection and the Life! . . .

Chorus: For ever and ever,

Congregation: Amen! Now shuts the senses feeble [sisters] each Handmaid [brethren], and disciple,

Chorus: As if this hour their Lover

Congregation: With his skirt them did cover.

[37] Here the names of those who have died since last Easter are mentioned.

This symbolic service with minor modifications is still observed and is one of the cherished traditions of Moravianism. Although the Brethren have never formulated a well-defined creed of their own, but have merely pledged their allegiance to the Augsburg Confession, this Easter Morning Litany approaches nearest to what may be called the Moravian Creed and is generally considered as such by them.

In addition to the foregoing rites there were Church festivals commemorating historical events which were exclusively Moravian. They are: March 1, celebration of the event in the year 1457, when the Ancient Brethren first assumed the name *Unitas Fratrum;* May 12, commemoration of several events of importance: the building of the first place of worship in 1724; the agreement of the Herrnhuters in 1727 to the code called "Statutes of the Congregation"; the election of twelve elders in Herrnhut; the recognition by Parliament in 1749 of the Brethren as an Ancient Protestant Episcopal Church and their exemption from taking oath;—August 13, the descent of the Holy Spirit on the congregation in Herrnhut in 1727;—August 27, the beginning of the hourly intercession;—November 13, commemoration of the day in 1741 when Jesus was made Chief Elder and Shepherd. At these great Church festivals, hymns and litanies were sung and special odes composed for the occasion. The daily program, the weekly schedule, and the yearly Church calendar were full to overflowing of devotional services, congregational meetings, Church celebrations, special religious rites, and solemn ceremonies.

The Brethren's continual celebration of the redemption kept alive in them the history of their vicissitudes, how God had led them from darkness into light, from persecution to peace, from poverty to moderate prosperity, *"Durch Sturm zur Stille,"* and they repeatedly sang one of their favorite hymns:

> Though waves and storms go over my head,
> Though strength and health and friends be gone;
> Though joys be withered all and dead,
> Though every comfort be withdrawn,
> Steadfast on this my soul relies,
> Jesus, thy mercy never dies.

CHAPTER VI

CHRISTOCRACY

THE policy of the Brethren made them exclusive in practice rather than in doctrine and belief. By this is meant not that they had no distinctive and peculiar beliefs, but that in doctrinal relationships with other creeds, they proceeded on a basis essentially broad and inclusive. The underlying conception of what Moravianism was to do allowed them to proceed on no other principle than "in essentials unity, in non-essentials liberty, in all things charity." On this basis, Zinzendorf tried to bring harmony among the German sectarians in Pennsylvania. For this reason we do not find a well-defined Moravian creed. They have never drawn up any articles of faith to set forth the respects in which they differ from other communions. They have never pledged their names to a denominational creed of their own. They adhered to the Augsburg Confession, not as a wall of separation, but rather as a doctrinal statement in which all denominations could unite. Zinzendorf himself declared they had no creed of their own, nor did they desire one; and whoever wanted to inquire about their beliefs should consult, in addition to the Bible, the doctrines of the Augsburg Confession and the Synod of Bern.[1] Nevertheless, we cannot fail to note among the Moravians several distinctive theological conceptions.

In this study of the theology of the Brethren, the reader must not forget that we are concerned here with a definite period in their history, approximately the middle of the eighteenth century, and not with the whole of the Renewed Church. We do not attempt in these pages to give an exposition of their later and present theological tenets. The similarity of modern Moravians to other denominations in this respect would make such a study unnecessary, to say the least.

[1] *Barbysche Sammlungen,* p. 188.

All the formal details of their faith are in practice so over-shadowed by the one doctrine of the vicarious atonement that this became their distinguishing mark in worship, belief, and conversation. The atonement was so mysterious to them that they shrank from any explanation of the controversial words, "this is my body." Their teaching and preaching were exclusively Christo-centric, not Christological, always directing their thoughts to the sacrificial death of Christ and his Passion. By faith in Christ the sinner was justified in the sight of God and received immediate and complete deliverance from the guilt and burden of sin. Christ made this possible not only through his vicarious death but also through the merits of his holy life. At the Synod of Zeyst in 1746, the Count said: "There is really no circumstance of human life, wherein he has not at times been our forerunner." [2] Thus under any and all circumstances Christ was the dominating figure in their thoughts and the theme of their discourses.

Since they emphasized the person of Christ above all else, disbelief in him was the greatest sin. But faith, for the Brethren, did not consist in an intellectual assent to a dogmatic statement about the person of Christ. The mystery surrounding Christ prevented them from any such speculation. Faith consisted rather in feeling than seeing him.

> To believe, is, without seeing,
> Jesus' death and life to feel:
> How they him on the cross lying,
> Mocked and bruised, his blood did spill.[3]

Faith was the ability to keep before them the blood, wounds, and agony of Christ, until it became real to their senses.

[2] *Ibid.*, pp. 108, 109.
[3] *Anhang*, XI, no. 1,735.
> *Glauben, das ist ohne sehen*
> *Jesu tod und leben fühl'n,*
> *Wie sie ihn am creuze schmähen,*
> *Wie sie sein gebein durchwühl'n.*

English trans. from *Collection of Hymns*, London, 1754, part II, no. 65.

How happy, that my heart can view
The Lamb in all that bloody hue,
Upon the cross outstretched!
If from my eyes this should depart,
My heart would feel a piercing smart,
Yea I should be most wretched.

If those dear wounds I did not know,
Which now with blood's juice overflow,
What else could satisfy me?
But Blood, that's good
Still to wash me, and refresh me;
In that Ocean,
I do ever find my portion.[4]

Away, ye painters, with your art!
The Spirit paints within the heart;
Draws to the life the bloody tree,
And lets us it in spirit see.[5]

The life of faith was this constant fellowship and communion
with Christ.   In a sermon the Count declared that the daily
fellowship with the Man of Sorrows, the confluence of our souls
with his, and constantly saluting all his wounds, will make us
so like him that his image can be seen in our eyes.[6]   "When I
have him, then I have what will make me everlastingly
happy." [7]   This personal acquaintance with their Saviour they
carefully nurtured, until they themselves believed it was their
peculiar blessing.   The Count said: "If I were to say what
really is the distinguishing mark of the Economy which I serve,
from other economies, it is the devotion to the person of
Christ." [8]   In a treatise called *Jeremiah*, Zinzendorf said:
"Fight not with Satan in his own way, but send him to Jesus for
his own answer, presently in prayer before the Saviour.   Have
you been guilty of an oversight, a mistake or neglect, a wrong
thought, word or deed? go directly to the Saviour, and bewail

[4] *Collection of Hymns* (1754), part II, no. 99.
[5] *Ibid.*, no. 113.
[6] *Einige der Letzten Reden des seligen Grafen Nicolaus Ludwig von Zinzendorf*, p. 11.
[7] *Ibid.*, p. 62.
[8] Unttendörfer and Schmidt: *Die Brüder*, p. 146.

it. He will bless you that you shall be able to do better. Have
you good success? do you stand strong, and does the devil fly
from you? Lay yourself then upon the heart of Jesus, and
learn that short doxology, which all the saints repeat and
which you will once repeat with them in heaven: Christ's blood
and Righteousness is my only spotless and glorious robe,
wherein I will appear before God." [9]

Awareness of such an experience of unbroken fellowship
with Christ was the sign of divine life in the soul; in fact it
was the unmistakable evidence of salvation and a foretaste of
the life hereafter. Thus the preachers were eager and the
hearers receptive; and the result was that the Christo-centric
religion of the Brethren was a "heart-religion." The chief aim
of the devout Brethren was to preach Christ, so that he might
be the vortex around which their lives revolved. Zinzendorf
declared: "We preach nothing but the crucified Christ for the
heart; and we believe that whoever lays hold of him, all the
evil in him will disappear, and all the good comes simultane-
ously from the living and abiding impression of the sympathetic Man, called the Lamb of God." [10]

In England the Brethren were called "a sort of Methodists
that affect to know of nothing but Christ." [11] In an introduction to a volume summarizing the theological ideas of Zinzendorf, a Moravian author states: "Christ crucified is the library,
which triumphant souls will be studying to all eternity. Other
knowledge than the knowledge of Christ is apt to swell men
into high conceits and opinions of themselves; this brings them
to the truest view of themselves, and thereby to humility and
sobriety. Other knowledge leaves men's hearts as it found
them; this alters them and makes them better. So transcend-
ent an excellency is there in the knowledge of Christ crucified
above the sublimest speculations in the world." [12] A hymn
written in 1745 gives a description of their attitude toward
theological preaching:

[9] Gambold: *Maxims*, pp. 4, 5.
[10] *Barbysche Sammlungen*, p. 108.
[11] Benham: *Memoirs of James Hutton*, p. 138.
[12] Gambold: *Maxims*.

The preachers enlarge on morality;
Of Jesus Christ their sermons are free,
Except on Good Friday—and sometimes in Lent
A great deal of power is uselessly spent
Condemning the Jews.[13]

In their hymns, litanies, and discourses, all of which deal with the vicarious suffering and the blood atonement, the language of scholastic theology is almost entirely absent. They were not interested in a syllogistic analysis of what happened on the cross when Christ died there. The theories of substitutionalism and ransom held little or no interest for them. This Christo-centric theology received its first impetus from the Ancient Brethren, who in an age of cold religious scholasticism cultivated a literature of purity and piety based on the New Testament. But the influence of Zinzendorf greatly intensified Moravian theology, making fellowship and communion with the Christ the central themes. Zinzendorf, although a pietist, was not long a follower of the pietism typical of Halle, because he could not correlate his own experience with the struggle of repentance which was emphasized there. Whereas they stressed repentance, struggle, fear, and an angry God, the Count emphasized love, peace, and fellowship with Christ. For him regeneration was instantaneous and complete; and with it the reign of love and fellowship with Christ began immediately, resulting in a gradual sanctification.

Furthermore, in view of the fact that the Brethren considered it their mission to vitalize the Lutheran and Reformed Churches in Europe, and in view of their attempt to form a Church of God in the Spirit in Pennsylvania, it was very expedient that they make Christ the central doctrine of their faith. Here at least was a common starting point for all sects bearing the name Christian. They believed they could enhance their work by stressing their points of agreement rather than their differences. This is one reason why they refrained from dogmatizing about the atonement. They could all agree on Christ as their Saviour.

[13] *Church Miscellany*, July 1852.

One significant illustration of the extremes to which Moravian Christocracy was carried is the fact that in 1741 in Europe and 1748 in America, Christ was actually elected the Chief Elder in their settlements. Previous to this time Martin Linner, and after him Leonard Dober, had been the General Elders in Europe, and Spangenberg in America. A little over a decade after this was done, one of the Brethren said: "Having been used to appoint a General Elder, who should inspect and be answerable for all things, this office in our congregation was found, at last, to be too much for a Mortal man, and so thirteen years ago in a Synod, we asked our Saviour whether he himself would fill this place, to which he consented." [14] They were assured that Christ himself approved of this new office which was bestowed upon him; for on Nov. 13, 1741, when his Chief Eldership was created, "some Brethren were led to notice in the course of the day, the phenomenon of a rainbow in the clouds, and the impression thereby made upon their minds was such that they could not help considering its appearance as an emblem and token of grace and favor from the Lord." [15]

To discover God's will, they had frequently used the lot. It was used, for instance, in the selection of their first elders in 1727; and after 1733, it was frequently used at marriages to determine the Lord's approval or disapproval. In 1735 David Nitschmann was chosen by lot to be consecrated the first bishop of the Renewed Church. The lot was used to decide questions at Synods and Conferences and to establish missions and make appointments for offices. But now, with Jesus as the Chief Elder, all questions were submitted for his decision by lot; and all decisions arrived at by this means were considered the will of God. A Moravian of later date writes: "In a word, 'faith being the substance of things hoped for, and the evidence of things not seen,' the Brethren sought a more direct medium of its exercise in an appeal to the lot." [16] Christ was thus the director of their practical affairs in everyday life, deciding their social, economic, and political questions. The lot was

[14] Benham: *Memoirs*, pp. 311, 312.
[15] *Memorial Days*, p. 221.
[16] Ritter: *Moravian Church in Phil.*, p. 118.

merely the visible, tangible method by which the Chief Elder, Christ, made his will known.

The further development of their Christology, in the first three or four decades under our consideration, was almost entirely under the leading and dominating mind of Count Zinzendorf. Since he had not received any theological training in the universities, except the instruction he got at Halle as a boy and somewhat later at the University of Wittenberg, which he left when he was only nineteen years old, he was a self-educated theologian. Being a pietist by nature, he was not interested so much in theology *per se,* as in its fruits made evident in saintly living. Having cut himself loose from the cold orthodoxy of his day, he followed his fanciful imagination, guided by feeling and emotion rather than reason, which led him and his followers into many vagaries, where outsiders and some of the Brethren themselves could not follow him. Consequently the early Christology contained much to which such contemporaries as Spangenberg and Böhler objected, and which the Brethren of a later age refused to accept.

Although Zinzendorf said that it would be well not to go too deeply into the innermost secrets of the mystery of the Trinity,[17] he nevertheless worked out a literal statement of the relations of the persons of the Trinity. The family idea of the Godhead was stressed in the development of his theology. "The family idea of the holy Trinity is the safest and most blessed for anything that has a spiritual life." [18] The offices of God as Father, the Holy Spirit as Mother, and Christ as Son were realistically explained in a novel way.

> O Christ's dear Father! be thou glad,
> We're thy Son's Crown and joy indeed:
> O tender Mother! kiss us,
> Nurse us poor children carefully;
> We are not so as we should be,
> And this indeed does grieve us.[19]

[17] *Barbysche Sammlungen,* p. 106.
[18] *Ibid.,* p. 199.
[19] *Zugabe* II, no. 2,257. Trans. *Collection of Hymns* (1754), part II, no. 418.

God is Father, but he is a "dear Father" because he is Christ's Father. In other words, in the development of the Trinity, Christ takes the position of pre-eminence.

> In the uncreated Family,
> Of the house thou only Son!
> That house which ne'er extinct can be,
> Because it ne'er begun;
> Head of the Court of Elohim,
> Arch-penitentiary thou!
> I worm would penance do.[20]

In the further development of this thought, Christ became the real father and God a kind of grandfather. In a sermon, the Count said: "Our Saviour is our father, according to Isaiah 9:6; Heb. 2:13, and his Father is our grandfather or father-in-law." [21] He insisted that the prayer "Our Father who art in heaven," could only be directed to Jesus. Christ was the father of the whole creation, believers and unbelievers, but God was the father by adoption of the believers only. "Prayer to the Father of Jesus Christ can be prayed by no one but children of God." [22] Eschenbach in Oley, Pennsylvania, said that it was not necessary to pray to God, but only to his Son, Jesus Christ.[23] The father of Jesus can become the father of believers by adoption, but he remains a sort of grandfather, since God gives himself only to those who are already children of his Son. Unbelievers are under the government of the Son only.

This relationship of Christ and God in the Trinity was frequently intimated and stressed. At the first Pennsylvania Synod, a resolution was unanimously adopted that: "The devotion among the children of God one toward another should be as great as that which exists between our God and his father." [24] In some annotations to the records of the minutes of these

---

[20] *Zugabe* III, no. 2,290. Trans. *Collection of Hymns* (1754), part II, no. 345.

[21] Gambold: *Maxims*, p. 86.

[22] *Nine publick discourses upon important subjects in religion preached in Fetter-Lane-Chapel at London 1746.*

[23] Fresenius, vol. III, pp. 186-187.

[24] *Auth. Rel.*, p. 7.

Union Synods, the writer, defending Zinzendorf against the accusation that the latter made a Father out of the Son, wrote: "That is true; he cannot do otherwise since Isaiah 9:6 reads: the child which was born unto us, and the Son which was given to us, is called the 'Mighty God' and the 'Everlasting Father.' " [25] In London, in 1746, the Count said: "In public meetings we don't often use the Lord's Prayer, because the hearers in general will join therein, meaning withal to call upon the first person of the Trinity, and yet our Saviour has positively declared, none can do this but Children of God." [26] In a Synod of 1745, he explained further: "The Father is the God of the congregation. Only real members of the congregation can say, 'My God.' The Saviour must remain God over all creatures unalloyed. In that sense he is God to the greatest monarchs, as well as to the smallest mole. The Saviour gave us the idea that he is God 'illative'; his humanity, however, is to be established. Whoever does not have him as his God, has none; instead he is an atheist. His incarnation is the greatest doctrine of our faith. One of us became the Logos, and told us that he had yet a Father in heaven. But this is purely a congregational matter, and absolutely not for the world. When those of the world accept the Father as their God, they lose sight of their Creator and fall into idolatry. The world cannot comprehend this, and if we should try to demonstrate this, we ourselves would become heretics." [27]

The Count even appeals to the history of Satan's work to prove his point. In Old Testament times Satan opposed God with idols and many false gods. But after Christ appeared he was willing to drop the idols and deceive men by a misapplication of the intrinsically true notion of the divine unity. Satan now is only too anxious to have men worship one God, hoping thereby to keep them from believing that he who was crucified is the true God. "We don't therefore disagree with the Socinians, that a common reasonable man ought to worship only

[25] *Auth. Rel.—Anmerkungen*, pp. 18, 19.
[26] Gambold: *Maxims*, pp. 188, 189.
[27] *Barbysche Sammlungen*, pp. 145, 146.

one God, but the dispute between us is: Who is that God?" [28]

Thus in the theology of Zinzendorf the Son was raised to the highest position in the Trinity family. The Count readily overcame the difficulties of those passages of Scripture where Jesus gives the Father the place of prominence, by saying that it was painful to Jesus' humble heart to receive worship, and that, wanting to withdraw and forget himself as much as possible, he placed his Father foremost. The Son was so willing to efface himself that he worshipped the other two—the Father and the Holy Spirit. The passage in Revelation wherein Jesus bows before the throne, was an instance of his homage to his own divine Nature. Christ must remain God and the Father of the whole universe. Zinzendorf said: "If it were possible that there should be another God than Christ, I would rather be damned with Christ than happy with another." [29]

For the Brethren, the Jehovah of the Old Testament was the Christ of the New. Christ was always understood as the presupposed foundation of the whole Old Testament. Under the old dispensation, Jesus was called Jehovah and was the only God known. Jehovah Elohim was the babe in Mary's womb, the infant in the cradle, the boy in the temple, the carpenter of Nazareth, and the one tempted in the wilderness. By these means Jehovah prepared the way for what he intended to do.

> By birth he is the Jehovah,
> And for his throne and Scepter
> His Sire hath in the eternal law
> Provided such a chapter.
> That he with him together reign
> Since in the Royal House divine,
> There can be no succession.[30]

Jesus was the Logos who was with God and was God; he was the first cause of all things. It was Jesus who spoke to Adam in the garden, who sent Moses, and who led his people in the

[28] Gambold: *Maxims,* p. 290.
[29] Hutton: *History,* pp. 179, 180.
[30] *Zugabe* I, no. 2,175. Trans. *Collection of Hymns* (1754), part II, no. 306.

wars against the Canaanites. It was he who said: Let there be light, and there was light. The idea that Jesus, not the Father, was the creator of the world, we find frequently in Zinzendorf's sermons [31] and the hymns of the Brethren.

> O Maker of my soul,
> My every hair's Creator!
> O Thou, who makest my tears
> Of sweet and joyful nature!
> My Manhood's only spouse,
> Prince of my ministry,
> Who hast in all thy house
> The sole supremacy! [32]

Jesus was creator, controller, and sustainer of the world. At the Synod of Zeyst in 1746, Zinzendorf said: "He the Saviour is the architect and father of the ages, and they are properly only so far in his father's hand as they have now been committed to him as the careful executor of the intentions of the Creator and Redeemer."

In carrying out the family idea of the Trinity, the Holy Spirit is spoken of as a mother.

> Thou Mother of God's Children all,
> Thou Sapience archetypal!
> He who all hearts doth search and try,
> And Soul and body purify.
>
> Thou didst fit up the poor Maid's womb
> For that awful conception,
> In order to bring forth that child,
> The Father of the ages stiled. [33]

The Holy Spirit is not only the Mother of the Son in the Trinity, [34] but also the Mother of all believers, and is therefore called the Mother of the Congregation, the *"Gemein-Mutter."* [35]

[31] *Pennsylvanische Reden* I, p. 47; and *Naturelle Reflexiones,* pp. 66, 195.

[32] *Collection of Hymns* (1754), part II, no. 406.

[33] *Ibid.,* no. 388.

[34] Zinzendorf's *Marienborn Reden* (1745), *"Eine Rede von dem Mutter Amte des Heiligen Geistes."*

[35] *Wunden Litaney Reden,* p. 232.

Thou Spirit of Jesus Christ our Lord!
Who long before there was a time,
Did'st stand with him in one accord;
And then his battles fought'st with him:
Thou art the Church's Mother dear,
And lov'st to dwell in temples blest;
That Church whose elder he is here,
Make thou a pattern of the rest.[36]

The offices of the Father and the Mother in the Holy Trinity were those of assistants to the Son. The Father executes his Son's will, and the Mother unites the members of the Church in a common fellowship. In a sermon at Herrnhaag, the Count declared: "As concerning the Father and the Holy Ghost, they rejoice over his [Christ's] creatures; and they assist the Son in quickening, preserving and sanctifying us. The whole blessed Godhead rejoices, that the loving Son has created so many worlds; that he has remedied so many evils; and that when he neither would nor could create Gods, but only imperfect beings, he has notwithstanding in so glorious a manner found out means to preserve the honour of the deity." [37]

When this blest flock of souls so weak,
Against the hostile squadron,
(Of whom we many things could speak)
Does need a mighty patron:
Then does Jehova's Father there
With his omnipotence appear,
And the Son's sheep protecteth.[38]

The Christological problem, which to the minds of the Brethren had never been a problem, and about which they refused to speculate dogmatically, had led them under the influences of the Count into its deepest mysteries. Like children absorbed in their play and suddenly realizing that they have gone too far in the woods to find their way back, the Brethren sang and conversed in a language of experience and feeling about the

[36] *Collection of Hymns* (1754), part II, no. 385.
[37] Gambold: *Maxims*, p. 21.
[38] *Zugabe* I, no. 2,175. Trans. *Collection of Hymns* (1754), part II, no. 306.

person of Christ and the Trinity, until they were lost in their self-made ramifications. They complicated the matter by carrying out still further the family idea. While in Jesus there was the unity of the Father, Son, and Mother Spirit, he was also the husband of all souls. But the wound in his side was spoken of frequently as the birthplace from which all souls are "dug" or born. Thus Jesus is both mother and husband, and his father is grandfather and father-in-law, of all souls.

> Within our Husband's pierced Side
> Where all his little hearts abide
> And where we're sure we have a seat;
> There we do now each other greet.
>
> He us hath chose, and made his own,
> His members, his true flesh and bone,
> Who then were formed from his Side dear,
> When it was opened by the spear.[39]

> The first male Person's wife and she
> Issued out of his heart;
> The sinless man's bride suitably,
> Through breach made by a dart,
> Was fetched out of one Side of his:
> The mistress of the house since this,
> The Pleura does in scutcheon wear,
> And in each draught of her.[40]

> Jesus' Sire consented,
> That to him cemented
> Thou should'st ever be;
> Jesus did it merit
> And the Holy Spirit
> Beautifieth thee.
> Through Christ's blood, the Three-One God
> Owns thee as his near relation,
> O Lamb's Congregation.[41]

[39] *Collection of Hymns* (1754), part II, no. 366.
[40] *Zugabe* IV, no. 2,340. Trans. *Collection of Hymns* (1754), part II, no. 428.
[41] *Collection of Hymns* (1754), part II, no. 372.

Her clothing is of wrought gold,
God Father's daughter-in-law exhibits clear the ray
Of the holy blessed Trinity,
To them, who her in the Side do see.[42]

The Married choir the conduct fair
Of the blest Trinity do share,
And every daughter-in-law of God
Unhurt goes on her Road.[43]

With the Son thou'rt joined in one,
And the Holy Ghost and Father
Love thee as a daughter.[44]

Since Christ is the husband of all souls, they are of necessity all female, whether of man or woman. Physically men are male but spiritually female.[45] That all souls are married to their one conjugal Lord Jesus was minutely set forth in song and speech. In this married relationship of souls to their God-husband, all aspirations and desires were fully realized. The married state, which is the most intimate connection between two individuals, was the state existing between them and Christ. Souls came forth out of his Side wound; they were once one with him; and now they must seek reunion with him by being his loving wives. What could be more blessed than being married to God himself? They were one; he would hold them. The Lord's Supper was spoken of as the "Embrace of the Husband." Upon this thought the mystic natures of the Brethren fed to their hearts' content, as we have told in the preceding chapter.

Although Christ was especially the husband of women, men were no less blessed by him, since he appointed them to be his vice-husbands. The men were to bear a charge in Christ's name. "A husband ought to be well acquainted with the

[42] *Zugabe* III, no. 2,284. Trans. *Collection of Hymns* (1754), part II, no. 377.
[43] *Zugabe* IV, no. 2,340. Trans. *Collection of Hymns* (1754), part II, no. 428.
[44] *Collection of Hymns* (1754), part II, no. 372.
[45] *Homily of Wounds,* pp. 83 f.

Saviour's heart, that he may know how to discharge this trust, for as the wife is to have the thought and disposition of the church, or of a human soul simply, so he is to think and deport himself in all respects like Christ the Husband of Souls. This is an arduous incumbency on the man; he himself is inwardly but a female spirit towards the divine bridegroom: but when he has finished his service with grace, and for his Lord's sake, he has the comfort that he also in eternity, where male and female cease, shall be a plain and common soul, whose part is only to be caressed and cared for." [46]

A great responsibility rested upon the men in the discharge of their office as Christ's representatives on earth.[47]

> O thou, within whose arms we were
> Predestined to have place,
> Before the fall's deep harm and scar
> In heaven noticed was:
> We blush at thy election kind,
> Which in such list to set us deigned,
> Vice-husbands of his maids to be
> And copies of his She.[48]

> 'Tis certain by the general plan,
> A Proxy-husband may
> Rejoice in his high trust as man;
> But more, that there's a day,
> When he shall lay it down, and be
> What sisters were unvariedly,
> Who knowing they were the Lamb's bride,
> Had nought to learn beside.[49]

> Our present proxy-marriages
> Are done in Jesus' holy Name! [50]

[46] Gambold: *Maxims*, pp. 243, 244.
[47] *Zugabe* II, no. 2,268.
[48] *Collection of Hymns* (1754), part II, no. 428.
[49] *Collection of Hymns* (1754), part II, no. 423.
[50] *Anhang* XI, no. 1843. Trans. *Collection of Hymns* (1754), part II, no. 268.

Whether Zinzendorf's theology was that of all the Brethren is a pertinent inquiry. Certainly it survived this dominating figure by a brief span of years, until the influence of Spangenberg made itself felt. Today, the Moravians claim him and not Zinzendorf as their theologian. Although in these years under discussion, men like Spangenberg and Peter Böhler took exception to Zinzendorfianism, it was in general the prevailing religious thought. The theology of the common people of those early years is to be found especially in their voluminous hymnals, not only because it was the people who sang the hymns, but also because the authors of many of them were artisans, farmers, housewives, missionaries, and preachers. The religious thought of almost every class and condition of the Brethren is there represented.

That the Zinzendorfian theology was commonly accepted by the Brethren is evident from the fact that they approved of the sermons and addresses of the Count. John Becker, a missionary in the West Indies, wrote of his conversion: "In my twenty-first year, I visited Wächtersbach, where I met with many awakened persons who stood in connection with the Church of the Brethren. In the evening meeting at which I was present, a most edifying discourse by Count Zinzendorf was read which made a lasting impression upon me. In this blessed hour, I entered into a new covenant with my Saviour, to live no longer to myself, but to him who loved me first, and gave himself for me. . . . I became by degrees quite convinced that these were the people among whom I should like to cast in my lot." [51]

The people urged that the Count's addresses be put into permanent form. A noted Moravian author writes: "These discourses were commonly taken down as he [Zinzendorf] uttered them, and the love and admiration of his brethren were so great that they urged the publication of them." [52] The Brethren were fascinated by the fluency of the Count, impressed by his

[51] *Church Miscellany*, June 1852.
[52] Benjamin La Trobe, in the preface to Spangenberg's *Exposition of Christian Doctrine.*

emotional fervor, and charmed by his protrusive personality. They could not escape his subtle influence; he was the molding genius of their lives and thought,—but only for a generation. After his death, as we shall see, many of his characteristic ideas were discarded.

Although the Moravian Church, through the influence of Spangenberg, has gained in orthodoxy, it has lost in originality. There has been nothing new and original in Moravian theology since the days of Zinzendorf, and the Church professes adherence to the broad doctrines of the evangelical churches. The theology of the Zinzendorfian era, on the other hand, bore the stamp of extreme pietism in both the organization of exclusive groups and the cultivation of "simplicity" of mind and heart (*Einfalt*). This spirit is well expressed in a hymn by Spangenberg still sung by Moravians: [53]

> *Heilge Einfalt! Gnaden Wunder!*
> *Tiefste Weisheit! gröszte Kraft!*
> *Schönste Zierde! Liebeszunder!*
> *Werk das Gott alleine schafft!*
>
> *Alle Freyheit geht in Banden,*
> *Aller Reichthum ist nur wind,*
> *Alle Schönheit wird zuschanden,*
> *Wenn wir ohne Einfalt sind.*
>
> *Wenn wir in der Einfalt stehen,*
> *Ist es in der Seele licht;*
> *Aber wenn wir doppelt sehen,*
> *So vergeht uns das Gesicht.*
>
> *Wer allein auf Jesum trauet,*
> *Wer in Jesu alles findt;*
> *Der ist auf den Fels erbauet,*
> *Und ein seligs Gnadenkind.*[54]

[53] *Hymnal and Liturgies of the Moravian Church* (1920), no. 636.
[54] *Gesangbuch zum Gebrauch der evangelischen Brüdergemeinen* (1778). English trans. from *Collection of Hymns* (1754), part II, no. 63:

> Simple mind, thou grace's wonder!
> Deepest wisdom, greatest might,
> Fairest jewel, love's defender,
> Most successful Christian Fight!

Liberty does walk in fetters,
Riches are but empty wind,
Beauty has some ugly features,
If we're not of simple mind.

When simplicity we cherish,
We've a whole and perfect light;
But that view away will vanish,
Soon as double grows our sight.

Who alone by Jesus holdeth,
And in him does all possess;
He it is, who on him buildeth,
He walks too in holiness.

CHAPTER VII

"THE SIFTING TIME"

THEORETICALLY, after 1741 the care of the Brethren was committed to the Chief Elder Jesus, but practically the Count had already taken over the Lord's responsibilities. He had made himself a dictator, a theocrat ruling directly under the Invisible King. By a gradual process almost unnoticeable to the Brethren, authority had become more and more centralized until at last it rested almost wholly in the Count. His forceful personality and pivotal position, which made him the natural leader of the movement, whetted his appetite for power.

At the beginning of the Herrnhut movement, he shared authority with twelve elders. Perhaps under the Count's influence, these elders began "to feel conscientious scruples, lest they themselves should suffer harm in their souls in consequence of the high regard which was paid them in their official character, and which they feared was carried rather too far." [1] During the next stage of Moravian government, authority was vested in four elders, of whom the Count was one. The others were Augustin Neisser, Christian David, and Martin Linner. Thus control was placed in fewer hands, but the number was still to be reduced. The Count was the first to resign his office as warden on March 15, 1730, saying "that he wished to commit the care and keeping of the congregation entirely to God and the bridegroom of his Church, the Lord Jesus Christ." Following his example, and in the same year, Christian David "felt himself induced to lay down his elder's office." [2] After

[1] *Memorial Days,* pp. 194, 195.
[2] *Ibid.* He had brought the first settlers to Herrnhut, and perhaps for this reason thought himself entitled to more authority. When Zinzendorf had tried to make Lutherans of the Brethren, David had objected and withdrawn to a little hut outside of Herrnhut. Perhaps there were additional differences between him and the Count behind his resignation.

his resignation Martin Linner became the Chief Elder, with Augustin Neisser as an assistant. The Chief Eldership was not vested in Zinzendorf because it was still too soon for him openly to assume control. But in spite of the Chief Elder, the place of priority was never denied to the Count. His financial resources, his title, and his brilliance naturally overshadowed the prestige of the newly created office of Chief Eldership. The Chief Elder became merely the mouthpiece of the Count and the screen behind which he hid.

The expulsion of Zinzendorf from Herrnhut in 1736 seemed to the authorities a prudent step to dissociate the Count from the Separatist movement, which he was suspected of fostering on his estate. They might have exiled the settlers instead of the Count, but the Saxon officials, remembering their troubles with the Count while he held his official position in the Court, had "an ax to grind." Furthermore, it was "better that one man should die than that the whole nation should perish." But his exile did not prevent the Count's making himself an absentee autocrat in the Moravian kingdom; it merely served to bring to the fore his extreme and extravagant forms of pietism.

In 1741, when Leonard Dober, who had succeeded Martin Linner as Chief Elder, resigned, no one could be prevailed upon to accept the position. Now at last the opportunity had come "to commit the care and keeping of the congregation entirely to God"; Christ was made the Chief Elder, and Zinzendorf's autocratic rule soon began.

This centralized control in the hands of the temperamental and imaginative Count led the Brethren into a new religious experience, which, after they had emerged from it, they called the "Sifting Time." It reached its height in the years 1746-1750. The Count, at the height of his power, so impressed his personal fanaticism upon Moravianism that, in the period we are here discussing, the spirit of Zinzendorf was more in evidence than the "Unity of the Brethren." But there were, in addition, external circumstances in the history of their Church that contributed to the rise of the extravagant theology and practices of this period.

When Zinzendorf was exiled from Herrnhut he went to Wetteravia, which was jointly owned by the three Counts of Isenburg-Büdingen, Isenburg-Meerholz, and Isenburg-Wächterbach. The latter permitted Zinzendorf, with the Pilgrim Congregation, to move into an old castle called Ronneburg.[3] This castle lay half in ruin and was a forbidding place. It is said that no door or window of the castle would close, no stairway was safe to use, and the place was infested with mice and rats. The dirty walls and ceilings were as unsightly as the surrounding grounds, on which there were huts, dilapidated barns, and buildings. But Zinzendorf, surrounded with political and theological enemies, had few alternatives.

The Counts of these estates were deeply in debt and therefore welcomed new settlers to improve the land. Since 1712 liberty of conscience had been granted to any who would come. As a result "the out-houses, and farms and stables were let out to fifty-six dirty families of Jews, tramps, vagabonds and a mongrel throng of scoundrels of the lowest class." [4]   In and around this castle there were persons from numerous creeds and beliefs. "On Sunday evenings or at other times in the week there could be heard from a near-by building where the Jews had built their school, their unpleasant songs which sounded into the cells of the Separatists where two or three had gathered for song and prayer, while the Inspired waited in silence until the spirit laid hold of some man or woman to place in their mouths a new revelation." [5]

The Pilgrim Congregation worked among this motley rabble, living in filth and poverty. These Separatists were decidedly different from the Moravians in Herrnhut and were indeed not Moravians at all. The Count provided free instruction to the children and on Sundays gathered all who would come for a religious service. The inhabitants at Ronneburg never understood why a person with his culture and prestige should have taken up his abode with them. Was he to be an object of pity or ridicule? His preaching and zeal to reform soon made

[3] Glaubrecht: *Zinzendorf in der Wetterau-Ronneburg.*
[4] Hutton: *History,* p. 165.
[5] Glaubrecht: *Ronneburg,* p. 7.

enemies even here, especially among the "Inspired," who disagreed with him on the sacraments and free grace. The Count and his followers were soon scorned and ridiculed, and their meetings were disturbed. Under such conditions, they looked about for new living quarters and moved.

Zinzendorf rented the castle Marienborn from Count Isenburg-Meerholz for three years. Here the Pilgrim Congregation established itself; and from this place as headquarters the missionaries went forth to preach. Also, from time to time, the Count summoned here those who held official positions for conferences which he called synods. The Brethren fared better than at Ronneburg. The castle at Marienborn and other buildings were soon crowded with persons who desired to cast their lot with these Brethren. Persons of various creeds and conditions assembled here: the religiously persecuted, exiled statesmen, tired business-men, married and single laborers, women as well as men, and even some persons of wealth.[6]

Because of this rapid growth at Marienborn, the Brethren negotiated with Count Isenburg-Büdingen and acquired a piece of land from him on which Herrnhaag was built. Herrnhaag was established in 1738 and grew so rapidly that within a few years its population was about one thousand. Some came from the strange mixture of Marienborn and settled here; others came from foreign countries and applied for entrance. Of seven who were taken into the membership of the settlement on a single day, one was from Poland, another from Hungary, a third from Switzerland, a fourth from England, a fifth from Livonia, a sixth from Germany, and the last from Sweden.[7] This promiscuous group, the Count by a stroke of genius welded into a unity. Herrnhaag then became the rendezvous where missionaries and labourers in home and foreign fields came on furlough to rest; here others were prepared and sent forth; and thus it became the official headquarters from whence all Moravianism was directed and controlled.

Although the Count was in exile, he had bettered his position, since in a few years' time he had established himself in a

---

[6] Glaubrecht: *Zinzendorf in der Wetterau-Marienborn.*

[7] Glaubrecht: *Zinzendorf in der Wetterau-Herrnhaag*, p. 79.

strange land with a large following. From the unsightly Ronneburg to the well-equipped Herrnhaag, where large and elaborate buildings for the various Choirs were built, was an achievement to which he could point with pride. The Brethren were no longer a poor Pilgrim Congregation. Prosperity had followed them into exile. They now lived in luxurious buildings such as they had never had at Herrnhut. It was a haven of rest which attracted even the well-to-do. The Brethren made their position here still more secure by lending large sums of money to the Counts Isenburg-Meerholz and Isenburg-Büdingen, who were in financial straits. These loans were given on a thirty-year contract and were made possible by financial aid which the Brethren received from some friends in Holland and England. By this contract they achieved security and made themselves the creditors of two of the Counts in whose realms they lived.

In this situation we see at work two external forces which were bound to bring forth "something new out of an old treasure," namely, the medley of beliefs and nationalities and the unexpected prosperity. The union of these two circumstances needed only to be fertilized by the extravagant imagination of Zinzendorf to give birth to what was an illegitimate child of Moravianism.

After his visit to America and his work among the sectaries of Pennsylvania, Zinzendorf inferred that the evils of Pennsylvania were due to the many methods of sanctification and salvation that had been built upon the general doctrine of the merits of Christ. He had hoped to bring harmony and good will to Pennsylvania by a general agreement on the person of Christ. On his return to Wetteravia he feared that the forces which caused the disharmony in Pennsylvania, if they were once aroused in Herrnhaag, might produce a similar situation. He therefore "laboured against it in his discourses and hymns, endeavoring fully to enthrone the merits and wounds of Jesus; and showing that not only the forgiveness of sins and eternal salvation were to be deduced from thence, but that the cleansing from sin, and our true sanctification and preservation, flowed solely from this fountain." [8]   As fanaticism usually consists in driving a truth to the extreme, so the Brethren at Herrnhaag became a group of enthusiastic fanatics on the subject of the atonement of Christ, to the exclusion of all else in their speech and practice.   This emphasis on a single topic, though it created unity, also produced a new extravagance which in turn caused the ruin of Herrnhaag, as we shall see.

The other external force which hastened the theological extravagances was the newly acquired prosperity.   The Brethren felt a new sense of security and believed that the "Lord had consented" personally to take charge of Moravian affairs. They now let the Lord do all the worrying for them and applied to themselves literally the words: "Except ye become as little children."   Although these Brethren had, until recently, worked hard for their daily bread, they were now resting securely and enjoying unaccustomed luxuries.   Most of the money with which the Choir houses, churches, and public buildings were erected had been lent them by friends on interest.   Of the financial status the common people had no knowledge.   They simply believed that it was the invisible Chief Elder who was thus smiling upon them.   This Moravian boom made others willing to lend them large sums of money. The Brethren enjoyed to the full this new sensation of public confidence in contrast to the burden of reproach they had borne for some twenty years.   The Count, sharing this confidence, kept on spending borrowed money with no thought of how to liquidate the debt.   The lot was continually used to ascertain the invisible Chief Elder's will in all these matters, but usually the Lord was in agreement with Zinzendorf, although there is no evidence that he manipulated the lot consciously.

Having cast their cares upon the Chief Elder, who had thus prospered them, the Brethren became irresponsible.   They spoke of themselves as "little fools, children, virgins that were only to enjoy themselves in the wounds of Jesus."   In his exposition of the Litany of the Wounds, Zinzendorf said that we should be children, because Christ himself was a child and

[8] La Trobe: *Cranz's History of the Brethren,* p. 356.

was childlike and rejoiced as a child. Christ ignored his danger on his flight to Egypt, when Herod sought his life. The honor and the pomp with which the three Wise Men honored him, he did not understand. He did not even know or at least he was unconcerned about his parents and his home, when for three days in all simplicity he stayed in the Temple. "Therefore we want to be children; we all together our whole life long want to live in such a blessed childlikeness, whenever thou shalt grant it to us; and be in such an innocence and ignorance of all unnecessary things, and in an easy contentment in all difficult circumstances, and continue to find shelter in the hole of thy wounds, as a child relies on his guardian or depends on his father or mother, in which they are superior to the rest in blessedness, and become an example in peace and joy." [9] Zinzendorf even organized a new order called *"Närrchen"* (little fools), which had as its aim simplicity and childlikeness. This society was to set forth the true character of a true Christian. The members of this order no longer had heads but only hearts. The mind was no longer necessary; they let God care for them; they spent their lives in blessed and happy play. The Count also allowed himself to be called "Papa" (*Herzens Papa*), and his wife "Mama" (*Mütterlein*).[10]

Zinzendorf suffered from a pathological condition which broke out in demonstrations of emotionalism, phantasies, and morbidity. In place of the pious exhortations of earlier days, his speech now resounded with word pictures of the merits of Christ's blood and wounds and an excess of sensual symbolism. This example of the cultured Count among these simple-minded Brethren was imitated until they used a language which was intelligible neither to themselves nor to others. It was a kind of "speaking with tongues" in which they strove among themselves for superiority. They called themselves by such diminutive terms as *"Närrchen"* (little fools), *"Herrchen"* (little lords), *"Hühnchen"* (little chickens), and *"Würmlein"*

[9] *Wunden Litaney Reden,* pp. 91, 92.
[10] Cammerhoff's *"Epistola Tertia."* Ms. Beth. Arch. Also his letters to Jonas P. Weiss, 1747, and to Peter Böhler, Jan. 17, 1751. Ms. Beth. Arch.

(little worms).[11] They spoke of themselves as "little doves flying about in the atmosphere of the cross," and "little fish swimming in the bed of blood," or "little bees who suck on the wounds of Christ,"[12] "who feel at home in the Side hole and crawl in deep."[13] To this can be added many other pet names.[14] The Count explained: "When the heart is right and whole, and one can say with truth: 'this is a heart, a little blood worm, one who is a little dove flying in the atmosphere of the cross, a little fish swimming around in the bed of blood, a sickly creature according to the Side Shrine of Jesus, a poor human soul that can not live without his merits,' then the bridegroom will say: 'Let me see your form for your form is lovely'; now you need distort your face no longer to express composure; you need no longer consult the spiritual mirror; you need no longer be careful about your strides and steps, how you will appear, how to hold your hands and set your feet, and how you will hold your eyes and move your mouth; of all this you need no longer think; but when you are full of bloody grace, when your mercy is besprinkled, when your heart swims in blood, then you will of necessity have carried away the stripes of blood and also the beauty of sinners."[15] In the stream of the wounds they "want to have little beds, and tables, and everything."[16] They are "doves in the cleft of the rock."[17]

This extreme sensuality found its expression in the Choir rites, especially in connection with the Single Brethren, Single Sisters, and Married Choirs. This extravagant fanaticism was never characteristic of Moravianism at its best, and although a residium of it remained for many years, the frequent subsequent revisions of the liturgies and hymnals deleted more and more of the sensual imagery.

[11] *"Conclusa oder Verlasz des Vom 3/14 bis 8/19 Sept. 1747, in Bethlehem gehaltenen Synodi der Brüder."* Ms. Beth. Arch.

[12] *Wunden Litaney Reden*, p. 198.

[13] Cammerhoff's *"Epistola"* (fifteenth letter). Ms. Beth. Arch.

[14] See *Zugabe* II, nos. 2,255, 2,269, 2,270; *Zugabe* III, no. 2,277.

[15] *Wunden Litaney Reden*, pp. 45, 46.

[16] *Ibid.*, p. 183.

[17] *Ibid.*, p. 198.

My dearest, most beloved Lamb
I who in tenderest union am
To all thy cross-air-birds bound,
Smell to and kiss each corpse's wound;
Yet at the Side-hole's part,
There pants and throbs my heart.
I see still, how the soldier fierce
Did thy most lovely Pleura pierce,
That dearest Side-hole!
Be praised, O God, for this Spear's slit!
I thank thee, Soldier, too for it.
I've licked this Rock's salt round and round
Where can such relish else be found! [18]

Symbolism of this kind, although not always so repulsive, flourished with morbid sentiments in most of the early hymns.

In time there came into use a whole list of meaningless words and phrases which were on all lips. The more holy and sacred the subject, the more unintelligible the language and the greater the challenge to the imagination for novel expressions. This new language is hardly translatable, and so a few examples are here submitted in the original.[19]

So immer seit-wärts-schielerlich,
So seiten-heimweh-fühlerlich,

[18] *Zugabe* III, no. 2,305. Trans. *Collection of Hymns*, part III, London, 1749. The original is as follows:

Mein allerliebstes Lämmelein,
Ein zart verbundnes herzelein
Mit denen creuz-luft-vögelein,
Beriecht und küszt dein Leichelein;
Doch übers Seit-revier,
Da zappelts herze mir.
Ich sehs noch, wie der kriegs-knecht
Stach das allerliebste Seitenfach,
Das Seiten-höhlgen.
Gott lob! für diesen speeres-stich,
Du kriegs-knecht, ich bedanke mich.
Ich hab as um und um belekt,
Das stein-salz! O wie hats geschmekt!
In dem punct ist mein seelgen verrükt,
Zum Seiten-höhlgen.

[19] For other examples see *Zugabe* III, nos. 2,277, 2,281, 2,282, 2,283.

So Lamms-herz-gruft-durchkriecherlich,
So Lamms-schweisz-spur-beriecherlich,
An der magnetschen Seit.
So Jesus-schweisz-tropf-haftiglich,
Vor liebes-fieber schütterlich,
Wie's kind voll Geistes,
So leichnams-luft-anzieherlich,
So wunden-nasz-ausprüherlich,
So grabes-dünste witterlich,
Auf's mensch-Sohns zeichen zitterlich,
Dem licht in Salem's gassen,
Wenn sonn und mond erblassen.

Indesz so Lammhaft seliglich,
Einfältig, taubenartiglich,
So sünder-scham-roth inniglich,
So sünder-mäszig spielerlich,
Worein's doch immer summ': "efflavit animum";
Vor creuzes-freuden weinerlich,
So brust-blat-jünger-mäsziglich,
Wie Sanct Johannes;
So Marter-Lamms-herzhaftiglich,
So Jesus-knabenhaftiglich,
So Marie Magdalenelich,
Kindlich, jungfraulich, ehelich,
Soll uns das Lamm erhalten,
Bis zum kusz seiner Spalten.[20]

Wie machts ein creuz-luft-vögelein,
Wenns will, wenns eben darf hinein?
Da nehmens die creuz-lüftelein
Und führens bis vors Leichelein,
Die flügel werden schlapp,
Das vöglein fiel herab,
Wenns nicht mit seinem schnäbelein
Sich zwischen fell und fleisch hinein gepikket hätte.
Da hängts nun an dem Ur-Magnet,
Da hängt das vöglein steiff und stät,
Verging ihm drüber stund und zeit,
Und mehr als eine ewigkeit,

[20] *Zugabe* III, no. 2,278.

Viel glüks zum ewgen leben!
Ihr heilgen, laszt mich kleben.

Wie machts das Ehe-herzelein,
Dasz es ein solches täubelein,
Wenns noch in diese zeit gehört,
In seinem sabbathismo stöhrt?
Das stellt der liebe Mann
Auf diese weise an,
Dasz er dem vor dem Seitenschrein
Vor lieb entschlafnen täubelein
Das eingebissen, aufs zugefallne äugelein
Und wie verschlungne schnäbelein
Auf einmal einen blut-strom geuszt,
Der übers ganze vöglein fleuszt.
Das losgeweichte vöglein
Macht wieder creuz-luft-seglein.[21]

"They began in such a manner to refine upon, and over-charge with various poetical figures and unintelligible expressions, the subject of the sacred wound made in the side of Jesus, that his precious merits were almost totally set aside. Each of this sort of people strove to out-do the other in strange and unintelligible new expressions and poetical productions, deviating very far from the pattern of the old church-hymns and the spiritual songs hitherto in use in the congregations of the Brethren. Others who had formerly read mystical books brought all manner of fanatical ideas upon the carpet. Many who had had a legal education, (and this was the most surprising of all), from a gloomy, self-working spirit still cleaving to them, fell at once into a liberty equally unbecoming children of God, which in some proceeded even to a licentious impudence."[22]

With transparent pictures, colorful illuminations, living pictures, and tableaus, they pictured the wounds, blood, and suffering of Christ. They interpreted in all its hideous literalness the conception of regeneration by the Holy Spirit in the blood of Christ. It is said that a niche covered with red cloth was

[21] *Zugabe* III, no. 2,280.
[22] La Trobe: *Cranz's Hist. of the Brethren,* pp. 370-371.

built into the wall of the church, into which children were placed to symbolize their lying in Christ's Side wound, and that Christian Renatus, Zinzendorf's son, built a "Side Wound" through which the congregation marched.[23]

To every deed and act of Christ, no matter how small, a great mystic significance was attached. Everything in connection with his body, the wounds, the blood, the sweat, the saliva from his mouth, the scars made by the pricks of the thorns, became objects of worship and were adored, and their mystic relation was expounded at great length. Thus, when Jesus appeared before Herod, he was given a baptismal garment to wear, for "the Saviour was now baptized, my brethren; he was saturated and vaporized with the sacrament of the baptism of anger [*Zorn-taufe*] and the covenant-dew [*Bundesthaues*] of his own death sweat." [24] When sweat appeared on Jesus' brow, they had no further reason to be anxious, for this was an indication that he sweated out all their sins.[25] They wanted Christ to dry their feet with his besweated hair so that a dampness from his bloody sweat might remain. "For it is a blessing for our feet, it is a grace for us, when the washing of this holy bath is always renewed by a residual of sweat drops, when we go about in a constant moistening from his tears of penitence and death-sweat drops." [26] As some have holes drilled in their noses and ears in which to carry rings, so the Lord allowed holes to be dug through his hands that the bride might have her name stamped in them with the nails that were hammered through them and etched in with his blood and sweat. And as one nation has the marriage ring on the small finger of the left hand, another on the index finger, so the Lord, the bridegroom of souls, carried his in the palm of the hand. In this marriage ring was the name of the bride, that is, of all the betrothed souls.[27] The disciples at the Last Supper literally ate his body, since "when this last distress had already seized him,

[23] Oskar Pfister: *Die Frömmigkeit des Grafen Ludwig von Zinzendorf,* p. 33.
[24] *Wunden Litaney Reden,* p. 189.
[25] See *Anhang* XII, nos. 1,945, 1,956.
[26] *Wunden Litaney Reden,* pp. 236-237.
[27] *Ibid.,* p. 270.

and he stood already half dead before his disciples, so that he could say: 'My soul is exceeding sorrowful, even unto death!' then he took bread in his hands which of course while he held it was so penetrated with his moist dying sweat, and partook of the ferment of his agony (the psalmist mentions his mingling his bread with ashes, and his drink with weeping Ps. 100:11) that when he blessed and broke it for his disciples, it was indeed mixed with his body and the 'Effluvia' thereof; and when he took the cup, some of his tears dropt into it, and also of the blood which was now ready through anguish everywhere to extravasate, Luke 22:44. Thus they ate not only bread, but therewith took in real particles of his death-struck and excruciated body; and drank not only wine, but a tincture of his blood therein." [28]

As an expression of this new religious feeling, the Brethren turned out hymns prolifically. The four supplements called the *Zugaben,* including the hymns numbered 2,157-2,359, dating from the years 1745-1749, were products of this time. Out of this strange and new spirit came such hymns as:

> Whilst yet the babe is in the womb,
> No damps it feels or bears,
> Which so impregnate all the Room,
> Where nurse its vestments airs:
> Constrictions sore, which do compel
> The babe to leave its mother's cell,
> Do cause it soon howe'er to breath
> The streams that round it wreath.[29]

> A little bee am I,
> Who on thy Side's shrine lie,
> And without cessation
> Thy fragrant wounds enjoy.
> With thy cross congregation.
> I can't have a thought,
> That one wanteth ought,
> When he thee hath got.[30]

[28] Gambold: *Maxims,* p. 175.
[29] *Zugabe* III, No. 2,293. Trans. *Collection of Hymns* (1754), no. 399.
[30] *Zugabe* I, no. 2,194. Trans. *Collection of Hymns* (1754), no. 440.

Our husband's Side-wound is indeed
The queen of all his wounds;
On this the little pidgeons feed,
Whom cross' air surrounds.
There they fly in and out and sing,
Side's blood is seen on every wing.
The bill that picks the Side-hole's floor,
Is red of blood all o'er.

Ye cross'-air birds, swell the notes
Of the sweet Side-hole song,
That fountain's juice will clear your throats,
And help to hold it long.
Each day and year shall higher raise
The Side-hole's glory, love and praise:
Hallelujah!   Hallelujah!
To the Side Gloria! [31]

In conversation, too, they expressed an extreme love for Christ. Thus the Lord's Supper was called an "embrace." "From the time of the sacramental embrace, each faithful and in the person of Christ truly enamoured heart, swimming by faith in his wounds, can count on his genuine blood stripe which truly shows itself in his face, in his deeds, nature, and in his external person and presence." [32] At nights they retired in the arms of their Husband (Jesus).[33] Christ kissed them with his "pale and dead lips" and with his "corpse," and the Brethren in return kissed the "four holes of Jesus' nail prints." [34] "It has happened and it happens daily that he approaches us with his lips, that he presses us on the heart . . . he loves us so much that we feel the urge in which he burns when our Creator embraces us." [35] This song of love became

[31] *Collection of Hymns* (1754), no. 460.

[32] *Wunden Litaney Reden*, p. 48.

[33] *"Das Chor Gemein Diarium in Christiansbrunn. July 7, 1754."* Ms. Beth. Arch.

[34] *"Umständlicher Bericht von den Herrnhutischer und Herrnhaagischer Reise Nach Pennsilvanian im Jahr 1743 von der einrichtung einer See Gemeine und andern dahin gehörigen Umständen. Abgefasset von Bruder G. Neisser der sie teils auf der Lande Reise, teils zur See bis Plymouth in England begleitet."* Ms. Beth. Arch.

[35] *Wunden Litaney Reden*, p. 48.

extremely sensuous. "When for example at the Lord's Supper we really bite into his death and martyr-corpse [*Marter-Leichnam*], when we attach ourselves to him, and would like to kiss ourselves to death on him, and he on us, so that he really kills, devours, gulps down, and tears everything on us that does not please him, and that also does not please us, with all this our bodily eyes remain shut and our bodily ears closed. Our natural taste is not allowed to taste the wound-sweetness [*Wundensüszigkeit*], nor can we become aware of the loveliness of the corpse-likeness [*Leichenhaftigkeit*] with the natural human sense of smell, as we at times would like to. Our souls and spirits, however, see, smell, taste, and have perception of it." [36]

"At certain times, when for example one leaves the body, or is engaged in special liturgical transactions, when one prostrates himself before him, before the wounded Side, when one is drawn into an astonishingly deep wound discourse, or has come into a deep thought about his martyrdom, and in that way with soul and heart buries himself deeply, or works himself into the hole in the rock, yes, wishes himself wholly into it, especially at the Holy Communion, when the mouth keeps the wound-covenant with the most undivided, then at times he can come so near that one can truly think: Now I will see him, now I will hear him, now I will lay hold of his body. And then one sees, hears and holds, however, not bodily, but in faith and yet corporeally." [37] In fact it was the duty of the Holy Spirit as Mother "to preach wounds and to hold open the Side and direct our thoughts to this cleft in the rock of his holy side until we have become a wound of Jesus in body and soul." [38]

For this morbid theology a special litany was dedicated to the wounds of Jesus, which celebrated the "bloody gore," "besweated hair," "pale lips," "bespittled cheeks," "shady wounds," "sun-like wounds," "purple wounds," "juicy wounds," "gentle wounds," "lodging wounds," and "beauteous

[36] *Wunden Litaney Reden*, p. 217.
[37] *Wunden Litaney Reden*, pp. 216, 217.
[38] *Ibid.*, p. 15.

wounds." [39] This litany was chanted at the congregational festivities [40] and also in the Choir devotionals.[41] Of Zinzendorf's son, Christian Renatus, it is said that he wrote: "In our congregation it constantly becomes bloodier, and the cross and blood themes become increasingly pleasanter and heart penetrating. We have a taste at every hour only for wounds and wounds and wounds and wounds." [42] What they "do and think and speak was mixed with his meritorious tears and blood." [43] "Every state among us, every regulation, yea every ruling idea must be first sprinkled with blood." [44]

Their aim was to present the picture of the blood and wounds until the hardest hearts would melt. Therefore they wanted to find in the Bible nothing but the blood and wounds.[45] Since the "only light they had shone from the wounds of Jesus," they had to "beware of everything that was not bloody." [46] Of the children in Bethlehem and Nazareth, Cammerhoff wrote: "Among them you hear nothing but wounds and wounds and wounds." [47] He rejoiced that "in America there were blowing bloody breezes of grace." [48] In respect to the blood and wounds they boasted of their sectarianism and called themselves the "visible Wound-Church." [49]

> *Des Wundten Creuz-Gotts bundes-blut,*
> *Die Wunden-wunden-wunden-fluth,*
> *Ihr Wunden! ja, ihr wunden!*
> *Eur wunden-wunden-wunden-gut*
> *Macht wunden-wunden-wunden-muth*
> *Und wunden, herzens-wunden.*

[39] See Appendix C.
[40] *"Diarium Bethlehem,"* Aug. 1754. Ms. Beth. Arch.
[41] *"Das Chor Gemein Diarium in Christiansbrunn,"* June 23, 1754. Ms. Beth. Arch.
[42] Pfister: *Frömmigkeit des Grafen,* p. 32.
[43] *Einige der letzten Reden,* p. 15.
[44] Gambold: *Maxims,* p. 140.
[45] *"Conclusa Synodi,"* Sept. 1747. Ms. Beth. Arch.
[46] *Ibid.*
[47] *"Epistola Tertia."*
[48] *Ibid.*
[49] *"Verlasz des Synodi der Brüder gehalten in Bethlehem vom 12/23 bis 16/27 October 1748."* Ms. Beth. Arch.

> *Wunden! Wunden! Wunden! Wunden!*
> *Wunden! Wunden! Wunden! Wunden!*
> *Wunden! Wunden! O! ihr wunden.*[50]

"Wounds and boils in fact are nothing pleasant, that is certain, but it so happens that all people who otherwise cannot bear the sight of blood, cannot remove a plaster, and who cannot think of an abscess without dread, laugh when in the Congregation they sing and think about the Saviour's gashes, boils, wounds, and pus."[51]   In short "his wounds are the Summum Bonum of all souls."[52]   This fanaticism brought upon the Moravians the ridicule of others, so that when they appeared on the streets in Philadelphia, their opponents began shouting: "Lamb, Lamb, Lamb, Lamb."[53]

In this morbid adoration of Christ's body attention was centered more particularly on the wound in his side.

> Holy Side-wound, pierced Pleura,
> Heart of Jesus, rent for me!
> Thou unfathomable Side-hole,
> Fain would I be lost in thee.
> Ever a sure rock-hole
> Art thou to my man-soul.
> Which from that hole of the pit
> Hewn and split,
> Always weeps and pants for it.[54]

This wound stood for everything that Christ was.[55]   "The pierced side of Jesus is a central point from whence all that is spiritual may be deduced; there we can find the square-root of all spiritual and heavenly matters, and can bring out something of a system."[56]   This wound had the power of giving birth to souls and was spoken of as the "true matrix."[57]

[50] *Anhang* XII, no. 1,945.
[51] *Wunden Litaney Reden*, p. 343.
[52] *Ibid.*, p. 53.
[53] Cammerhoff's *"Epistola"* (fifteenth).   Ms. Beth. Arch.
[54] *Zugabe* III, no. 2,281.   Trans. *Collection of Hymns* (1754), part II, no. 447.
[55] *Zugabe* IV, no. 2,343.
[56] Gambold: *Maxims*, p. 230.
[57] *Ibid.*

"Adam fell asleep, and the Creator in the meantime opened his side, and took out of it his future spouse; and when he awoke he saw her before him, Gen. II. Just so our Saviour likewise falling asleep, soon after came one and pierced his side, it having been so decreed, because the human soul, as happy, was to be taken and dug out thence." [58]

The theological implication of this strange religious dialect was the centricity of Christ's atonement in God's plan of redemption. "The holy five wounds must be for me clefts in the rock into which I can flee like a dove, so that the hellish inauguration may not rob me." [59]

> *Wir Sünder Sünderine*
> *Um Seinen Seiten Schrein*
> *Sind alle eine darinn.*
> *Nur da daheim zu sein*
> *Da wo sein Busz-Lamm-Blut*
> *Den Boden durstig machte.*[60]

These wounds were to shine into the whole world for the salvation of all.[61] "What shall convince mankind of sin will be the sign where they have pierced him; these wounds which some of his creatures gave, and others would not help to heal." [62] There sins are to be forever drowned. "I suppress them [sins] so assiduously with the corpse of Jesus, and drown them so often with the blood out of his holy Side that they shall be far distant from me till my dying days, if only I will not be a day out of the arms and lap of the Saviour, even as he shall not permit me as long as I remain a poor sinful man and not become a proud devil or rather a fool of the devil." [63]

The blood was also a mediator, "for his blood speaks more powerfully and effectually than that of Abel. For that called for vengeance against his brother. But the blood of Christ intercedes for grace as well for those who actually shed it as

[58] *Ibid.*
[59] *Naturelle Reflexiones,* p. 104.
[60] "*Verlasz der Synodi,*" Sept. 1747.
[61] *Barbysche Sammlungen,* p. 149.
[62] Gambold: *Maxims,* p. 305.
[63] *Naturelle Reflexiones,* p. 112.

for us who had as truly a hand in it." [64]   His bloody death also sanctified and made them holy.   "All those who know what sin is and have obtained permission not to sin any more, refrain from sin and lead a godly life, but that this is only the benefit of the most precious privilege, which Jesus has purchased for them with his own blood, and which no body will part with, who is in his right senses." [65]   And finally, the blood had the power to unite all believers.   "It is known what a strong cement the ancients used in their buildings, so that a whole wall was like one stone.   But ours excels all.   When our house is joined together by the Lamb's blood, and not the least pebble put in without having the moisture of his wounds upon it, we shall be indissoluble." [66]

As the Athenians erected an altar to the unknown god, so Zinzendorf, for fear of committing the gross sin of overlooking a single thorn-prick or bruise on Jesus' body, spoke of the unknown wounds.   He said it was one of the treasures in Christ, that when we think we have viewed, pictured, and meditated about the Saviour from head to foot, we discover that there is still this and that which we have forgotten.[67]

That this theology was early implanted into the minds of the young is illustrated in a catechetical hymn for children.

Question: Ye children; where do you dwell? Where is your ground? Where is the best care for such little ones found?

Answer: We dwell in the wound holes, in Jesus' flesh made: The holy church cares for, and lends us her aid.

Question: What is now to children the dearest thing here?

Answer: To be the Lamb's lambkins and chickens most dear: Such lambkins are nurished with food which is best; Such chickens sit safely and warm in the nest.

Now when you know so much, dear children! then see That each on the wound-holes do suck as a bee:

---

[64] *Sixteen Discourses on the Redemption of Man,* pp. 38, 39.
[65] Preface to *Sixteen Discourses on the Redemption of Man,* p. 3.
[66] Gambold: *Maxims,* p. 173.
[67] *Wunden Litaney Reden,* p. 302.

The grace got in baptism right value and hold,
So will be more myst'ries unto you unfold.[68]

Another excess to which all this enthusiasm led was an immoderate exaltation of marriage. Christ's marriage to the soul was vividly portrayed in sexual terminology, and the idea of the Bridegroom and the bride pictured to the point of sensuousness. Only by reason of this marriage relationship had they the right to holiness and salvation. "Whereby out of a creature that was but a walking sink or sewer, there is formed a temple of the Holy Ghost; and he that has found salvation in Jesus' wounds becomes as holy as those wounds by right of compact and matrimonial provision.[69]

The marriage contract between Christ and the soul made earthly marriage a "proxy marriage," anticipating the final wedlock of the Bridegroom with the bride. Earthly marriage was merely an "interim," a time of preparation for what will be. In the development of this thought the married relationship was fantastically idealized in discourses and hymns for the married Choir, the Single Brethren, and the Single Sisters. To sanctify sexual relationships the "First Wound" (circumcision) of Jesus was honored. The Single Brethren in Bethlehem held a special service to honor this wound.[70] "Through the merit of his wound of circumcision, we trust to sanctify the choirs or conditions of life, to keep the bodies of the youth and virgins shut up from dissolute nature, and reserve to the Creator alone the right of using them hereafter (if, and when it shall be his will concerning any) for his service. And then, in the state of marriage we also trust, agreeably to his original plan, in the authority of the only virgin-like man Jesus Christ, to disenchant and rid the act of begetting children from that voluptuous luxury, which otherwise by a kind of magic has been interwoven with it; and to free our lying in women from the usual dread of child-bed, and make this act, though at-

---

[68] *Anhang* XII, no. 1,917. Trans. *Collection of Hymns* (1754), part II, no. 411.

[69] Gambold: *Maxims*, p. 156.

[70] *"Die Erste Wunde Jesu kriegte heute ihre Ehre von unserm Chor."* *"Diarium des Ledigen Brüders Chors,"* Jan. 1745. Ms. Beth. Arch.

tended with pain, appear such a venerable piece of divine worship as they can rejoice at in soul and body." [71]

The exaltation of marriage was sung in hymns, some of them having twenty-five or more stanzas. In the year 1743, four hymns which are representative of this language and thought, were written for the widows, the married people, the Single Brethren, and the Single Sisters.[72]

It is not our intention here to make a psychological analysis of this symbolism. Students of psychoanalysis will readily recognize in this extravagant enthusiasm common symbols of common psychopathic fixations. This type of sexual pathology is by no means unique. What makes this particular form especially interesting, however, is the extensive use of theological symbols for sexual themes, and the fact that these abnormal traits dominated the whole community. In the Orient such religious eroticism is common and traditional, and Hindu symbolism analogous to Zinzendorf's can be found in the extreme forms of Bhakti and in the Tantric literature; but in the Christian tradition they are comparatively rare.

It is commonly understood that this extravagant theology flourished only in the years 1746-1750, known as the "Sifting Time." But earlier and later documents and hymns abundantly prove that it persisted for a longer time. In a hymn written as early as 1741 love was lavished on Christ in terms of "kissing," "blood sweat," "their dear Man," and "Side wound." [73] Hymns for the adult Choirs containing extreme exaltations of marriage were written in the year 1743. In 1742, Zinzendorf spoke of the Brethren as "little blood-worms in the sea of grace." [74] In 1740 one of the unmarried Brethren wrote that if he were unconscious and heard something said about the cross, he would be immediately revived.[75] As early as 1740 Anna Nitschmann, before her sailing to America with Zinzendorf, in a letter to all the Brethren's congregations

---

[71] Gambold: *Maxims*, p. 229.
[72] See *Anhang* XI, nos. 1,842, 1,843, 1,844, 1,845.
[73] See *Anhang* X, no. 1,656.
[74] See preface to *Anhang* XI.
[75] *Büd. Samm.*, vol. II, p. 539.

wrote: "I want to lock myself in his wounds and scars like a poor little worm. . . . Let it be your element to swim and bathe in the sea of grace that is in Jesus' blood." [76]   From America she wrote: "I am happy in Jesus' Side-hole." [77]   Even the tendency to play appears as early as 1741. In that year the Count said: "Even our whole sanctification and following of Jesus is not a serious enterprise but a happy child's play." [78]

Because of these excesses, of which Herrnhaag was the source, this place was disrupted in 1750 by the government of Büdingen. By this jolt the Count was somewhat shocked into sobriety, and he now reprimanded the Brethren in a circular letter [79] for the extravagances of which he himself was the instigator. But he could not immediately stop the movement. It continued for some time by the force of its own momentum. The Chief Eldership of Christ was retained and the use of the lot was continued until the end of the nineteenth century. However, soon after the evacuation of Herrnhaag, the extremely sentimental and objectionable language was greatly modified.

On Oct. 17, 1749, the Count of Isenburg-Büdingen died. His successor was suspicious of the Brethren and wanted them to renounce allegiance to Zinzendorf and swear allegiance to the Büdingen government. Accordingly the new Count sent them a form of homage which they refused to sign. Consequently, according to the Peace of Westphalia, the Brethren had to vacate the land in the period of three years which the law allowed. At the end of this period, Herrnhaag was a desolate and deserted place. The creditors of the Brethren, who had made possible the erection of the large buildings and the loans to the government, now became anxious about their money, especially in view of the controversial writings of Rimius, Whitefield, and others. This financial crisis was at its height in 1753, when George Whitefield, who accused the

[76] *Ibid.*, III, pp. 46, 47.
[77] *Ibid.*, p. 88.
[78] Gambold: *Maxims*, p. 24.
[79] "A letter to Choir Leaders and Elders' Conferences. London, Feb. 10, 1749." Ms. Beth. Arch.

Count of robbery and intrigue, published his *Expostulatory Letter to Zinzendorf,* which almost ruined the Brethren financially. By a very narrow margin, the Brethren again established confidence in their creditors. The burden of liquidating the debt incurred in Herrnhaag was imposed upon all the congregations in Europe and in America, and after many years was paid.

The fanaticism in England and in the Wetterau provoked the hostile pen of Henry Rimius, who was interested in having the Brethren driven from the country. In a work dedicated to the Archbishop of Canterbury, he said the Brethren were a danger to church and state, and were setting up an empire within an empire. He accused them of having their own secret service men to plot against the government. He denounced them for their independence of the civil government, since they had their own magistrates, secret laws, and courts. He assailed their community life, in which the Count and the elders exercised arbitrary authority to marry and divorce couples and to separate children from their parents. The Brethren, according to Rimius, were immoral and sensuous, delighting in filthy expressions.

"The opposition soon took serious form. The rumour that they cherished secret principles aroused popular alarm. At Broad Oaks, in Essex, where they had established a boarding school, a mob of three hundred surrounded the building under the impression that the Brethren were 'papists' harbouring the Young Pretender, and that they had even stored ammunition to set fire to Thaxted. At Pridsey the Brethren were searched for arms and ammunition, and Ockershausen, a Moravian preacher, was arrested and imprisoned in York Castle. At Dukinfield the Brethren were forbidden to preach, and all young men who attended their meetings were threatened with impressment into the royal navy. At Swindon, John Cennick was drenched with water from a fire engine, and at Stratton, on account of his Blood Theology was squirted with blood saved up by a butcher. If the Earl of Stair had not intervened several other Brethren would have been imprisoned. In the 'Universal Spectator' Count Zinzendorf was accused of kidnapping young women for Moravian convents; and in London the Brethren suffered so severely that they were compelled to make an arrangement to keep their trade to themselves." [80] In answer to all these attacks, Zinzendorf made a reply in the newspaper called, "Reply to all the Controversial Writings," and in 1754 he published a pamphlet called, "Plain case of the Representatives of the *Unitas Fratrum*," in which he defended himself and the Brethren.

Many of these irregularities were introduced into America, although they were not carried to such extremes as in Herrnhaag. When Zinzendorf came to America, he immediately planted the seed. In his Pennsylvania addresses, the sentimental expressions and fancies were numerous, and at the Union Synods he admitted speaking in a manner that others could not understand. His daughter's letters back to Europe were full of "blood" and news of the "blood congregation" in America.[81] In 1743 when Zinzendorf was about to return to Europe, a brother wrote: "I am poor dust, through grace a poor child, a poor sinner washed in the blood of the slaughtered Lamb in which I live; and to swim and bathe in Jesus' blood is my element, that is to say briefly, my enjoyment." [82]

The Herrnhaagian theology then came to America "in a flood of hymns." [83] The extravagant hymns found in the *Zugaben* and *Anhänge* were available to the American Brethren. Cammerhoff wrote from America to Peter Böhler, asking him to send at once *Anhang* XII, which contained some of the extremest compositions, "because the souls were hungry for that kind of hymn." [84]

This new theology had a personal representative in America when John Frederick Cammerhoff came to be Spangenberg's assistant in 1747. He came directly from Herrnhaag and had thoroughly imbibed the new spirit. He indulged in the worst sentimental eroticism. He spoke of the rest of the Brethren

[80] Hutton: *Contributions to the Revival in England*, pp. 429, 430.
[81] *Büd. Samm.*, vol. III, p. 69.
[82] *Ibid.*, p. 103.
[83] Reichel: *Early History*, p. 180.
[84] Letter from Cammerhoff to Peter Böhler, Sept. 30, 1747.

as being little children, and of Henry Antes as a "juicy (*saftiges*) and happy heart." [85] He was well fortified by a large group in America who shared his views. Various groups of Herrnhaag enthusiasts had come over whose speech and practices both astonished and disgusted Spangenberg. Of the second Sea Congregation in 1743 seventy-eight were from Herrnhaag and Marienborn, while only twenty-six were from Herrnhut, and thirteen from England. [86] In the next five years, five other small groups [87] came to America, culminating in the group of nineteen single men who came from Herrnhaag in 1748. [88] These groups worked as a leaven among the Brethren. But when John Nitschmann came in 1749 with his colony of about 120 Brethren, the third Sea Congregation, [89] the American communities were inundated with Herrnhaagianism. A still stronger Herrnhaagian influence was represented in a group of eighty-one single men who came to America when Herrnhaag had to be abandoned. [90]

The American Moravians, under the Chief Eldership of Christ and the example of John Nitschmann, now cast all their worries upon the Lord and cultivated childish play, like their sisters and brothers in Herrnhaag. They forgot the frugality and thrift that had been insisted upon by Spangenberg. It was John Nitschmann's purpose to pattern the Bethlehem Economy after that of Herrnhaag. Therefore elaborate buildings had to be erected like those in Herrnhaag, while the fields, which they had so diligently cultivated, were neglected. The result was that they had to buy what hitherto had been produced on

[85] Cammerhoff's *"Epistola Tertia."* Ms. Beth. Arch.

[86] Levering: *History of Bethlehem*, pp. 167, 168. See *"Die Namen der Geschwister so sich auf unserm Schiff:* The Little Strength, *befinden."* Also *"Namen Verzeichnis der Geschwister so im Jahr 1743 auf dem Schiff,* Little Strength, *nach Pennsylvanien gereiszt sind."* Ms. Beth. Arch.

[87] *Pa. Mag. of Hist. and Biog.*, vol. XXXIII, p. 228.

[88] Erbe: *Bethlehem*, p. 98.

[89] *"Verzeichnis der lieben See Gemeine an Bord Deal."* See also *"Catalogus der Geschwister des See Gemeinleins auf dem Schiff Irene."* Ms. Beth. Arch.

[90] *"Diarium der Ledigen Brüder."* See also Levering: *History of Bethlehem,* pp. 253, 254.

their own land. In the year 1749, the Brethren bought 6,832 pounds of butter, 4,032 pounds of flax, 974 bushels of rye, 16,264 pounds of meat, and 1,442 bushels of wheat.[91] The cultivation of the fields and management of the farm were neglected.[92]

When Zinzendorf finally realized, from his forceful expulsion from Herrnhaag and the financial crisis following closely upon its heels, to what lengths all this enthusiasm had led them, he recalled John Nitschmann to Europe, in 1751, and sent the faithful and capable Spangenberg back to replace him. Spangenberg, now, not only had to rebuild what had been allowed "to play itself out" under Nitschmann, but also had to work against the odds of a well-rooted mania. Fortunately other forces were soon at hand that made the Brethren willing to surrender their excessive enthusiasm; but with it went also many other customs, traditions, and beliefs that Moravianism at its best had greatly cherished. To this reaction we now turn.

[91] Erbe: *Bethlehem,* p. 99.
[92] Ledderhose: *Life of Spangenberg,* p. 67.

CHAPTER VIII

THE END OF THE GENERAL ECONOMY AND EXCLUSIVISM

THE Moravian theocratic community with Christ at its head was theoretically approaching realization. This co-operative unity could not have been thought of as temporary. Certainly if, as the Brethren say, their original purpose in coming to America was missionary and the Economy was established to support this work, they could not have thought of their work among the Indians as temporary; at least, it is improbable that they expected to conclude their work of evangelizing the Indians within the twenty years that the General Economy prevailed. This Economy was a practical realization of the *Unitas Fratrum,* and they could not have considered it, as they later claimed, a passing phenomenon to bridge the time until the colony became economically stabilized. The reasons for its dissolution are other than its supposedly temporary purpose.

The Moravians in America at first were held together as one large household by their enthusiasm, the mutual feeling of strangeness in the new world, the missionary ideal, and a vigorous religious fervor. The group movements to America, especially the Sea Congregations, of which the members were carefully selected on the basis of their devoutness, must have awakened in them the spirit of Crusaders sent out on a holy errand for the Lord. That such a feeling should fill their hearts was only natural; but it was equally natural that the novelty should wear off and the first enthusiasm gradually subside as they faced such conditions as they could not have imagined, tempting them to more individualistic living. Being a member of a single large household was constantly becoming less novel, less interesting, and less necessary. The feeling of strangeness in a strange land was rapidly waning. They soon adapted

EXORCISM OF BAPTIZED CHILDREN AMONG THE NEGROES

(A) The Pastor performing the ceremony. (BB) The Deacons assisting him. (CCC) Three baptized Negro boys. (DDDD) Four baptized Negro girls. (EE) The Negro Congregation.

themselves to their new habitat. Furthermore, conditions were not so strange as they might have been, for they soon found themselves surrounded by emigrants from the same country, whose manners and customs were similar in many respects, and whose common mother-tongue broke down religious barriers. Outside of the fact that some of their neighbors taunted them because of their peculiar community life, they began to feel at home. They felt a new sense of security.

By 1747 the industries and responsibilities of the community had grown so much that they taxed the faithful Spangenberg beyond his strength. In that year John Frederick Cammerhoff, a young man of twenty-five, who was sent from Europe to be his assistant, took over the tasks of chief diarist in Bethlehem and correspondent with the European authorities. But he caused more trouble to Spangenberg than he gave assistance, for he introduced the Herrnhaagian fanaticism. In spite of Zinzendorf's support of it, Spangenberg protested against this tendency. He gently remonstrated with Zinzendorf,[1] but the latter, as a modern Moravian writer puts it, "was impatient at any opposition, and disposed to treat with contempt the advice of others."[2] The election of Christ as Chief Elder in America served as a convenient ground for deposing Spangenberg from his office of General Elder. A Moravian historian writes that Spangenberg was called from his duties in America in "hot haste" because he was needed by Zinzendorf in Europe.[3] Another historian professes not to know the reason for the sudden recall of Spangenberg,[4] while a third suggests that there "was a desire to have him disconnected from . . . the new régime."[5] Clearly the last is the true reason, since at the "high festivities" of the inauguration of Christ as Chief Elder, "Spangenberg was a quiet, unofficial participant."[6] Spangenberg not only yielded his position but was entirely separated from the work, although there was no man so capable as he or

[1] Hamilton: *History*, p. 125; also Levering: *History*, p. 228.
[2] Hutton: *History*, p. 395.
[3] *Ibid.*, p. 379.
[4] Hamilton: *History*, p. 169.
[5] Levering: *History of Bethlehem*, p. 228.
[6] *Ibid.*, p. 229.

with such thorough knowledge of the problems and the needs.

Spangenberg's successor, Bishop John Nitschmann, introduced the novelties which Spangenberg had refused. As an obedient tool he followed instructions, without regard to the methods suitable under circumstances so different from those in Europe. He lacked both tact and vision. Saner minds were repelled by the new régime with its distasteful practices. Henry Antes saw the trend and the difficulties into which the Brethren would be led. Their enemies would have new reasons for slander, gossip, and ridicule.

The sudden expulsion of the Brethren from Herrnhaag by the government of Büdingen shocked the Count sufficiently to open his eyes to the extremes to which the extravagances had led them. Cammerhoff, who had been broken in health since his long missionary journey to the Six Nations, died April 28, 1751. In November 1751, John Nitschmann was recalled, and when he set sail for Europe, Spangenberg, who was in Europe at the time, was already on the sea to resume his duties in America, not as General Elder but under the title of Vicar General of the Ordinarius Zinzendorf, who was superintendent of all the Brethren everywhere. Bishop Matthew Hehl came as an assistant to Spangenberg.

Upon his arrival, Spangenberg immediately called a Synod as a first step to reorganize the General Economy. During the superintendency of John Nitschmann, the Brethren's economic status had declined. In the long up-hill work back to normalcy, Spangenberg's executive ability and capacity for an abundance of hard work gradually won the day. Under his leadership the Brethren were efficiently organized. Diplomacy and tact were essential requirements of the leader at this juncture, and in these Spangenberg was not lacking. But the restoration of the General Economy was thwarted by the financial crisis that hit all the Brethren in Europe, England, and America in 1753. The Brethren suffered heavy losses as the result of the forced abandonment of Herrnhaag. The numerous elaborate buildings and all the investments they had made there in those years were now a total loss. After the evacuation of Herrnhaag many careless transactions were made to meet the obligations of some of their creditors. The Brethren had gone into a debt of far over a million dollars, which took them half a century to liquidate.[7] The heavy losses in Europe and the financial straits of the central directing board of the Brethren in Europe meant that the Brethren in America not only had to be self-supporting, but also had to carry the added responsibility of liquidating the debt incurred across the sea.[8] Some of those who held a lien against the lands in America pressed the Brethren, but Antes and a few others went to Philadelphia and finally succeeded in allaying the fears of some of the creditors by explaining the conditions and correcting false reports.

Meanwhile there were several accessions from Europe. In 1752 two small companies arrived, one under the leadership of Anthony Lawatsch and the other under John Töltschig.[9] In the same year, there arrived with Peter Böhler, who was temporarily taking Spangenberg's place, a small company, of whom twenty-three were single men. Nine of these had studied in universities; one was a surgeon and another a surveyor.[10] When Spangenberg returned from Europe in 1754, he brought back with him a notable company of men and women.[11] In it were Bishop David Nitschmann; Rev. John Ettwein and his wife (he became noted for his work among the children and also as a correspondent); Rev. Francis Christian Lembke, a school teacher who became a leader at Nazareth; John Haidt, a painter and a preacher; Andrew Höger, architect; Rev. Christian Thomas Benzien; Rev. Paul Daniel Bryzelius; and John Heckewelder, who became a famous missionary among

---

[7] Levering: *History of Bethlehem*, p. 270.

[8] *"Vesprochene Gelder von den Geschwistern zu abtragung der Unitäts Schulden von Bethlehem."* Ms. Beth. Arch.

[9] *Pa. Mag. of History and Biog.*, vol. XXXIII, p. 228. Also Levering: *History of Bethlehem*, pp. 272, 273.

[10] *"Catalogus der Geschwister welche mit dem Gemein—Schiff Irene, Captain Nich. Garrison den 23 Juni von England abgesegelt den 9 Sept. bei New York angelandet und den 13-14 Sept., hier in Bethlehem angekommen sind."* Ms. Beth. Arch. Also *"See Diarium von London in Engeland Nach New York in North America von fünfzig Jahren, Nämlich von 9 Juny bis 21 Sept. Anno 1753."* Ms. Beth. Arch.

[11] *Pa. Mag. of Hist. and Biog.*, vol. XXXIII, p. 228.

the Indians; and his parents, who went as missionaries to the West Indies. John Heckewelder mastered the Indian language and became famous as a linguist and archæologist.[12]   In the same year Gottlieb Pezold had gone to Europe to fetch a group of over fifty single men, who were farmers and mechanics, representing sixteen trades.[13]   Some of these were to go to new settlements in North Carolina and at Lititz.   From the personnel of these accessions, it is at once evident that the recent arrivals were, so to say, hand picked.   Not every one who had a fancy to go into a strange land "for the Lord" was allowed to come to America.   Promiscuous groups had been allowed to cross the sea, with the hope that somewhere they would find their respective places according to their unknown abilities. Many of them were fanatics and enthusiasts, with a burning desire to lay their lives upon some kind of an altar as a sacrifice.   Uneducated men preached the gospel, and the unlearned tried their hand at ruling.   Spangenberg, in his new attempt to guide the Brethren under the difficulties of a bad reputation and a heavy debt, saw the immediate need of trained leadership and an educated ministry.   Accordingly, Böhler, Spangenberg, and Pezold returned with selected companies to work as a leaven among the Brethren and to counteract the last vestiges of the John Nitschmann fanaticism.

In August 1752, Spangenberg, Antes, and four others set out on horseback for North Carolina to examine a tract of 100,000 acres that was offered for sale by Lord Granville, the Speaker of the House of Commons.[14]   The Brethren were interested in the purchase of this land, since it offered them opportunity to work among the Cherokee, Catawba, Creek, and Chickasaw Indians.   It would also give added property and opportunity to the new arrivals, while, at the same time, the Brethren hoped by such a stroke to restore their financial prestige among their creditors.[15]   In the spring of 1753, Spangenberg was in Eu-

[12] Levering: *History of Bethlehem*, p. 278.
[13] *Ibid.*, p. 279.   Also *Pa. Mag. of Hist. and Biog.*, vol. XXXIII, p. 228.
[14] Letter from Spangenberg to the *Junger Collegium* from Philadelphia. Ms. Beth. Arch.
[15] Hamilton: *History*, p. 170.

rope, counciling with authorities there concerning the debt and urging the purchase of more land. The territory in North Carolina, named Wachovia, was bought, and on it was established another Economy, having "a common housekeeping, each member doing the work for which he or she was best fitted, the income going into the general treasury, and food, clothing and lodging being furnished to all alike." [16] Bethabara was established as the place of the Pilgrim Congregation; in 1759 Bethany was founded; in 1766 Salem; and later Friedberg, Friedland, and Winston. The title of this land was placed in the name of James Hutton, making him the sole proprietor. In Pennsylvania until 1751 the estates were held in the names of those individuals who made the purchases for the Brethren, there being as yet no corporation. After that all the lands were sold nominally to David Nitschmann, in whose name the estates were held for the Brethren. After Nitschmann, Seidel became the proprietor in 1759. This system was continued for about a hundred years.

After Spangenberg returned from Europe in 1754, an undertaking similar to that in North Carolina was begun in Lancaster County, Pennsylvania. George Klein donated a tract of 500 acres as the site for a new settlement to be named Lititz.

During these years the lands and roads were improved and the creditors were satisfied. The school system was enlarged and extended in accordance with the division of the Choirs. The boys, girls, little children, and nursery were in separate departments, which, in these years, were frequently shifted from one place to another, according to needs and circumstances in the overcrowded buildings. The various industries were flourishing, and the many articles which the Brethren had for sale outside their community [17] became famous for their high quality.

Their success was due to several causes. First of all they were a thrifty people who literally adhered to the words of Scripture: "By the sweat of thy brow shalt thou eat thy bread." The mutual support which all the members pledged in this co-

[16] Fries and Pfohl: *The Moravian Church,* p. 35.
[17] Erbe: *Bethlehem,* p. 124.

operative union accomplished in those pioneer conditions what could not have been done individually. In addition to this, they were not wholly without financial resources, as were many of the other settlers. They were a company, members of an institution. The Church bought land for them and established them in their industrial pursuits. These financial resources made it possible to buy large tracts of land, and because they could buy extensively, they came into possession of some of the best land. Although we cannot call the Brethren wealthy at this early stage, there was soon sufficient prosperity to allow them more comfort and luxury than they were getting under the rigid system of the Economy. Increasing prosperity was accompanied by a growing feeling of self-sufficiency and a waning sense of dependence upon the Economy for every enjoyment. The Brethren were now sufficiently established and self-confident to gain for themselves more than the Economy was offering them in a material way. With the first measure of success, their individual instincts to appropriate, to hold, to possess, and to dispense their profits according to their pleasure, asserted themselves.

But an unlooked for difficulty was at hand. The Brethren, who were then on the frontier, could not flee from the scene of struggle between the French and the English. Many of the Indians who had allied themselves with the French committed atrocities in Pennsylvania and the Susquehanna valley. Many companies of troops marched through Bethlehem, to protect it or in search of hostile Indians. Bethlehem soon came to be considered as an outpost against the savages, being barricaded and well protected by the Brethren. Although the Moravians refused to bear arms they declared their willingness to protect their settlements and prevent incendiarism, atrocities, and murder.[18]

The severest attack by the Indians occurred on Nov. 24, 1755, at the Indian mission at Gnadenhütten. On that day while the Moravian missionaries were gathered for their evening meal, they were suddenly surrounded by war-whoops, tomahawks, knives, and guns. In self-defense they barricaded

---

[18] *"Der Brüder Erklärung wegen des Soldaten."* Ms. Beth. Arch.

themselves in the upper story, but when the enemy set fire to the building, some leaped through the burning roof hoping to escape.   Worbas, Sensemann, Sturgeon and his wife, and Parsch and his wife made their escape and fled into the forest; but Fabricius, Martin Nitschmann and his wife, Anders and his wife and child, Sister Sensemann, Gattermeyer, Lessly, Presser, and Schweigert, eleven altogether, were shot, burned, and scalped.   The converted Indians took to the woods for their safety.   Of the Gnadenhütten mission, the barns, the dwellings, the school, and the church were heaps of smouldering ashes.[19]   Spangenberg estimated the financial loss to have been about £2,000.[20]   An exact appraisement of the total loss, consisting of horses, cattle, oats, hay, flax, hemp, wheat, rye, barley, butter, buckwheat, corn, beans, salt, beeswax, harness, furniture, clothes, watches, tools, and buildings, at £1,914.19.3 was affirmed by Timothy Horsfield, the Justice of the Peace.[21]

The unprotected women and children in the outlying villages of the General Economy were now moved to Bethlehem and Nazareth, which the Brethren barricaded and guarded against similar attacks.   The workers in the fields carried guns to protect themselves against lurking Indians.   Other atrocities occurred among the frontier population, and the fear-stricken people fled to the protected Moravian settlements.   Thus Bethlehem and Nazareth became cities of refuge for many defenceless persons.   The Moravians had been the victims of hatred on the part of the English, who accused them of being in league with the French and Indians.   The grounds for these suspicions were the converted Indians at Gnadenhütten and the fearlessness with which such a missionary as Frederick Post worked among the hostile Indians.   However, these suspicions were allayed after the massacre at Gnadenhütten.   The Brethren were also hated by the Indians, who were unsuccessful in persuading converted Indians to join them and the French.

[19] *"Bruder Joseph's Bericht von der Begebenheit an der Mahoni am 24 Nov. 1755.   Diarium Bethlehem 1755."*   Ms. Beth. Arch.
[20] Letter from Spangenberg to Isaac Norris, April 5, 1756.   Ms. Beth. Arch.
[21] "Appraisement of the United Brethren's loss suffered by the Indians at the Mahoni and Gnadenhütten, Feb. 4, 1756."   Ms. Beth. Arch.

Fresh outrages occurred from time to time, and more refugees continued to arrive. To shelter them the rooms in the dwellings were crowded, and available space in the barns was utilized. In 1756 the total number of refugees with the Brethren were 626, including the 70 Indians who escaped from the Gnadenhütten Massacre.[22] The Moravians themselves in that year numbered 1,041 in the General Economy, and we can imagine the inconvenience and hardships it must have caused them to add 626 to their number. Spangenberg relates the difficulty in obtaining food, clothes, and shelter.[23] The account books of these years show that many provisions had to be bought. The refugees provided nothing for themselves. Not only did the Brethren have to provide for these refugees and patrol the settlements day and night, but also for that reason they were unable to attend to their trades and farming properly. Therefore Spangenberg asked that they be partially relieved from the heavy taxes.[24] In these troublous times, the congregations outside the Economy sympathized with and assisted the Brethren at Bethlehem and Nazareth.[25]

In 1759, the danger from the Indians ceased, the refugees left, the industries resumed their normal stride, and the women and children returned to their former places. Much of the work of the missionaries was undone during these hostilities, but the great missionary, David Zeisberger, had not been idle. During these years he worked on the materials for his seven-volume lexicon of the German and Onondago languages, an Onondago grammar, a Delaware grammar, and a German-Delaware dictionary.[26] Once more peace reigned and the

[22] "A list as under of familys from the frontears above Nazreth Irish settlement, escaping the barbeity of the Indians, fled to and now residing in Bethlehem, Jan. 6, 1756." Ms. Beth. Arch.

[23] Letters to Anthony Benezet, Jan. 18, and Jan. 21, 1756. Ms. Beth. Arch.

[24] Letter to Isaac Norris. Beth. April 5, 1756. Ms. Beth. Arch.

[25] Letters to Van Vleck in New York, Dec. 22, 1755, and from D. Brinkerhoff to Spangenberg, Dec. 16, 1755. Ms. Beth. Arch.

[26] Zeisberger also prepared other volumes for the Indians which were translations from their hymns, litanies, sermons, Spangenberg's *Bodily Care of Children*, Lieberkühn's *Harmony of the Four Gospels,* and also Scripture verses and the Lord's Prayer.

Brethren were able to continue the busy life of the Economy. In 1761 the total income of the Economy amounted to 38,000 dollars. The settlement of the Brethren had become a thriving center of trade and business, with ninety-seven buildings, flourishing trades and businesses, productive fields, and profitable gardens and orchards. Many curious visitors could not help expressing their surprise at what they saw. But on every hand there were indications that the régime could not last much longer.

The greatest cause for discontent was the difficulty which family life entailed under the existing system. To meet the difficulties of pioneer conditions, the Brethren insisted that the majority of those emigrating to America should be young married couples or single men and women of marriageable age. In the second Sea Congregation (1743),[27] there were thirty-three young couples from Herrnhaag and Marienborn, of whom twenty-four had been married at the same time. The wedding anniversaries of these twenty-four couples were celebrated with a Love Feast at Nazareth, and the day was known as "the Great Wedding." A similar large wedding occurred in 1749, when thirty-one couples of the third Sea Congregation[28] were married at Bethlehem. In this colony there were thirty-one single men and forty-eight single women. All of the single men married upon their arrival in Bethlehem.

In those early years while there were few children, the large household of the Brethren could be managed very simply, but as the families grew complications increased, especially because of the lack of housing facilities. Until 1759, the married people lived together according to the Choir classification. Such an arrangement was possible only by mutual agreement to a strict code of rules and regulations. Children of parents in these overcrowded buildings had to be placed in a nursery as soon as they could be separated from their mothers, and later in a boys' or girls' boarding school. The General Economy

[27] *"Namen Verzeichnis der Geschwister so im Jahr 1743 auf dem Schiff Little Strength nach Pennsylvanien gereiszt sind."* Ms. Beth. Arch.

[28] *"Catalogus der Geschwister des See Gemeinleins auf dem Schiff Irene."* Ms. Beth. Arch.

broke up the family circle and took children from parents in the most impressionable years. In addition to this, the crowded dormitory life of these married people gradually began to appear absurd in America with its wide and open spaces. Three years before the General Economy was dissolved there was such a demand for more family privacy that some of the buildings were turned into apartment houses.[29] With the growing interest in private family life there was a corresponding decrease of interest in the large household, and with this shift of interest, the basic principle in the social structure of the Brethren upon which the whole General Economy rested began to crumble.

Those in authority realized that the rigidity of the system had become irksome, and they introduced numerous Love Feasts in connection with the various occupations to afford sociability and fellowship. These Love Feasts for various groups of workers impressed the laborer with the religious character of his work and made him willing to continue, believing it was "unto the Lord."

Under a system already severe enough, the faithful Spangenberg had to urge his people to still more thrift and sacrifice to save the Brethren's Church in Europe from ruin. The American share of this debt, as well as the support of the whole Economy and the Pilgrim Congregation, became the burden of the farmers and the tradesmen. It is not surprising that, under these trying circumstances, the artisans began to chafe; for in the year 1756, 236 of the adult population of 480 belonged to the Pilgrim Congregation and were therefore unproductive. In that year there were 188 married people, 225 single men, 67 single women, and 418 children. Of the adults, 48 were missionaries, 54 were itinerant preachers, 62 were employed in the education of the children in the Economy, and 72 were employed as bishops, elders, deacons, and supervisors. The active support of the whole Economy, therefore, fell to the remaining 244 adults.[30] In the year 1759, the unproductive

[29] Levering: *History of Bethlehem,* p. 366.
[30] *Pennsylvania Archives,* vol. III, pp. 69, 70.

members numbered 665, of whom 228 belonged to the Pilgrim Congregation.

The grievances were brought before the elders in 1754.[31] Some asked for better living accommodations and more comforts, while others preferred to leave and live for themselves.[32] Some had already left by their own choice, and a few had been expelled.[33]   Thus, in 1750, a Mr. Hohmann left the Brethren because of personal grievances,[34] and the Germantown newspaper reported that "many people left Bethlehem because they did not want to submit to Zinzendorf's domination." [35]   Spangenberg had received an anonymous letter in which the discontent of these Brethren was expressed.[36]   The burden was heavy and believed to be unfairly distributed.   Outsiders misrepresented the Economy and instigated certain expressions of dissatisfaction among the Brethren.   There was misunderstanding within and without, and the Economy was in imminent danger of breaking up.

Accordingly a meeting was called of all the members of Bethlehem and Nazareth in August 1754, to deal adequately and thoroughly with the new crisis.   Bishop Spangenberg read a long carefully prepared document, setting forth the purpose of the General Economy and their relationships to it.   This document was adopted and signed by the people of Nazareth and Bethlehem as the first "Brotherly Agreement," [37] indicating that the rebellious spirits had been pacified and that the Economy was to continue for a short time.   The Co-operative Unity might have dissolved then and there had it not been for the war between the British and the French.   This danger from without made them forget their troubles within, and for the five years that the Indian hostilities continued, the Brethren

[31] Levering: *History of Bethlehem*, p. 292.
[32] *Diarium Bethlehem, July 10, 1754."*   Ms. Beth. Arch.
[33] Levering: *History of Bethlehem*, p. 292.
[34] *"Diarium der Ledigen Brüder, Jan. 1750."*   Ms. Beth. Arch.
[35] *Pennsylvanische Berichte*, May 16, 1751.
[36] *"Diarium Bethlehem, July 16, 1754."*   Ms. Beth. Arch.
[37] *"Einige Zur Bethlehemschen und Nazarethschen Gemeinschaftlichen Brüder Öconomie gehörige Momenta.   Diarium Bethlehem, Aug. 19, 1754."*   Ms. Beth. Arch.   See Appendix A.

stood together as one large family and succeeded in protecting themselves by constant vigilance, while many of the other settlers fled, were massacred, or came to the Brethren for protection.

After 1754, the General Economy was continued for eight years under the stipulations of the Brotherly Agreement and under a legal contract [38] in which the members or applicants for membership were required to endorse the Brotherly Agreement, to refuse to be prejudiced by outsiders, to make known in advance their intention of leaving or to leave upon request, to accept the existing rules and regulations, and to promise to sign a written instrument surrendering any claim to property or wages.   The contract was easily enforced as long as the Indian hostilities lasted; in fact, during these years the General Economy could have been maintained without such a contract.

Spangenberg saw the many forces at work undermining the foundations of their system.   The deciding factor that now made the abrogation of the Economy advisible was Spangenberg's departure from America, necessitated by the death of Zinzendorf on May 9, 1760.   Spangenberg was now needed on the central directing board in Europe.   Nathanael Seidel and Frederick von Marschall were put in charge of dissolving the General Economy, and they completed their task in 1762.

Under the new procedure the property of the General Economy still remained the possession of the entire Unity of the Brethren.   When this religious communism broke up, the wealth they had amassed was not distributed among the members.   Although the members had made no investments in it except their time and labor, the Church owed much to the individuals through whose diligence the original investments had increased so plentifully.   The abrogation of the Economy would have been less difficult if the property could have been offered for public sale.   But the abolition of religious communism did not imply the surrender of exclusive Moravian

[38] "*Copia des an Gemein-Rath den 12 Nov. sub Signo a. No. 10 mentionirten Reverses.   Diarium Bethlehem, Nov. 12, 1754.*"   Ms. Beth. Arch.   See Appendix B.

settlements. The right to membership in these settlements continued to be determined on the basis of membership in the Moravian Church. Consquently the various industries were to be conducted by Moravians, though under private management; each was to earn for himself and to contribute liberally to the public institutions of the Church, as in Europe. But almost all of the Brethren were wholly without means to commence businesses of their own, since under the government of the General Economy they could not earn for themselves. The Church had even given them free transportation across the sea. The main concern was, therefore, to carry on the various industries of the Church under private managements and at the same time to provide homes for and give employment to all the members.

It was therefore necessary, until the time came when the Brethren could buy their own businesses, that some of the establishments of the Church be conducted on a salaried basis, while others were taken over and continued by those who could lease the grounds and the buildings. The farms were leased on a share basis. A certain percentage of the crops was retained by the lessee; the remainder was the Church's share and was delivered to the large barns built for the Economy.[39] The Church made contracts with those who conducted the various industries for her.[40] For example, Matthew Otto was to manage the drug store for the Church, for which he received £60 in wages, free heat and light, and an additional £6 for his child in school.[41] Similar contracts were made in relation to the other trades and industries.

The managers of the Church's industries had to keep accurate accounts of the business transacted. These account books were given to the salaried bookkeepers every four weeks,

[39] *"Die Veränderung der Öconomie der oberen Plätzten betreffend, Juli 1764."* Ms. Beth. Arch.

[40] *"Abschlusz mit denen Handwerks Meistern, 1763."* Ms. Beth. Arch.

[41] *"Heuto dato Friederich Marschall von Bethlehem in der County of North Hampton in der provinz Pennsylvanien in Namen Nathanael Seidel eben daselbst wohnhaft auf der einen Seite und Matthias Otto ebenfalls in Bethlehem wohnhaft chirurgis und Apotheker auf der Andern Seite folgende Vergleich getroffen worden."* Ms. Beth. Arch.

of whom there were two in Bethlehem and one in Nazareth. They carried the figures into a general account book, which was sent to the governing board in Europe now called the General Diacony.[42]   This central board, of which Spangenberg was now a member, was the final authority in all matters and supervised the churches, the missions, the schools, and the industries.   American Moravianism was now even less autonomous than before.

To insure the exclusivism and orderliness that had existed under the General Economy, the Brethren mutually agreed to have a board of arbitrators to enforce the following rules: that only Moravians were to live in the settlements; there should be no teaching contrary to the principles and doctrines of the Unity of the Brethren; there was to be obedience to the government and the Church laws; grievances were to be brought to the committee of arbitrators; taxes were to be paid punctually; everyone was to support the public interests of the community; there was to be a quarterly meeting of the supervisors of Choirs, heads of houses, and the trade masters; no one was to wrangle and dispute, much less carry his grievances to court but rather to the board of arbitrators; each member must be diligent and the congregation must care for those who cannot provide for themselves; guilds of trade masters must supervise the quality and price of their products; honesty must be exercised in business and conduct; any damage done must be righted; all animals must be kept within fences, and dogs were not to be kept without good reason; the streets must be kept clean by the residents; peddlers must not be allowed; the Brethren must get home on time at nights, there was to be no loitering on the streets, and parents must keep their children at home; people were not to meet in the dark, and there was to be no drunkenness and disorderly conduct; intermingling of the sexes must not be permitted; no marriage must be contracted without the knowledge of the elders and the parents; whoever did not observe these rules was to move out; no one was to keep Negroes or other servants without the knowledge

[42] "*An das Unitäts Vorstehers Collegium, July 31, 1765.*"   Ms. Beth. Arch.

of the committee; they were not to give lodging except in the inn; they were not to leave the settlement without the knowledge of the committee; no one could lend or borrow money or start a new trade without consulting the committee; they should not consult a doctor, midwife, or nurse other than those authorized by the congregation; they were requested to make wills; any who wanted to join the Brethren had to consult the committee and give evidence that he had settled any debts he might have incurred; whoever built a house had no right to rent, sell, or bequeath his property without consulting the committee; each house, especially the chimney, must be built according to the requirements; the committee must notify undesirable members to leave, and if they have property the Church was to buy it.[43]   The large household arrangement was thus officially ended.   This required many changes in the large buildings to arrange them for private family life, and some houses were erected as dwellings for separate families.   This was not so large a task as it may seem at first.   Among the 1,140 persons in Bethlehem and Nazareth in 1761, there were only 123 married couples.[44]   The remaining widows, widowers, single women, single men, boys, and girls continued to be housed in the large buildings according to their ages and sex. Thus fifteen years after the abrogation of the General Economy, there were in Bethlehem, not including the Nazareth settlements, only sixty-four private families; while one hundred and twenty single men and boys lived in a three-story building, 50 by 80 feet; one hundred and fifty single women lived in a building 42 by 100 feet; and thirty widows lived in a house 45 by 80 feet.[45]

In 1762 Spangenberg returned from Europe to make a final announcement about the abrogation of the General Economy and the management of American affairs by the General Diacony.   The consequence of the centralized European con-

[43] "Abstract of the rules agreed upon by the inhabitants of Bethlehem, and subscribed by all house keepers and masters of trades when the Family Economy ceased."   Ms. Beth. Arch.

[44] Levering: *History of Bethlehem*, p. 378.

[45] *Pa. Mag. of Hist. and Biog.*, vol. X, p. 368.

trol was that the American settlements were closely patterned after those of Europe. Bethlehem, Nazareth, Gnadenthal, Christiansbrunn, and Friedensthal became separate centers, like Lititz in Lancaster County and the settlements in North Carolina, with local organization and supervision of their industries. The settlements of the Economy took Lititz, which was an exact reproduction of Herrnhut, as a model. Under the central directing board in Europe the American Brethren were compelled more than ever to pattern after Herrnhut, without regard to the different conditions of the New World and the atmosphere of freedom and the growing demand for liberation from foreign domination. The abrogation of the General Economy in 1762 thus did not mean that the walls of Moravianism were being broken down; on the contrary, the philosophy of exclusivism was tenaciously adhered to for the next eighty years.

The rigid and severe discipline of former days was strictly enforced under the Church-village plan. One of the Brethren who lived in the Choir house stated that church discipline was driven to extremes and was even more severe than in the Catholic Church.[46] Young men and women did not even have the privilege of choosing their partners in marriage at their own pleasure and convenience. The elders had to be told of their intentions, and they, in turn, submitted the question to the Lord by the lot. The elders would also judge as misdemeanors such acts as going for a walk to a neighboring village without permission, or young men strolling along a way which had been designated for the Sisters, or familiarity with a Sister.[47] The Choirs were patrolled by the supervisors and assistants, who reported the slightest deviations from the rules laid down by the elders. The Single Brethren had to retire for the night immediately after the evening blessing; they had to present a valid excuse for absence from any services; at the sound of the first bell in the morning they had to rise and dress, and at the second bell they had to assemble for morning prayer; no one

[46] Author of remarks to Spangenberg's *Kurzgefaste Nachricht von der Brüderunität,* p. 73.
[47] *Ibid.*

was to be in a room with another without a light burning; they were not allowed to smoke in their rooms, nor to sleep on their beds before it was time to retire, and no one was to leave the premises without due notification.[48]   These rules were unalterable, for the Lord had spoken through the lot.   The walls of these Church-villages became constantly higher.   The children were trained in their own schools, and read only literature approved by the elders.   Any questioning of the prerogatives of the elders was considered a sin.

But toward the end of the eighteenth century there was evidence of a new spirit.   Political revolt was abroad in the land.   The salvation of the thirteen colonies became more important than the salvation of souls, and deliverance from political oppression than deliverance from sin.   The Brethren, because of their exclusive village settlements, succeeded in keeping themselves comparatively "untainted."   Furthermore, they were in large measure of the uneducated type who were more interested in an experience of the heart than an experience of the mind.   "They were mostly simple and unlearned persons, not at all prepared to undertake scientific disputations.[49]   But the new critical spirit began to undermine even exclusive Moravianism.

While the Church authorities tried to preserve their unity and keep the Brethren aloof from a wicked world, personal enterprises in business under the new régime took some of them beyond the confines of Moravianism.   Slowly but unmistakably they began to feel the spirit of the Revolution.   They found a new world of freedom and adventure, in which everyone was trying to say that man was not made to be lorded over and to be chained down to a prescribed course by tradition.   Thus, among the Brethren, nationalism replaced church-ism and community-ism, and they began to find their interests in secular patriotism and external affairs as well as in religion.

Many Moravians of the late eighteenth century ceased to be preoccupied with the faith of their fathers.   Since faith could not be inherited, the elders surrounded the rising generation

[48] *"Diarium des Ledigen Brüder Chors. Dec. 1744."*   Ms. Beth. Arch.
[49] *Church Miscellany,* July 1852.

with many religious safeguards. Their many devotional services, by which they hoped to pass on their experiences, proved in time to work the exact opposite.

The emphasis upon their hymns, while it apparently unified them externally, left them without an intellectual grasp of their belief. They largely replaced religious instruction and the study of the Bible itself. These hymns were supposed to be expressions of hearts already "set on fire" for the Lord, but the fact was that many who sang those hymns were not "set on fire." Later generations did not share the sentiment which those hymns presupposed. With the breakdown of the General Economy the individual pursuit of business afforded the Brethren less time for participation in these liturgical services. In short, the Brethren were no longer imbued with the piety to which a previous generation had given expression. They now dared to question the traditions and beliefs of their Church without being stricken with the sinfulness of such an attitude.

One of the first customs to be thus scrutinized was the use of the lot. The local government at the head of each settlement had used the lot mechanically. "Why," they argued, "will not God guide us as he guided the apostles?" The lot decided many issues harmfully to the Church; some were put into offices who had no talent for such work, and others were sent into the mission fields who were not capable. The constant use of the lot in the smallest details made it a mere oracle instead of an instrument of faith. Through it Christ decided all questions for them, and this casting of every burden upon him resulted in irresponsibility. Before the lot came to be used mechanically, there had been a searching in Scripture for the will of God; but now the lot arrested sober thinking on the problems of church and religion. Another evil from the use of the lot was the belief in their institutions as even more unalterable than "the laws of the Medes and the Persians," since Christ's judgments through the lot were infallible. Thus the Brethren's Church assumed a rigid and static character, when changing times were demanding changes.

The early Brethren had resorted to the lot because of their belief in the absolute insufficiency of man. The widening of their horizon and outlook in the New World made them more and more "this-worldly." Instead of "worms in the dust," they were potential angels, whose judgments the Almighty respected. And although the belief in the total depravity of man was re-affirmed by later Synods, it was subordinated to the practical pursuit of business. Under these circumstances the lot seemed less and less an evidence of faith in God, and more and more a lack of faith in business sense.

As early as 1782, the Synods began modifying its use. In 1818 it was discontinued in connection with marriages, and in 1889 the General Synod abolished it entirely. While this was good news for the majority, some of the fathers lamented the evil times into which they had fallen. One of them wrote: "This requirement [the use of the lot in connection with mar-riages] was annuled some forty years ago, and the rule applied to ministers only, and this now is compromised for the taste, the fancy, or the judgment even of the minister. Congregations seeing this dereliction of the fathers, claim the right of choice of pastor, and the lot to them is of none effect. And now, extreme necessity only reserves the use of the lot for its direc-tion. What that extreme may dwindle to ten more years will show, for the children of this world are wiser in their genera-tion than the children of light." [50]

The less exclusive these Church-villages became, the more difficult it became to preserve the uniqueness of the Choirs. The members of the Choirs, especially the young men and women, began to see the absurdity of their exclusive Choirs and villages when an inclusive world was beckoning to them. The confines of the Choirs became irritating. A normal and free relationship with members of the other sex was denied them. Even their manner of dress was prescribed, and all in all there was little room for originality. They became depressed by the despotic rule. The cry for freedom on the part of the young women and the boys and girls was hushed, but the more vehe-ment reactions of the young men were not so easily disposed of. The former discipline could no longer be enforced. The num-ber of recruits for the mission fields from the Choirs was de-

[50] Ritter: *Church in Philadelphia*, p. 127.

creasing. They began to take on the character of lodging houses, and the young men began to resent the reproach that outsiders attached to these institutions. The many features of the system that resembled Catholic monasteries and nunneries drew upon the Moravians the charge that they were as bigoted as Roman Catholics. The custom of confidential communications ("speakings") between the superintendents of the Choirs and the members was a kind of Protestant Confessional peculiar to Moravian Church discipline and seemed to justify the outsiders in their charge. These "speakings" were gradually given up. "We may naturally suppose that this devotional regimen in the earlier stages of Moravianism was highly conducive to its advancement in true piety, and that such communings with a Superior were sought after and valued as precious moments; but as the community enlarged its limits, and the heart lost its purity, many repaired to the place of visitation with alloyed natures and feelings." [51]

From year to year it became increasingly harder for the Choirs of the Single Brethren and the Single Sisters to maintain themselves. After the abolition of the General Economy, these Choirs were independent institutions in which the members paid for their lodging and meals.[52] Also, the Single Sisters [53] and the members of the widows' Choir [54] were provided work and garden ground for their support, but it was very difficult for them to be self-supporting, since they could not engage in the trades and farming like the men. As a result they ran into debt.[55] Not only had the number in the Single Brethren's Choir in Bethlehem been reduced from 100 in 1783 to 38 in 1806,[56] but the debt had increased from year to year. In 1781,

---

[51] James Henry: *Sketches,* p. 127.

[52] *"Die Projecte und Vorschläge zur Künftigen Veränderung der Bethlehemischen Economie in spezie aber das Ledigen Brüder Haus betreffend. Beth. Dec. 16, 1761."* Ms. Beth. Arch.

[53] Ms. Beth. Arch.

[54] *"Vorschläge wie das Witwen Chor in Nazareth einzurichten und für sich seine Wirtschaft zu führen."* Ms. Beth. Arch.

[55] *"Schreiben an das Unitäts Vorstehers Collegium und Directorien Collegium. Aug. 27, 1764."* Ms. Beth. Arch.

[56] Erbe: *Bethlehem,* p. 153.

the debt amounted to £46.1.3; in 1797 £707.17.1; [57] in 1812 $11,447; [58] and in 1815 $15,672.74.[59]   The Single Brethren's Choir in Nazareth was discontinued in 1812, and the one in Christiansbrunn as early as 1796, because of the intemperance and drunkenness of the Brethren there.[60]   The decadence of these Choirs was brought before the General Synod in 1825, and it was decided to allow these institutions to continue or disband according to local conditions.

The debts of these Choirs were assumed by all the Brethren in each settlement and became congregational debts.   The total debt of the whole Unity was increased every year by the business enterprises carried on for the Church.[61]   The privately owned businesses were operating at a profit, but some of those managed for the Church suffered a loss each year.   Also the farms were carried on at a loss.[62]   Thus in Bethlehem, the Brethren had a deficit of £803 in 1764,[63] £1,800 in 1765,[64] and $4,839.38 in 1821.[65]   In 1815, the total indebtedness of the Bethlehem Church was $42,136.68.[66]   The Brethren, therefore, were exceedingly anxious that all business be put under private management as rapidly as possible.

With the abrogation of the General Economy, the numerous Love Feasts that had been instituted for the various groups of workers became obsolete.   Gradually Love Feasts were observed only in connection with the Choirs, Church festivals, and services of a purely religious character.   When later the Choir houses broke up, the Choirs and Choir Love Feasts were

[57] *"Jahres Rechnungen der Chor-diaconie der Ledigen Brüder in Bethlehem."* Ms. Beth. Arch.

[58] Levering: *History of Bethlehem*, p. 598.

[59] *Ibid.*, p. 609.

[60] *Ibid.*, p. 540.

[61] Erbe: *Bethlehem*, p. 147.

[62] *"An das Unitäts Vorstehers Collegium Bethlehem, Oct. 6, 1765."* Ms. Beth. Arch.

[63] *"Schreiben an das Unitäts Vorstehers Collegium und Directorien Collegium, Aug. 27, 1764."* Ms. Beth. Arch.

[64] *"An das Unitäts Vorstehers Collegium Bethlehem, Oct. 6, 1765.* Ms. Beth. Arch.

[65] *"Jahres Rechnungen der Gemein—diaconie in Bethlehem."* Ms. Beth. Arch.

[66] Levering: *History of Bethlehem*, p. 609.

maintained with difficulty, since the tangible groupings had disappeared and the unity of previous days had been lost. Even in the Love Feasts of a purely religious nature, irreverence crept into the services. Therefore "many modern Moravian churches have never introduced Love Feasts, and some old ones have abandoned them where they could not be continued with decorum and dignity or in an appreciative spirit." [67]

The "kiss of peace" was successfully maintained as long as the community retained its solidarity, especially under the General Economy. But with the shift of love and affection to the members of the private family, the practice became not only undesirable but hypocritical. In 1836, the General Synod substituted "the right hand of fellowship" in its place, wherever there was objection to it.

Likewise the custom of foot-washing was continued by the Brethren under circumstances which falsified the spirit of it. The custom fell into disuse, except among the devout, and in 1818 the Synod allowed the practice to be optional according to local desires.

Concomitant with the corruption of these traditions, there was a decadence of church music. In the early years in America there were constant accessions to the colonies of those who had received musical training in Europe. Free instruction was given, especially in the Single Brethren's Choirs, which were the first to break up. The hours otherwise spent in the practice of music were now used for diversion or to earn a livelihood. And as they became interested in profits and gains, the willingness to render voluntary music slackened.

The traditional German *"Gemeindechor"* became constantly a greater problem, because of the musical skill required on the part of the organist. "Such organists were required to know about 400 church tunes, and be able to play them in any key the officiating minister might start them. (The Minister generally commenced the singing of the hymn without announcing the words, the organist and the congregation joined in as soon as they could catch the words and the tune.) They were re-

[67] Levering: *History of Bethlehem,* p. 67.

FOOTWASHING OF THE SISTERS

(A) The Pastor reading the Liturgy.   (BB) Deaconesses washing feet.

quired to perform concerted music at sight." [68]   Skillful organists with the decadence of musical instruction became fewer. In addition, the succeeding generations were not familiar with the old church hymns and tunes, and the traditional singing had to give way to modern church music. One of the fathers writes: "What would brother Latrobe say were he a worshipper in some churches of the present day, where snatches of song, operatic flirts and unfledged, fanciful jets of disconnected apologies for ideas are dealt out boldly, and most self-complacently palmed upon a congregation to amuse instead of edify, corrupting taste and good manners, and in a great measure 'Making the Word of God of none effect.' . . . Whilst on this subject I cannot forego the opportunity of protesting against the light, trifling and even vulgar perpetrations in the musical department of many of our sister churches; their constituents not only permitting but encouraging, aiding and abetting the tritely called young America to victimize the sanctuary to the worldly begettings of Belial; desecrating the noble instrument of prayer, praise and supplication to the lowest degree of a street hand-organ, and subverting this happy medium to the heart, to the influences of a vain show of a sickly if not a depraved appetite, of an experimenting and irreligious candidate for worldly fame and popularity, altogether inconsistent with the place and the trust committed to him. . . . Popular melodies hatched from operatic fancies dragged into the church are but meagre apologies for plucking Satan of his so-called superior musical taste, and cannot fraternize nor sympathize with those emotions which the heart should encourage in God's Holy Temple, to come out from the world and be separate. If the Devil has the best tunes, let him keep them. What has light to do with darkness, or Christ with Belial?" [69]

In the beginning of the Renewed Church, the elders kept it true to its original aims and motives on the basis of a membership well sifted. They did not swing wide their doors to whoever had an inclination to join. For them the Church was something altogether too holy and divine to be desecrated by

[68] Martin: *Historical Sketch of Bethlehem, Pa.*, p. 161.
[69] Ritter: *Church in Philadelphia*, pp. 152-156.

unrepentant members.   Zinzendorf held that if the Church "permits unconverted persons, both men and women, whose hearts are not right with God to become members, whom on account of their wealth or social position, everybody will try to please, and should it become the policy of the church to be (in a bad sense) all things to all men—this would certainly be the direct road to ruin." [70]   In the early years the growth of the Church depended on accessions from without.   It was easy to keep the membership pure, since only those who could prove their piety or claim a heart experience were allowed to join. But when the enlargement of the Church became more and more a growth from within by their own children, the purity of the Moravian Church became endangered.   With the increase in the number of children born in the Moravian community, they had to choose between two dangers, either of losing the purity of the Church, or of sacrificing the unity of the community by distinguishing between the Church and the settlement.   Since the Brethren from the very first thought of their settlements as churches, they refused to make this distinction. Thus, since by birth the children could claim membership in the settlement, they automatically became members of the Church at a certain age, although many were without the religious experience on which the elders insisted.

In the Synods of the late eighteenth century there was much discussion of how the spiritual life of the Church could be revitalized.   At the General Synod of 1818 a distinction between an outer and an inner membership was made.   Members entered the outer by birth, baptism, and confirmation and had the right to partake of communion four times a year.   A confession of faith and the approval by lot was required for the inner circle.   These observed the Lord's Supper every four weeks and were eligible to the responsible positions in the Church.   After the Synod of 1825, the distinctions between the two circles of membership were no longer observed.   Instead, the practice of having those born and baptized into the congregation present themselves for membership when grown was observed as long as the exclusive Church-villages continued.

[70] Hagen: *Old Landmarks,* p. 81.

Baptism of a Child

(A) The Pastor baptizing. (B) The child being baptized. (C) The godfather holding the child. (D) The sponsors. (EE) The children. (FF) The Brethren and Sisters of the Congregation.

Since the abrogation of the General Economy, the population of the settlements had decreased. While the Brethren in Bethlehem, not including the settlements on the Nazareth land, numbered 669 in 1761,[71] in 1771 they had decreased to 560; [72] in 1798 they numbered 601,[73] and in 1808, 593.[74] Thus, over a period of forty-seven years, the Brethren in Bethlehem had actually lost seventy-six members. At the time of the General Synod of 1825, the total membership of the entire Unity had decreased 1,200 since 1818,[75] while other denominations in the wide virgin fields of America were growing rapidly.

With such astounding facts to support their contentions, the more rebellious and progressive spirits demanded a surrender of the exclusive policy. Reluctantly the Church fathers had to submit to the increasing force of this demand. In 1844, the Moravians started upon a new era, when Bethlehem threw off the yoke of exclusivism, in which she was soon followed by the other settlements; and by 1856, this Herrnhut policy had disappeared from all the Moravian Churches in America.

This brought about the separation of the settlement and the Church, which hitherto they had refused to make. In the place of the exclusive policy, which had prevailed for a whole century, church extension was substituted, and with this emancipation from the philosophy of Herrnhutism, the American Moravian Church began to grow. One year later the Brethren in Bethlehem had already increased their membership to 808,[76] and to 945 in 1849.[77]

When the exclusivism ceased, strangers who were not members of the Moravian Church moved into these Moravian villages. Hitherto these settlements had been carefully guarded against such an invasion. If a tradesman or merchant wanted to sell his business, it had to be sold to a Moravian, and if such

[71] Levering: *History of Bethlehem*, p. 378.
[72] *Ibid.*, p. 425.
[73] *Ibid.*, p. 567.
[74] *"Diarium Bethlehem"* (1808). Ms. Beth. Arch.
[75] Hamilton: *History*, p. 343.
[76] Levering: *History of Bethlehem*, p. 682.
[77] *Church Miscellany*, March 1850.

a buyer could not be found, then to the Church.[78]   A year after this exclusivism was given up, 150 strangers had already moved into Bethlehem.[79]   From a Church report of Bethlehem we read: "This circumstance of strangers settling among us, some of whom attend our public services, and occasionally commune with us as guests at the table of our common Lord, enlarges our sphere of useful activity; opportunities for scattering the good seed being afforded by the baptism of children, the visitation of the sick, the interment of the dead, the religious instruction imparted both in the district and Sunday schools, and the confirmation of applicants, baptized in their infancy within the pale of other Christian denominations; while a more extensive field offers in the country around for preaching regularly as at Freemansburg or occasionally as at Sunday school anniversaries and funerals, or in exchanging pulpits with the ministers of other evangelical churches, some of whom have edified our congregation with their discourses in our own sanctuary. At the same time, other places of worship have been opened in this borough by resident members of different persuasions, for occasional or regular services to be conducted by the ministers and agreeably to the usage of their respective churches." [80]

In 1848 there was a further modification of Church membership.   Hitherto the Moravian children had to present themselves for membership when grown, but now the baptized and confirmed were counted full-fledged members.   With this new and easier basis for membership, the Church grew rapidly.   In 1857 the membership in America was 8,000, while in 1892 it had increased to 19,000, and in 1921 to a total of 32,650.

Under the Church-village plan, the Brethren had no power to act independently.   In 1855 at the American provincial Synod they made a demand for full authority in matters purely local, which the General Synod of 1857 reluctantly granted, with the privilege of Church extension according to local requirements.   It was from this very year, as we have just no-

[78] "*Auszug aus dem Protocoll des Aufsehers Collegii in Nazareth von January 1787 bis 20ten Febr. 1788.*"   Ms. Beth. Arch.
[79] Levering: *History of Bethlehem*, p. 682.
[80] *Church Miscellany*, March 1850.

ticed, that the Church membership began to increase rapidly.

In outlining the stages of exclusive Moravianism and the resultant reactions to it, we have at the same time suggested the evolution of the Brethren's conception of their Church.   In these concluding paragraphs we must point out the stages of this evolution.

We have seen that the Brethren at first made no practical distinctions between the Church and the settlement, nor between the secular and the sacred.   Every group movement in their society was a religious movement, and every individual act was "unto God."   All duties were religious duties.   Their religion welded the society into a unity.   This feeling of the "Unity of the Brethren" was a direct result of the persecutions that afflicted them.   They began to compare themselves with the apostolic church, many of whom willingly became martyrs for their faith.   Because of the sense of their apostolic character and their growth in numbers, they instituted certain customs and a church discipline that were to safeguard their apostolicity.   The introduction of foot-washing, the "kiss of peace," the Love Feasts, and the lot are evidences that they had the apostolic church as their model.

Because of their uniqueness, they believed the Lord had something special in mind for them.   As Israel, who had also been persecuted, was a favoured nation on all the earth, so they were a favoured church.   They began to think of themselves as the "favoured little sinner congregation." [81]   They were a chosen people, a theocracy under a new covenant.   As the high priest of old appeared before God with the Urim and Thummim, so they now appealed to him by the lot.   The Count said that the system of the Brethren consisted in a society of chosen people for a communion of grace.[82]   The Chief Elder Jesus, himself, was leading them.   They were "the little church of the cross," [83] "the blood congregation," [84] "the cross congre-

---

[81] *Manual of Doctrine* (London, 1742), Introduction.
[82] *Wunden Litaney Reden*, pp. 152, 153.
[83] *Manual of Doctrine* (London, 1742), p. 271.
[84] *Pennsylvanische Nachrichten,* p. 44.

gation," [85] and the "precious and tenderly beloved blood and cross church of the Lamb of God." [86]   Their persecutions, their apostolic customs, and their discipline gave them the conception of their church not merely as "a" church among others but as "the" church.

Zinzendorf quoted Luther as saying that the true evangelical method of church order was still lacking, and that he (Luther) himself could not establish it since he did not have the people for it, but when such a people did arise, he would help them faithfully.[87]   Now Zinzendorf's adherence to Lutheranism and the fact that he did "not differ from other evangelical Brethren in doctrine but in the application, not in the word but the dividing of it," [88] is evidence that he believed that he had the people for "the true evangelical method of church order" of which Luther had spoken.   The Count believed that the Moravian Church was a wonder of God's grace and an indispensable part of God's whole Church Economy.[89]

The Brethren believed that the members of the Invisible Church were to be found in all communions, and that this Invisible Church could become visible to the world through the united members, but that it could not be held together without special and peculiar regulations.[90]   In a *Manual of Doctrine* [91] questions 1,119 and 1;120 are:

Question: What is properly the church?
Answer: The Church of God in the Spirit.

Question: How is she called when she becomes visible?
Answer: The light of the world; a city that is set on an hill.

The Brethren considered themselves such a visible form of the Invisible Church.   Henry Antes in a letter to the people of Pennsylvania, in speaking of the first Sea Congregation which

[85] *Naturelle Reflexiones*, p. 267.
[86] *Büd. Samm.*, vol. III, pp. 67-71.
[87] *Naturelle Reflexiones*, p. 267.
[88] Gambold: *Maxims*, p. 140.
[89] *Naturelle Reflexiones*, p. 310.
[90] *Büd. Samm.*, vol. I, p. 41.
[91] London, 1742.

had just arrived, wrote: "Today, at last a visible church of the Lord was seen and recognized in Philadelphia." [92]

But gradually the reasons for calling themselves "the little persecuted flock" had been removed. In a land of religious liberty like the State of Pennsylvania, the Brethren lost all the characteristics which they once believed essential to "the" church of Christ. In fact they had become like their brethren of other denominations. In what sense were they better or on what grounds could they claim to be "the" church? They lost the conviction of their primitive apostolic character and made no effort to renew their former claims. They began to speak of themselves as "a" church among the others. Thus a Moravian of the middle of the nineteenth century said: "When we remember that we are but one among so many, we have abundant cause to wonder that God hath so increased us, but we have as abundant cause to be humbled in the very dust because He did not more increase us. We have of course no cause to be ashamed that we are but one among so many, but we should be ashamed that we are not more of a proselyting church! I do not mean by this that we should engage in the practice of drawing away members from other churches. . . . Think of certain other Christian churches! Think of the Presbyterians, of the Episcopal, of the Methodist, of the Baptist Churches! How much good are they doing! And though we differ from them on different points, yet they as well as we, and we as well as they, preach redemption purchased by the death of the Son of God, and applied by the renewing of the Holy Ghost! . . . And look at our Lutheran and Reformed Brethren, who in fact are one, or almost one with us in doctrine. . . . They toil and toil on and work and preach and visit, generally having from three to six or eight congregations, and it is not they who in most cases are to blame that they have so many. . . . Let us learn still more self-denial and diligence from them!" [93] The glory of "the" church had passed into the mediocrity of "a" church.

The fathers and elders, however, still hoped for a renewal

[92] *Büd. Samm.*, vol. I, p. 41.
[93] *Church Miscellany*, August 1852.

of the olden days.   One of the Brethren wrote: "If the mutilated remains of Jerusalem's second temple needed renovation
in Herod's time, the Renewed *Unitas Fratrum* of 1728 needs it
no less at this time.   If any marvel at this and ask: 'How can
this be done?' (John 3:9) The Holy Scriptures and Moravian
history answer: With God nothing shall be impossible." [94]

[94] Hagen: *Old Landmarks,* pp. 239, 240.

CHAPTER IX

MODERN MORAVIANS

WHERE once the Pilgrim Congregation went forth, "their feet shod with the preparation of the gospel of peace," today stands the thriving city of steel. These grounds, hallowed by the incarnation of the Invisible Church, have been defiled by the smoke and sordidness of American industry. The rule of Spangenberg has given way to the rule of Schwab; and Bethlehem, though it cherishes its religious origins as the seat of Moravianism, now lives on steel. The spirit that prevailed when the foot-washing and the "kiss of peace" were significant symbols, has yielded to the principles of competition and mechanical progress necessarily adopted by modern Moravian business men. The exclusive brotherhood has lost both its former holiness and its communal régime. The quiet devotional atmosphere of the old Choir houses, still standing, is displaced by the clanging and grinding of the wheels of industry.

Also in Europe, both on the continent and in England, the exclusive settlements have been abandoned.[1] In Herrnhut itself non-Moravians are residents and property owners. In Germany some of the pietistic ideals of Zinzendorf are still in force. The Diaspora work, which is the direct opposite of church extension, is enthusiastically pursued. The Choir system still lingers, with all the festivals, and is more than a mere convenient classification of the congregation. Superintendents and assistants in each Choir are responsible for the spiritual nurture of their wards. In Great Britain, the Moravians have adopted church extension as in America, and the Choir houses have been abandoned. In the more recent congregations in England, Choir divisions, Love Feasts, and Choir festivals are unknown.[2]

[1] Hamilton: *The Moravians and their Faith,* p. 10.
[2] Hutton: *History,* p. 493.

American Moravianism has undergone a radical transformation. The Brethren persistently requested home rule for the American branch of the Unity, which was finally granted, because they saw that the principles enforced in Germany were not applicable to America. Had this request not been granted, American Moravianism would still be confined to exclusive settlements, or perhaps be extinct. However, once given the liberty to adapt methods to local conditions, the American branch hastily adopted the methods of their sister denominations. The opportunities they missed in those early years to extend their borders, especially among the large German element in Pennsylvania, among whom the Moravians were active as an organized church even before the Lutherans and the German Reformed, can never be retrieved. When church extension was finally adopted, the preaching places were organized into Moravian churches. Thus the work of home missions was begun.

When the American Moravians began church extension, they did not surrender the basic principles of the Moravian Church, for the ideal of *"ecclesiola in ecclesia,"* which proved to be the most serious obstacle to the numerical growth of the Brethren, was a child of the pietistic movement and was injected into Moravianism largely by Zinzendorf. While the Moravian Unity has continuously been loyal to what they consider to be the real mission of their church, in America many traditions and peculiarly Moravian customs have been sloughed off under American traditions and influences.

The division of the congregation into Choirs according to age, sex, and station in life, has never been introduced in some of the newer congregations and is no longer observed by many of the older ones. Especially is this true of Great Britain and America. Sunday schools, Christian Endeavor, the Order of the King's Sons and the King's Daughters, Boy Scouts, Y.M.C.A. groups, State and County Councils of Religious Education, women's societies, and brotherhoods have very largely taken their place. Although the Choir houses have long been abandoned in America and Great Britain, the division of the congregation into Choirs is considered a practical help to the life of the Church. Where the Choir festivals are still observed they fall on the same days as in the earlier period of the Church.

The churches still hold services that consist almost entirely of singing and responses. At such Singing Services on festival days and celebrations, the choir usually sings chorals and anthems. There may be short prayers or Scripture verses interspersed in these services but no sermons or addresses.

The Love Feasts, which are held previous to the Holy Communion and in preparation for celebrations and festivals, are a distinct feature of the liturgical order. Their purpose is to cultivate fellowship in Christ, symbolized in the breaking of bread together. These impressive services are largely choral. Those who serve at the Love Feasts distribute buns and coffee to the congregation, while a chorus sings or the organ is played. The song service and fellowship are the main features of the service. "The Moravian love feasts are intended to set forth by a simple meal of which all partake in common, that there is no respect of persons before the Lord, and that all believers are one in Christ, united among themselves by the closest bonds of Christian love." [3] These Love Feasts are not observed by all Moravian congregations. Some have never introduced them, and others have given them up.

In place of the consecrated Choir houses where once the young men and women were impregnated with "the faith," today the younger generation have higher educational institutions and instructors who have availed themselves of the methods and research at centers of learning. The instructors are urged and given opportunity to do graduate work in state and other universities. Some of the instructors in the men's and women's colleges in Bethlehem commute regularly to avail themselves of such courses as are offered at the University of Pennsylvania and the universities in New York City. Their denominational colleges are the Moravian College and Theological Seminary at Bethlehem; the Young Ladies Seminary and College for Women, also at Bethlehem; and the College for Women in Winston-Salem, North Carolina.

[3] H. E. Stocker: *Moravian Customs*, pp. 72, 73.

The liturgical character of the church persists, but the liturgy has been modified and modernized. The Moravians belong decidedly more to the liturgical than to the evangelical churches. They have an established liturgical system in which singing is still a prominent feature. Since the publication of the first Church hymn-book in 1735,[4] there have been frequent revisions; the most important of them from a doctrinal and historical point of view was the collection prepared in 1778 under the direction of Christian Gregor.[5] The present *Hymnal and Liturgies of the Moravian Church* (1920), containing 952 hymns, is not a mere abridgement of the early hymnal with its eighteen supplements and 2,357 hymns. This new hymnal is a collection from many sources from the time of the Church Fathers to the present. Some of the authors belonged to obscure sects, but many of the hymns are by Moravian composers. James Montgomery, the Moravian poet, is the author of fifty-two, the largest number by any one composer. The characteristic theme of the early Moravian hymns dealing with the blood wounds and passion of Christ has been greatly modified or at least subdued. The present hymnal deals no more with morbid themes than the hymnals of other churches. It is significant that only 38 hymns of Zinzendorf are included, while there are 43 from the pen of Charles Wesley. The temper of the early blood and wound theology is still recalled in such hymns as:

> Wounded head, back ploughed with furrows,
> Visage marred: "Behold the Man!"
> Eyes how dim, how full of sorrows,
> Sunk with grief: "Behold the Man!"
> Lamb of God, led to the slaughter,
> Melted, poured out like water;
> Should not love my heart inflame,
> Viewing Thee, Thou Paschal Lamb! [6]

[4] In 1725 Zinzendorf made a private collection of hymns.

[5] This hymnal, which appeared in the same year with Spangenberg's *Idea Fidei Fratrum,* marks the beginning of the Spangenbergian era.

[6] *Hymnal and Liturgies of the Moravian Church* (1920), no. 222.

Streams of comfort, rich, unceasing,
From the wounds of Jesus flow.[7]

The spirit of Zinzendorf at his best is commemorated in his famous hymn: "Jesus still lead on." [8]

The Holy Communion is generally celebrated once a month but at least on the first Sunday after Epiphany, the first Sunday in Lent, during Passion Week, Whitsunday, the Sunday nearest August 13,[9] and the Sunday nearest November 13.[10] These services, consisting of the singing of hymns, kneeling in silent prayer, the words of Scripture at the Last Supper, and soft music, are conducted solemnly and reverently. The officiating minister wears a white surplice with full sleeves, symbolic of the righteousness of Christ in whose name he presides at this service.[11] Their custom is to receive the unleavened bread in the open palm of the right hand and to partake of it while standing, in contrast to communicants of those churches who bow to the floor because they worship the bread and the wine as the real body and blood of Christ. The "right hand of fellowship," which was substituted for the "kiss of peace," is given at the beginning and at the end of the service.

The Moravians practise infant baptism and confirmation. An infant is usually baptized within a year after birth and by this rite becomes a baptismal member of the Church. While the water is sprinkled or poured over the infant's head a man holds the child if it is a boy and a woman if a girl. At the rite of confirmation the candidates become communicant members of the Church.

The chief liturgical services of the Church calendar are: the

[7] *Ibid.*, no. 515.

[8] *Ibid.*, no. 696.

[9] In commemoration of the spiritual baptism of the Herrnhut congregation at the Lord's Supper in the church at Berthelsdorf on Aug. 13, 1727.

[10] Commemoration of the introduction of the Eldership of Christ on Nov. 13, 1741.

[11] The robe is worn also at the rites of baptism, confirmation, and ordination. Until 1769 a red girdle was worn with the surplice to symbolize that it was through the blood of Christ they had the right to wear the white surplice.

First Sunday in Advent, Second Sunday in Advent, Christmas Day, Epiphany, Lent, Easter, Ascension Day, Whitsunday, Trinity Sunday, All Saints' Day, and Thanksgiving Day. There are other liturgies for special services, missionary, patriotic, for schools and colleges, a day of humiliation and prayer, the office for the service preparatory to the Holy Communion. The seasons especially sacred to Moravians are Christmas and Passion Week. The Christmas season extends from Christmas Eve to the Eve of Epiphany. On Christmas Eve a service for the children is held and sometimes a Love Feast. At the morning service on Christmas Day the Christmas Litany is chanted, and in the evening of the same day there is usually a program by the Church School.

At the daily services during Passion Week the acts of Christ as they occurred day by day in the week of his crucifixion are read from the *Passion Week Manual*.[12] On Palm Sunday morning there is a confirmation service, and in the evening an antiphon "Hosannah" composed by Christian Gregor is sung. On Maundy Thursday there is a Holy Communion service, and on Good Friday a series of services if possible. The acts of Christ on this day are read from the *Passion Week Manual* as nearly as possible at the hours when they occurred, interspersed by responses and antiphonal singing by the congregation and the choir.

The Easter services bring a joyous climax to the vigil of the Passion Week. Where the churches have trombone choirs, the trombonists meet long before break of day. At the church and other selected places they play chorals proclaiming the Resurrection and finally return to the church to announce the early service, in which the beautiful Easter Morning Litany is chanted and which is concluded in the cemetery. "All assemble reverently around the graves of the departed, and pray to be kept in everlasting fellowship with the Church Triumphant, giving glory to Him who is the Resurrection and the Life. This service hallowed by many tender associations, is one of the

---

[12] The *Passion Week Manual* is especially prepared for this purpose and contains the last discourses and acts of Christ as found in the Harmony of the Gospels.

OSTER-LITURGIE.
Gehalten die abgeschiedenen Brüder und Schwestern
am Oster-morgen auf dem Gottesacker zu Herrnhuth.

Commemoration des Decedés
Le Matin de Pâques.

EASTER LITURGY AT SUNRISE IN MEMORY OF THE DEPARTED. THE CONGREGATION
GATHERED AROUND THE GRAVES AT THE HUTHBERG IN HERRNHUT

most impressive of the whole year." [13]   Many people who are not Moravians come from long distances to attend this impressive and unique service.   For example, 20,000 people attended the 1932 service in Winston-Salem, North Carolina.   Their march to the cemetery grounds was accompanied by the music of three hundred musicians grouped in eight bands.[14]

There is now comparatively little interest in dogma or creed among the Moravians.   They have always centered their devotions, beliefs, and practices around the "Crucified Saviour," without requiring definiteness on disputed points of doctrine such as the sacraments, election, freedom of the will, the Trinity, and the "mysteries of the Scriptures."   Today there are other communions which are equally tolerant, and from a doctrinal point of view the modern Moravians are not unique in this.   But historically they are, since they held these views before the Reformation, when the hand of Rome dominated, and during the Reformation, when doctrinal disputes raged. When other Protestant churches became interested almost wholly in creed and theology and followed in the way of rationalism, the Renewed Moravian Church reasserted the simple doctrine that "Christ not only died but that he also lives for us, and that his holy life is meritorious for us and is our model and encouragement."   They declare their adherence to the Augsburg Confession and the Apostles' Creed, and further statements of their beliefs are to be found in their Easter Morning Litany and in the *Results of the General Synods*.

The death of Zinzendorf in 1760 and the leadership of Spangenberg were the forerunners that heralded a more conventional theology.   The publication of Spangenberg's *Idea Fidei Fratrum,* of which the first edition appeared in 1778, made him the official Church theologian.   This publication was written to defend the Brethren against the attacks of their enemies and to clear them of the fanatic proclivities of the preceding years.   In the preface of this volume La Trobe wrote: "Having an open and generous mind, and being conversant with various sincere persons and sects in Christendom,

[13] Stocker: *Moravian Customs,* p. 58.
[14] *New York Times,* March 28, 1932.

he [Zinzendorf] sought for the truth in each, though more or less covered with rubbish, and was frequently led either in sentiment or expressions to adopt for a season the manner of utterance used by the party with whom he was at that time engaged. . . . Whether what is said above may appear necessary on presenting this book to the public, or no, we apprehend it may be useful, as those into whose hands some of the above mentioned discourses, or of the hymns which were in a peculiar style and badly translated, or of the false and mutilated quotations often found in the writings of the adversaries, have fallen, might allege them as speaking otherwise than the doctrine contained in this book, by making it known that the Brethren do not and will not receive the said discourses and hymns as an exposition of the doctrines and phraseology of the *Unitas Fratrum,* but that they heartily agree with those contained in this Exposition, and here their sense of the Christian doctrines may be found."

Spangenberg was commissioned to write not only an exposition of doctrine, but also a biography of Zinzendorf in which his undesirable characteristics were not to be mentioned.[15] The exposition of the Brethren's doctrine in Spangenberg's *Idea Fidei Fratrum* was translated into English, Danish, French, Swedish, Dutch, Bohemian, and Polish. It contains none of the novel Christological ideas of Zinzendorf; in fact, its purpose was to show the public that the Brethren's theology was not Zinzendorfian but Scriptural.

While Zinzendorf was the organizer of the Renewed Church, to Spangenberg belongs the credit of having remained true to the ideals of the Ancient Bohemian-Moravian Church. The Zinzendorfian Christocracy is not to be found in the hymns of the Ancient Bohemian-Moravian Church. The first hymnal (1501) of the Ancient Church was compiled by Bishop Lucas. In 1531 Michael Weisz issued their first German hymnal. These were revised by Johann Horn in 1540. The Bohemian-Moravian Church was then acquiring new hymns from German and Swiss reformers, which made a revision of their hymnal

[15] "*Verlasz des General Synodi Marienborn, Mense Jul. et Aug. 1764.*" Ms. Beth. Arch.

desirable. This revision in 1566 contained many of Luther's hymns.[16] In the light, therefore, of what we know of the spirit of the reformers, and of those hymns which the Renewed Church took over from the Bohemian-Moravian hymnals,[17] it becomes clear that the Zinzendorfian theology, with its striking Christological ideas, was not the theology of the Ancient Brethren.

The General Synods, at which Spangenberg was now the leading spirit, declared that the law of Christ must be preached as well as his love, and that much harm had been done in their church by an empty "blood babble" (*blut geschwätz*).[18] The Litany of the Wounds of Jesus [19] was to be discontinued wherever it was not understood or could no longer be properly conducted.[20] Christian Gregor was put in charge of revising the hymnal, in which the extremes of Zinzendorfian Christocracy were to be omitted.[21] Although Christ was to remain the Chief Elder in the Brethren's congregations, the lot was to be used more carefully and not mechanically as in the past. They were to use the lot only when they had no clear statement by Jesus in the Scriptures.[22] The stress of the family relationship in the Holy Trinity disappeared. The Brethren were urged to be careful in the use of the word "Mother" in relation to the Trinity.[23] Instead of God the Father being remote and having the relationship of a grandfather to the world, the General Synod now requested that He be made the special subject of theological thought and doctrine. The Fatherhood of God was to be emphasized, and a day was appointed when this was to be made known in all the Brethren's congregations.[24]

[16] *Historische Nachricht von Brüder-Gesangbuche des Jahres 1778.*

[17] *Christliches Gesang-Buch* (1735). Also *Gesangbuch zum Gebrauch der evangelischen Brüdergemeinen* (1778).

[18] "*Verlasz des im Jahr 1775 zu Barby gehaltenen Synodi der evangelischen Brüder Unität.*" Ms. Beth. Arch.

[19] See Appendix C.

[20] "*Verlasz des General Synodi zu Marienborn 1769.*" Ms. Beth. Arch.

[21] *Ibid.*

[22] "*Verlasz des General Synodi Marienborn Mense Jul. et Aug. 1764.*" Ms. Beth. Arch.

[23] *Ibid.*

[24] *Ibid.*

The Brethren now deplored the fact that they had not properly educated the youth in the faith. They blamed themselves for having stressed a "heart" theology at the expense of a proper understanding. Samuel Lieberkühn was, therefore, commissioned to publish a catechism for the instruction of youth.[25] Instead of allowing the uneducated to preach, the Brethren now insisted on an educated ministry,[26] who were not to preach with an oratorical flourish that moved the emotions but left no lasting impressions.[27]

In 1775, fifteen years after the death of Zinzendorf, the theology of Spangenberg had gained a sufficient foothold to allow the General Synod to make a clear statement of the following doctrines: (1) A belief in the atonement and the satisfaction made for us by Christ; that he gave himself for our sins and bore our guilt. Forgiveness and sanctification are a free gift from him. (2) A belief in the general corruption of mankind; that there is no health in man, nor strength in his fallen nature whereby he can help or improve himself. (3) A belief in the deity of Christ; that God the Creator of all things has been revealed in the flesh, and has reconciled the world to himself; that he was before all things, and by him all things consist. (4) A belief that the Holy Spirit convicts us of sin, establishes our faith, and sanctifies us. (5) A belief that obedience to the will of God is an evidence of faith. These doctrines were reaffirmed at later Synods and are still today an orthodox statement of Moravian theology.

The principle laid down at the General Synod of 1857 that the "Holy Scriptures of the Old and New Testament are and shall remain the only rule of our faith and practice" has been reiterated at the later Synods. "We regard them as God's Word, which He spoke to men of old time through the prophets, and at last through the Son and by His apostles, to instruct

[25] *"Verlasz des General Synodi zu Marienborn 1769."* Ms. Beth. Arch. The catechism was called: *Der Hauptinhalt der Lehre Jesu Christi zum Gebrauch bey dem Unterricht der Jugend in den evangelischen Brüdergemeinen.*

[26] *Ibid.*

[27] *"Verlasz des im Jahr 1775 zu Barby gehaltenen Synodi der evangelischen Brüder Unität."* Ms. Beth. Arch.

them unto salvation through faith in Christ Jesus. We are convinced that all truths that declare the will of God for our salvation are fully contained therein." [28] The intent of this statement is inclusive rather than exclusive. It is not narrowed by clauses as to infallibility, inerrancy, or verbal inspiration. They declare "it is not our business to determine what Holy Scripture has left undetermined or to contend about mysteries impenetrable to our human reason." [29]

Faith in Christ consists in a personal devotion to him rather than in conceptions about him. And the fruits of such a faith are sought in piety and godly living, rather than in formal creeds.

The Moravians are Trinitarians,[30] but they regard the Trinity as such a mystery that they decline expounding at great length what confounds even their imagination and are content with the phraseology of their Easter Morning Litany: "I believe in the One only God, Father, Son, and Holy Ghost, who created all things by Jesus Christ, and was in Christ, reconciling the world unto Himself." [31]

"They hold that in the Lord's Supper the believer receives a divine seal of the covenant which was ratified by the blood of Christ, and that he is thereby drawn into the most intimate communion with Jesus Christ." [32] Without defining the nature of Christ's presence in the bread and the wine, this sacrament is to them a pledge of Christ's continued personal presence.[33]

Although they are evangelical, there is a willingness to wel-

---

[28] *Results of General Synods* (1914), p. 10. The General Synods meet about every ten years. There were no General Synods between 1914 and 1931 due to the war, which practically annihilated the fund invested in Germany, the interest of which defrayed the costs of the General Synods. A further reason for this long interval between the General Synods was to wait until sufficient time had elapsed to disclose the effects of the war on their missions, so that they might adjust their missionary administration accordingly. The results of the General Synod of 1931 re-affirm the doctrinal statements of the Synod of 1914. See *General Order of the Moravian Church*, 1931, p. 49.

[29] *The Book of Order of the Moravian Church in America* (1911), p. 7.

[30] Schultze: *Christian Doctrine*, pp. 34-40.

[31] *Hymnal and Liturgies of the Moravian Church* (1920), p. 24.

[32] Schultze: *What do Moravians Believe?"* p. 5.

[33] Schultze: *Christian Doctrine*, p. 223.

come liberal theology. One can be a member of the Moravian Church and think as he pleases on disputed theological issues.[34] The emphasis is put on the broad principles of the Christian religion and not on distinctive doctrines. The fact that the family of evangelical churches can take opposite positions on some of these questions is an evidence to them that these questions are of minor or of little importance. They do not hesitate, therefore, to instruct their theological students in the results of critical research.[35]

The Moravian Church is still a missionary church, with thirteen mission provinces: Labrador, Alaska, California, Jamaica, West Indies, British Guiana, Surinam, South Africa (West), South Africa (East), East Central Africa (Nyasa), East Central Africa (Un-Yamwezi), West Himalaya, and Nicaragua-Honduras. In these provinces they have 303 congregations, with a total membership of 138,318, of whom 45,337 are communicant members.[36] "Whilst in the Protestant churches at large the proportion of missionaries to members is about 1 to 5,000, among the Moravians it is 1 to 60." [37] In addition to this heavy missionary program the Moravians alone as a church are maintaining two homes for lepers, one called "Jesus Help" just outside Jerusalem, and "Bethesda" at Groot Chatillon in Dutch Guiana (Surinam). Before the World War this entire missionary enterprise was the work of the whole Unity, managed by a central mission board responsible to the General Synod. Since the War, however, the administrative control of the mission fields has been divided, making the American Moravian Church responsible for Alaska, California, and Nicaragua-Honduras. The general principles of mission work are determined by the General Synod, and each of the four independent Provinces reports to this body whenever it convenes.[38] All the Provinces are also united in reviving their Church in Czecho-Slovakia (Bohemia and Moravia),

[34] Hutton: *History,* p. 484.
[35] *Ibid.*
[36] *Daily Texts* (1931), p. 230.
[37] *Encyclopedia of Religion and Ethics,* vol. VIII, p. 839.
[38] *General Order of the Moravian Church* (1931), p. 54.

the birthplace of the Ancient Church, where they have a total membership of 6,741.[39]

The Moravians have not only been first in Protestant missions but have persistently held their place of pre-eminence, so that their "missionary work is the marvel of the world even down to our day." [40] William Carey, who went to India in 1793, may justly be named "the father of modern missions," but to the Moravians belongs the honor of having preceded him in this work by 61 years. Carey himself acknowledged his inspiration by the Moravian missionaries.[41] In 1900 at the Ecumenical Missionary Conference in New York, John R. Mott said: "The most striking example of achievement on the home field in the interest of foreign missions is that of the Moravians. They have done more in proportion to their ability than any other body of Christians." [42]

If the modern Moravian Church has any distinguishing feature from other communions it consists in the fact that it is the only Protestant church which is united organically throughout the whole world. This makes it an international church, whose unity is made secure by the freedom it allows politically and doctrinally. Anyone acquainted with Moravian history knows that this is not a unity with many loose ends, but a unity that is closely knit. Although at times the Moravians are nationally divided because of international conflicts, religiously they remain a unity. The ideal of the modern Moravian Church is to extend the spirit of this unity into the political domain in order to avoid future international clashes as well as sectarian bigotry.

In setting up such fraternal relationships among all persuasions and communions, the Moravian Church in America is taking an active part. The American Moravians were allocated two delegates to the Universal Christian Conference on Life and Work held in Stockholm in 1925, but contingencies arose that made their representation impossible. At the World

---

[39] *Daily Texts* (1931), p. 230.
[40] A. D. Mason: *Outlines of Missionary History*, p. 57.
[41] Hutton: *History*, pp. 251, 252.
[42] *Ecumenical Missionary Conference* (New York, 1900), vol. I, p. 97.

Conference on Faith and Order at Lausanne in 1927, the Moravians were represented by a European delegate. At the International Missionary Council that met in Jerusalem in 1928, they were represented by their Secretary of Missions who has been a member of this Council since its organization in 1920. In the Foreign Missions Conference of North America there are 88 foreign mission boards and societies, of which the Moravian Society for Propagating the Gospel is the oldest incorporated missionary society in America. Of the Federal Council of the Churches of Christ in America, with which 28 denominations have affiliated themselves, the Moravian Church has been a member since its beginning. They also participated in the organization of the Home Missions Council, founded in 1907, and are represented on this Council by the Moravian Country Church Commission and by the Board of Church Extension of the American Moravian Church. Likewise their Christian Endeavor Societies, Sunday-schools and similar organizations are associated with and participate in the state, national, and international conferences and conventions of these organizations.[43]

The Unity of the Moravians was seriously threatened when the General Synods enacted laws that were contrary to the policy and opinion of the Provinces. Under the exclusivistic policy the Brethren in America and Great Britain had meekly obeyed the central authority of the European directing board. But when American conditions began to differ from those of Europe, the American Moravians demanded home rule and were finally forced to rebel, though they were regarded by the directing board as dangerous radicals who were more interested in separation than in unity. At the American Provincial Synod of 1817 the demand was made for self-government in affairs that were strictly American in nature and not understood by those in Europe. The following year the General Synod flatly refused the request. In 1855 the American Brethren renewed their request, and again the General Synod of 1856 denounced their proposals. But in 1857 the General Synod saw that to save the Unity, the American demands could

[43] *Journal of the Provincial Synod* (1930), pp. 104-109.

not be ignored. The constitution of the General Synod was revised, the changes in the main giving the Provinces the right to elect three delegates to the General Synods. The others, who were Germans, were "ex-officio" members, thus keeping the balance of control in their hands. Each Province now held its own property and was allowed to have its own Provincial Synods to make its own laws, provided they were in accord with the spirit of the Unity as represented in the General Synod. But the Provinces demanded even more independence from time to time, and the constitution underwent frequent changes.

According to the present constitution the four Provinces, the Continental, the British, the American North, and the American South, hold their own Provincial Synods, enact their own laws, and elect their delegates to the General Synods. The Provinces are subordinated to the General Synod which is the highest legislative body. The General Directing Board, which is the administrative board during the interval between the meetings of the General Synods, consists of the four governing boards of the Provinces, which are called the Provincial Elders' Conferences and which have administrative power during the interval between the meetings of the Provincial Synods. Under this system each local church is congregational and democratic in its government. It manages its own affairs according to the spirit of the Provincial Synod, and each member over eighteen years of age in good and regular standing is entitled to vote.

The Moravians are an episcopal church, having received their episcopacy from the Waldensians in 1467. The orders of the ministry are bishops, presbyters, and deacons. They are different from other episcopal churches in that the bishops do not have administrative power. Their prerogatives are in the spiritual and inner life of the church rather than in the external. The bishops, as well as the presbyters and deacons who are ordained by them, are subordinate to the Board of Directors of the local church and to the Elders' Conference. They attach no divine prerogatives to their episcopal standing, and therefore they recognize the ordination of other ministers not in the apostolic succession as valid and welcome them to preach in their pulpits. What they aimed at when they succeeded in obtaining recognition of their episcopacy from Parliament in 1749, was to obtain legal standing among the state churches, and especially among those churches which insisted on a ministry in the apostolic succession.

The Moravians are still a comparatively small denomination. The total membership of the Northern and Southern Provinces in America is 37,838. The total membership of the entire Unity, including 138,318 on the foreign mission fields, aggregates 226,489.[44]

[44] *Daily Texts* (1931), p. 230.

APPENDIX A

"BROTHERLY AGREEMENT" [1]

1. It is not to be forgotten at any time that Bethlehem and Nazareth and the remaining communities thereto belonging were established, and developed in the manner in which they now appear, for no other purpose except that the Saviour's work not only in Pennsylvania but in all America, as well, particularly, in the English Provinces, may thereby be given the hand of assistance. The purpose of the said Economy, if one is to speak plainly, has in view, of course, that we conduct ourselves unitedly in an honorable manner and well pleasing to God, that we rear our children according to His will and guard our young people, sisters as well as brethren, until they are trained so as to be of use to Him, that we care for our poor and weak, aged and infirm and faithfully minister to them, that we regulate, also, our wedded state so that we may doubly care for that which belongs to the Lord. But something further is intended therewith, we have, indeed, agreed with one another that we would each, according to gift and skill the Lord has granted him, be faithful and industrious so that we may be helpful when and where the Saviour may need us, be it that we give up people from our midst whom the Saviour designates for His service among heathen or Christians, among young or old, among neighbors or those far distant, for preaching, visiting, conducting school, or whatever other name the service may have, which is done for the Lord; or to serve the people of the Lord in their going and coming, during their tarrying among us or when they are in their fields of labor, because they cannot undertake anything for themselves, so that they could support themselves, if they are not to neglect the work for which the Saviour has separated them; or to receive the children of those brethren and sisters who are employed in this manner by the Saviour and to care for them in our institutions as we do for our own children, to support them and rear them to His joy and honor; or in other circum-

---

[1] *"Einige Zur Bethlehemschen und Nazarethschen Gemeinschaftlichen Brüder Öconomie gehörige Momenta." "Diarium Bethlehem,"* Aug. 1754. Ms. Beth. Arch. Translated by Dr. W. N. Schwarze.

stances where something is done for the sake of the Lord, *e.g.*, when Conferences or Synods are held, to assist heartily in whatever way we can do so, and in anything else of similar nature which might be specified which may have connection with service of the Gospel.

2. We all belong to the Saviour, as He is our Lord, and what we have, that all belongs to Him, and He shall dispose of it as pleases Him. Our worthy Brother David Nitschmann, whom we love and honor as a father among us, is, indeed, in the eyes of the world for the sake of good order recognized and known as the Proprietor of Bethlehem and its appurtenances and the possession goes under his name and the names of his heirs and shall be administered by his executors, after his death for the same objects as hitherto. Yet he is, in truth, as are his heirs, the one who possess in fee for the Saviour. We, however, will, at the same time, regard him, his heirs, assigns, executors and administrators as tutors given us by the Saviour and carefully avoid all appearance of arbitrary appropriation.

3. As no one among us can say with truth that he was forced by men to go into the said Economy, or remain in it, since, on the contrary, we have agreed to it ourselves, not without previously understanding the matter, nor in haste, but with good cause and conviction; Therefore, our mind is that we will govern ourselves according to the said purpose of the Economy of Bethlehem, Nazareth, and the remaining communities thereto belonging, as outlined in Par. 1. We do not, accordingly, regard ourselves as men-servants or maid-servants, who serve some man for the sake of wage, and who have for this reason joined the aforesaid Economy in order that they might demand hire or pay for their labor; but we are here as brethren and sisters, who owe themselves to the Saviour, and for whom it is, indeed, a token of grace that they may do all for His sake. We declare, therefore, not only in general but, also, in particular, each one for himself, that we do not for this time nor for the future pretend to any wage or have reason to pretend to any. We were received into the said Economy with no idea of having, taking, or seeking wage, the Economy having dedicated itself to the service of the Saviour, and with no promise that wage or pay should be given; we, on the contrary, regard it a mark of grace that we are here and may labor according to the above stated intention.

4. Although we look upon ourselves and our children as free people, and not as men-servants and maid-servants of a man, whatever name these may bear, and would be so regarded by everyone, we would not therewith say that we would live without order according

to our own notions. No, far from it. But since God is a God of order and has designated among His people and in His Church, from time to time, the persons who shall be leaders of the whole or its parts and govern the affairs we carry on together; therefore, we declare that we will not only not oppose those persons who have been appointed our leaders but through a hearty obedience lighten their burden, and this so much the more, as it is evident and comprehensible that the said Economy must perish and cannot continue, and would, therefore, fail of its purpose, if a willing and childlike subordination does not continue among us.

5. We will, also, yield a willing obedience to the arrangements which are either, from time to time, made among us, or are again renewed, as in accordance with the word and mind of Jesus as through His grace we have found in the Bible, and then, also, be willingly obedient to the laws of our government, under which we may lead a quiet and peaceable life in all godliness and honesty. Hence, we will not only be satisfied with that which is regulated, according to our special circumstances, in our Church, Choirs, and Economy, but, also, ourselves support it and by no means allow it to go unreproved if by anyone it should be set at nought.

6. Inasmuch as in accordance with the above named purposes of the Economy there may be many an item of expense, which otherwise would not be reckoned among the expenditures of ordinary house-keeping (though we may believe that the Saviour will not suffer the service of the brethren, which they accomplish in His work, to be unrewarded in externals, not to take into account the fact that it is for us a mark of grace, if He deems us worthy to share in His work), so we will be content with that which we have and joy in our Saviour. For until this day He has suffered no one of us to be naked or hungry a single day, if one excepts that which the pilgrims have now and then experienced, because of circumstances, in connection with the service in the Gospel, wherewith they have been heartily satisfied, for it is a sign of grace to be made like unto their Master in this matter.

7. As we all stand for one, so shall and will no one among us borrow anything or take up money, whether for his own person or on account of the Economy, without consent and power of attorney from the leaders. So far as the ordinary needs of the congregation are concerned, these will be cared for by the brethren and sisters whose office this is. If, in addition, anything were to be borrowed, this should be announced to the congregation council at the proper

time and thoroughly investigated by deputies before it comes to execution.

8. Should anyone among us have the misfortune to get into such affairs, which are opposed to the former point and he could not, therefore, be tolerated among us, he shall be interviewed by the Committees for Outward Affairs on this account and, according to findings, be dismissed from our Economy. If anyone has cause of complaint against anyone, he is to appear with notification before them, but not to the hurt of other souls to bear a grudge. Whoever may be dismissed from our Economy shall before leaving declare in the presence of said Committees whether he has a claim against anyone, and, if there be nothing of the kind, execute a quit claim instrument.

"DRAFT OF AN INSTRUMENT TO BE SIGNED BY EACH ONE ADMITTED INTO THE BETHLEHEM ECONOMY" [1]

To all people, to whom these presents shall come, we whose Names are here unto subscribed send greeting.

Whereas each One of Us in particular have received permission of and from these officers and persons whom it concerns, being of the congregation residing at Bethlehem in the County of Northampton in the province of Pennsylvania and of the Church of the *Unitas Fratrum* or United Brethren, to live together with the aforesaid Congregation in One Family, labouring with our hands according to each one's Faculty and Ability under such Rules, Regulations and Orders as the Wardens or Officers shall from Time to Time order, direct and appoint.

Now we do hereby declare, that we have received this permission at our own special Instance and Request, and without any persuasion, incitement or allurement of any person or persons whatsoever, and without any particular View or Expectation of worldly advantage save only for our own Souls, Health and spiritual advantage, and the Immolument of the Community or Congregation aforesaid, And hereupon we do hereby promise during the Time of our Continuance in the Economy or Congregation aforesaid to be subordinate and obedient to such Rules, Regulations, Orders and Directions respecting the Economy and government of the aforesaid Congregation as the Governors, Wardens and Directors thereof shall from Time to Time ordain, direct and appoint.

And we do each of us for him and herself come under this solemn engagement and covenant, and do for each of us and each of our Heirs, Executors and Administrators respectively For and in Consideration of our Food, Clothing and Accomodations, according to the Economy, Way and Usage of the aforesaid Congregation hereby cov-

[1] *"Copia des an Gemein-Rath den 12 Nov. sub Signo a. No. 10, mentionirten Reverses."* Appendix to *"Diarium Bethlehem,"* Nov. 12, 1754. Ms. Beth. Arch.

enant, promise and grant to and with all the rest of the Members of the aforesaid Congregation, and to and with every of them, and more—especially to and with the aforesaid Wardens, Directors and Officers for the Time being (Andrew Anton Lawatoch being at present the Warden), That if any of us shall at any Time hereafter think fit to withdraw ourselves from the aforesaid Fellowship or Economy, whereunto we are permitted, as aforesaid, which at present we do not intend, Then and in such case we will give a reasonable and timely notice thereof unto such persons or officers whom it doth or shall and may concern. And also if the Wardens, Officers or persons whom it concerns shall be dissatisfied with our Conduct or think fit to order us to withdraw from their Economy or Congregation, whereunto we have received permission to join ourselves respectively, Then on timely and reasonable Notice thereof we will withdraw ourselves accordingly and peaceably depart from the aforesaid Congregation with our Clothing and proper Effects.

And further that we will not on any Occasion whatsoever have demand or sue for any Wages or Hire for our Labour or Services which we shall do in or for the aforesaid Family or Congregation, promising therefore to be content with our Food, Clothing and such other Accomodations as aforesaid.

And that we will sign, seal, deliver and execute unto any such Warden or Officer as aforesaid such an Acquittance or Release of and for all Wages, Duties and Demands for our Particular Labour and Services as aforesaid and generally of, for and from all Actions and causes of Action as by such Officer or Warden, shall be reasonably devised or required, so as such Warden or officer shall at the same time, in like manner, For and in the name of the Congregation aforesaid, Release, acquit and Discharge such person so releasing as aforesaid, If, required, In witness whereof we have hereunto respectively set our Hands and Seals.

APPENDIX C

"LITANEY ZU DEN WUNDEN DES MANNES" [1]

(*Erstes Chor.*)	(*Zweytes Chor.*)
Ave!	Agnus Dei.
Christe,	Eleison!
Gloria,	Pleuræ!

HERR GOTT VATER IM HIMMEL!
Gedenk an deins Sohns bittern tod: Sieh an seine heilige fünf wunden roth; die sind ja für die ganze welt die zahlung und das lösegeld. Desz trösten wir uns allezeit, und hoffen auf barmherzigkeit.

HERR GOTT SOHN DER WELT HEILAND!
Wir wären all verdorben per nostra crimina; so hast du uns erworben cölorun limina. Pleurä gloria, et memoria.

HERR GOTT HEILIGER GEIST!
Seinen Creuz-Gemeinen, die ihn gefunden, predige täglich des Lammes wunden. Es ist dein amt.

Du heilige Dreyeinigkeit!
Sey für das Lamm gebenedeyt.

Lamm Gottes, heilger Herr und Gott! nimm an die bitt von unsrer noth! erbarm dich unser aller.

Vor aller eigenen gerechtigkeit,
Vor aller zucht-trokkenheit,
Vor der unblutigen gnade,
Vor unbebluteten herzen,
Vor aller schönheit ohne blut-strich,
Vor der gleichgültigkeit gegen deine Wunden, } Behüt uns,
Vor der entfremdung von deinem Creuze,   lieber Herre
Vor der entwehung von deiner Seite,   Gott!
Vor ungesalbtem blut geschwätz
Vor der ewigen tod-sünde,

Deine schmerzliche erstgeburt   Mach uns unsre menschheit lieb!
Deine heilige erste wunde   Helf uns zur beschneidung des
                                     Herzens!

[1] *Anhang* XII, no. 1,949. Translations to be found in *The Litany Book* (London, 1759) and in *A Collection of Hymns* (London, 1754).

235

Deine kinderhaftigkeit
Dein erstes exilium
Deine erste mannbarkeit
Dein fleisz bey deiner lection

Deine heilige jünglingschaft
Dein theuresarbeits-schweisz
Deine handwerk's-treue
Deine erstaunliche einfalt
Dein richtiger bibel-grund
Deine verdienstliche unwissenheit
Deine exemplarische tempelandacht

Deine ohnmacht und schwächlich-
keit
Deine Creuz-theologie
Dein recht zum letzten willen
Dein mit dem tod bestätigtes testa-
ment
Deines Testaments Erfüller

Deine leidens-und todesfurcht
Dein verlasz mit deinem himm-
lischen Vater, zu leiden und nicht
zu leiden,
Deine willige passion
Deine heilige blut-tauffe

Dein schweisz im busz-kampfe
Ihr ritzen von der dornencron,
Blasse lippen,
Speicheltrieffender mund,

Bespiene wangen,

Gebrochene augen,
Blutiger schaum vom rükken,
Zerschwitzte harre,
Offne arme,
O ihr heiligen fünf Wunden,

Durchgrabne hände,

Durchbohrte füsse

Du Zeichen des menschensohns,

Du grosses Seiten-loch,

Helfe uns zur kinder-freud!
Lehr uns überall daheime seyn.
Heilige unsre knabenschaft!
Mach uns gelehrt zum himmel-
reich!
Sey der ledgen Chöre cranz!
Mach uns alle mühe leicht!
Mach uns treu in unserm theil!
Mach uns bei vernunft verhaszt!
Mach uns alle bibelvest!
Zäune unsre einsicht ein!
Mache uns zu treuen religions-
leuten!
Mach uns unsre schwachheit recht!

Bleibe unser glaubens-bekentnisz!
Mach uns deinen willen theur!
Bleibe die regel deiner erben!

Bringe die zerstreuten kinder Got-
tes in die arche der heiligen
Christenheit!
Beschäme der zeugen groszmuth!
Sey unser macht-spruch von deiner
selbständigen Göttlichkeit!

Lehre uns die leidsamkeit!
Zünde hin durch Gottes erdbo-
den!
Dünst uns über leib und seel!
Zeichnet uns an den stirnen!
Küszt uns aufs herz!
Dasz du niemand ausspeyen müs-
sest!
Dasz uns der Vater nicht anspeyen
dürfe!
Seht uns zum augen heraus!
Wasch uns unsre füsse!
Troknet sie!
Nehmt uns!
Machts wie Elisa, wir wollen dasz
kind seyn,
Weist uns, wo wir geschrieben
stehn!
Wenn steht ihr wieder auf dem öl-
berge.
Erscheine dem Israel nach dem
fleisch, ehe du in den wolken
kömmst!
Beherberge die ganze welt!

B. Doch Seiten-Spalts, Dich bitt ich sonderlich, ach behalte dein Volk und mich! Dein durchstochenes herze Klopfe und hüpfe dir über uns!

Ihr ungenanten und unbekanten Wunden,	B. Seyd alle gegrüszt!
Würdge Wunden Jesu,	Wer Wills uns wehren, dasz wir euch hier und dort ewig ehren? Ihr habts verdient.
Bundes-Wunden Jesu,	Man musz Gott loben, der uns auf eure zeit aufgehoben; da man was hat.
Liebste Wunden Jesu,	Wer euch nicht liebet, und euch nicht gänzlich sein herze giebet, der hat nichts lieb.
Wunder-Wunden Jesu,	Ihr heilgen löcher, macht sünder heilig, aus heilgen schächer. Wie wunder—lich!
Kräftge Wunden Jesu,	So nasz, so blutig; blut't mir aufs herze, so bleib ich muthig, und wundenhaft.
Geheime Wunden Jesu,	Ich danks dem Pfarren,* der mich mit meines Lamms beuln und schmarren bekant gemacht.
Klare Wunden Jesu,	Bey euren strahlen wolln wir noch manch crucifixbild mahlen, nur herzen her!
Funkelnde Wunden Jesu,	Ihr macht mein herze zu einer blendenden gnadenkerze vor strahl und blitz.
Hole Wunden Jesu,	In euren horten sitzen geräumlich viel tausend sorten von sünderlein.
Purpur-Wunden Jesu,	Ihr seyd so saftig, was euch nur nah kömt, wird wundenhaftig und trieft von blut.
Saftge Wunden Jesu,	Wers stäblein spitzet, und euch damit nur ein wenig ritzet, und lekt, der schmekt.
Nahe Wunden Jesu,	Ich bin nicht gerne nur ein gespaltenes haar breit ferne von eurer hohl.
Schmerzens-Wunden Jesu,	Dem Lamm empfindlich, und eben darum zur cur so gründlich und so probat.
Niedliche Wunden Jesu,	So zart, so zierlich, ihr seyd so kindern proportionirlich zum bettelein.

* 1. Pet. 11, 11.

Warme Wunden Jesu,

In keinen pfühlen kan sich ein kindlein so sicher fühlen für kalter luft.

Weiche Wunden Jesu,

Ich lieg gern ruhig, sanfte und stille, und froh: was thu ich? ich kriech zu euch.

Heisse Wunden Jesu,

Fahrt fort zu hitzen, bis ihr die ganze welt könnt durchschwitzen mit eurer gluth.

Wunden-Schatz Jesu!

Zu dem die sclaven, bettler und könige, baurn und grafen wahlfahrten gehn.

Ew'ge Wunden Jesu,

Mein haus zu wohnen: in allen millionen Eonen seyd ihr noch neu.

Unsre Wunden Jesu,

Die alle schaaren, jung und alt, grosse und klein' befahren; wer glauben hat.

Meine Wunden Jesu,

Meine, ja meine! mir ist, als wäret ihr ganz alleine für mein herz da.

Um ende aller noth

Ölt uns ein, ihr wunden roth!

Bis dahin gläube ich der augen todten strich, des mundes speicheltrauffe, des leichnams feuer-tauffe des hauptes dornen-schrikken, die fürchen auf dem rükken:

Bis ich zu seiner stund den leib fur mich verwundt, da wir so fest auf bauen, in meinem fleisch kan schauren, und innig herzlich grüssen die maal an händ und füssen.

Ave!

Agnus Dei.

Christe,

Eleison!

Gloria,

Pleuræ!

BIBLIOGRAPHY

This bibliography does not exhaust the literature on the subject of this volume. Additional manuscript and printed sources are to be found in the archives at Herrnhut, Germany. The bibliography here submitted constitutes, in the main, the sources available in America. Much of the printed literature and almost all of the manuscript sources are in the German language.

MANUSCRIPT SOURCES

I. THE MORAVIAN CHURCH.

Diarium der Hütten, 1747-1756; from 1756-1760 it was called *Jüngerhaus Diarium;* from 1761-1764, *Gemeinhaus Diarium;* and from 1765-1818, *Gemein Nachrichten;* 156 vols. This work contains a complete account of what Zinzendorf and his helpers did from day to day and reports from every mission in Christian and heathen lands.

Nachrichten der Unitäts Ältesten Conferenz, 1764-1858, 11 vols. Reports and proceedings of the *Unitäts Ältesten Conferenz,* the governing board of the whole Unity between the meetings of the General Synods.

Synodal Verlasz ("Results of the General Synods"), 23 vols., of the years 1746, 1764, 1769, 1775, 1782, 1789, 1801, 1818, 1825, 1836.

II. THE MORAVIANS IN AMERICA.

Amerikanische Provincial Synoden, 1748-1835, 20 vols.

"American Revolution documents." Political papers and letters to Congress and Assembly; petition for the Brethren by Ettwein in relation to militia laws and the oath; caring for the wounded in Bethlehem; letters of Ettwein to Washington, to Franklin, etc.

Authentische Relation (1742). Minutes and proceedings of the Seven Pennsylvania Union Synods to form a "Church of God in the Spirit." Also in print.

"Early History of the Brethren in America." Papers in relation to the founding of Bethlehem, the General Economy, the division of the Brethren in the various trades and occupations, and the abrogation of the Economy.

"Early Immigrants to America." Letters and diaries of the early Moravian immigrants, journals of the various Sea Congregations, and a register of their names.

Nachrichten aus der Helfer Conferenz, 1802-1843. This conference was the governing board in America between the meetings of the Provincial Synods.

Pennsylvanische Synoden, 1742, 1743, 1745, 1747, 1748, 5 vols. The Synods after 1742 were also considered as Union Synods, but they became more and more Moravian so that in 1748 only Moravians were present.

Ledgers and account books in the time of the General Economy and after its abrogation, of the farms, trades, and businesses still carried on for the whole Unity of the Brethren. There are over a thousand volumes, giving in minute detail the receipts and expenditures of the trades and businesses, the number of animals on the farms, the bushels of grain harvested, the number of eggs and pounds of meat eaten, and the gain or loss for the current year.

III. BETHLEHEM.

Diarium Bethlehem, 1742-1871, 50 vols. Contains daily accounts of the outstanding events of the Bethlehem settlement.

Diarium der Ledigen Brüder, 1744-1817, 6 vols. A relation of their social and religious life, with interesting accounts of their meetings, Love Feasts, and of the administration of the Choir house.

Diarium der Ledigen Schwestern, 1748-1841, 5 vols. Contents are similar to that of the above.

Protocolle des Ältesten Conferenz, 1764-1862, 30 vols. These are the proceedings of the local Elders' Conference, consisting of ordained men and their wives and those in charge of the Choir houses, which composed the governing board of the village.

Protocol des Aufseher's Collegium, 1780-1849, 19 vols. Contain the proceedings of the *Aufseher's Collegium*, which was a board elected by the voting membership, whose function was to supervise the trades, business, and manufacture according to the religious principles of the Brethren.

IV. Congregations and Settlements.

Diaries, letters, reports, and registers from the following congregations: (1) Rhode Island: Newport; (2) Connecticut: New London and Pachgatgoch; (3) New York: Camden, Camden Valley, New York City, Shekomeko, Sichem, Staten Island, and Zauchtenthal; (4) New Jersey: Camden, Hope, Old Man's Creek, and Woolwick; (5) Pennsylvania: Christiansbrunn, Languntoutenunk on the Beaver, Lawunakhannek on the Alleghany, Machilusing, Meniolagomeka, Nain, Tschichschiquannunk, Wechquetank, Allemongel, Bethel, Hebron, Lebanon, Donegal, Mt. Joy, Emmaus, Maguntsche, Salisbury, Frederickstown, Friedenshütten, Germantown, Gnadenhütten on the Mahony, Gnadenthal, Heidelberg, Hopedale, Lancaster, Yorktown, Graceham, Lititz, Lynn, Nazareth, Schoeneck, Philadelphia, Shamokin, Tulpehocken, and York; (6) Maryland: Baltimore, Carol's Manor, Graceham; (7) North Carolina: Salem; (8) Ohio: Beersheba, Canal Dover, Gnadenhütten on the Muskingum, Sharon, Goshen, Lichtenau, New Salem on Lake Erie, Pettquottink on Lake Erie, Salem Schönbrunn or Welhik Thuppek on the Muskingum; (9) Illinois: Olney, and West Salem; (10) Wisconsin: Sturgeon Bay; (11) Iowa: Blairstown, and Moravia; (12) Kansas: New Fairfield, Osborn, and Westfield; (13) Canada: Fairfield, and Jongquakamik.

Auszüge aus den Kirchen Büchern der Landgemeinen in Penn., Md., and Ohio, 2 vols.; in North Carolina; in New York, Philadelphia, Staten Island, and York; in Lititz and Nazareth; in Salem, N. C. (1818-1848); *Berichte des Westlichen stadt und Landgemeinen 1776-1789*. These volumes contain extracts and reports from city and country congregations.

General Catalogus von denen Seelen die in der Brüder Pflege sind in America. These are registers of the members of the settlements in the early years of the Brethren in America. (Other lists of this period and later years are to be found in the *Beylagen* of *Diarium Bethlehem.*)

Miscellaneous letters from town and country congregations to the Provincial Synods and Boards.

Records of defunct Congregations, 68 vols.

V. Indians and Indian Missions.

Documents containing accounts of their work; Indian conferences; registers of marriages, baptisms, and deaths; statutes and rules agreed upon at the Indian stations; substance of conversation between Teedyuscung and the Brethren at Bethlehem; receipts by Indians for work; treaty council held at Easton; minutes of the Indian Treaty at Pittsburgh; diaries of Moravian missionaries; catalogues of Indian congregations; letters to and from the Indians; the Indian wars; Indian atrocities; etc.

"Indian Department." Containing letters, diaries, journals of travels, Indian dictionaries, translations of hymns, and sermons, filed away under the following subject heads: Massacre at Gnadenhütten, French and Indian War 1755; Gnadenhütten, Ohio; Pontiac conspiracy and Paxton insurrection; Tschichschiquannunk and Wechquetank; Pachgotgoch; Meniolagomekah; Nain and Shamokin; Lawunakhannek on the Alleghany and Languntoutenunk on the Beaver; Wyalusing or Friedenshütten; Schönbrunn and Lichtenau; Tuscorawas Reservation, Ohio; Pettiquotting Second, White River, Indiana; Gnadenhütten on Mahony; Goshen, Ohio; New Fairfield, Kansas; Shekomeko, Fairfield and Chippewas, Canada; Pettquottink at the mouth of Detroit; Cherokees; Gnadenhütten on Huron; Cayahaga; Captivity of Missionaries: Treaties; Journeys; Catalogues and letters; Miscellaneous.

VI. Correspondence.

Correspondence with public authorities in America, Moravian authorities in Europe, and many other letters to and from such persons as Zinzendorf, Spangenberg, Nitschmann, de Watteville, Cammerhoff, Seidel, Böhler, Ettwein, Marschall, Zeisberger, Hehl, Horsefield, Antes, etc.

VII. The Society for Propagating the Gospel.

Account books. Stated rules of the Society. Circulars to the members of the Society. Minutes of the general meetings for the years 1787, 1789, 1792, 1804, 1810. Reports of the Directors of the Society for the years 1814, 1815, 1832, 1841.

PRINTED SOURCES
I. Histories.

Authentische Relation von dem Anlass, Fortgang und Schlusse der am 1sten und 2ten Januarii Anno 1741/2. In Germantown gehaltenen Versammlung einiger Arbeiter Derer meisten Christ-

lichen Religionen Und Vieler vor sich selbst Gott-dienenden Christen-Menschen in Pennsylvania Aufgesetzt in Germantown am Abend des 2ten obigen Monats. Philadelphia Gedruckt und zu haben bey B. Franklin. The seven Conferences bound in one volume with a different title page for each. A report or minutes of the Seven Pennsylvania Synods.

Bost, A.: *History of the Moravians,* London, 1862. A history of the origin of the Bohemian-Moravian Brethren and the renewal of the Church under Zinzendorf.

Burkhardt, G.: *Die Brüdergemeine,* Gnadau, 1893. A history of the origin and progress of the Moravian Church.

Clewell, J. H.: *History of Wachovia in North Carolina,* New York, 1902. A study of the origin and growth of the Brethren's settlements in North Carolina and the effect of and reactions to the Revolutionary and Civil Wars.

Cranz, D.: *Ancient and Modern History of the Brethren; or a succinct narrative of the Protestant Church of the United Brethren or Unitas Fratrum, in the remoter ages, and particularly in the present century; written in German by David Cranz, author of the "History of Greenland"; now translated into English with emendations and published with some additional notes by Benjamin La Trobe,* London, 1780.

Cröger, E. W.: *Geschichte der erneuerten Brüder-kirche,* Gnadau, 1852-1854. In three volumes: the first dealing with the rise of the evangelical Brethren; the second with the spread and the growth of the Church; and the third with the Church from Zinzendorf's death (1760) to 1822, especially missions.

De Schweinitz, Edmund: *The History of the Church Known as the Unitas Fratrum,* Bethlehem, 1885. An extensive history beginning with the times preceding John Hus to the present.

Erbe, Hellmuth: *Bethlehem, Pa., eine Kommunistische Herrnhuter Kolonie des 18 Jahrhunderts,* Stuttgart, 1929. A very valuable book giving an accurate account of the settlement in Bethlehem, based largely on European manuscript sources.

Fries, A. L.: *Moravians in Georgia,* Raleigh, 1905. An account of the events that led to the settlement in Georgia and the consequent withdrawal.

—— *Publication of the North Carolina Historical Commission,* Raleigh, 1922, 4 vols. Records of the Moravians in North Carolina, chiefly from diaries of 1752-1783.

—— and Pfohl, J. K.: *The Moravian Church Yesterday and Today,*

Raleigh, 1926. A treatment of the movements and doctrinal positions of the Brethren since the days of John Hus.

Glaubrecht, O.: *Zinzendorf in der Wetterau. Ein Bild aus der Geschichte der Brüdergemeinde dem Volke dargestellt,* Frankfurt A. M. und Erlangen, 1852-1853. A narrative account of Zinzendorf and the Brethren in the Wetterau.

Gradin, Arvin: *A Short History of the Bohemian-Moravian Church of the United Brethren,* London, 1743. "In a letter to the Archbishop of Upsal primate of Sweden." Trans. from the Latin.

Hacker, H. H.: *Nazareth Hall,* Bethlehem, 1910. An historical sketch and roster of principles, teachers, and pupils.

Hamilton, J. Taylor: *A History of the Church Known as the Moravian Church,* Bethlehem, 1900. A comprehensive history of the whole Unity of the Brethren.

—— "A History of the *Unitas Fratrum,* or Moravian Church," in vol. VIII, American Church History Series.

Holmes, J.: *History of the Protestant Church of the United Brethren,* 2 vols., London, 1825. A detailed history from the introduction of Christianity into Bohemia and Moravia to 1825.

Hutton, J. E.: *History of the Moravian Church,* 2nd ed., London, 1909. A very comprehensive history from the burning of John Hus to the present.

Levering, J. M.: *A History of Bethlehem, Pennsylvania 1741-1892 with some account of its founders and their early activity in America,* Bethlehem, 1903. A valuable work, based on sources.

Martin, John H.: *Historical Sketch of Bethlehem in Pennsylvania with Some Account of the Moravian Church,* Phila., 1872.

Memorial Days of the Renewed Church of the Brethren, Ashton-Under Lyne, 1822. Trans. from the German.

Pennsylvanische Nachrichten von dem Reiche Christi Anno 1742. A second title is: *B. Ludewigs Wahrer Bericht, de dato Germantown den 20 Feb. 1741/2 . . . zu prüfung der Zeit und Umstände ausgefertiget; nebst . . . erläuternden Beylagen.* Contains verses composed by Zinzendorf and others, a letter from Spangenberg to him, a letter by Zinzendorf to the whole of Pennsylvania after two months in America and accounts of the first four of the Seven Pennsylvania Union Synods.

Pescheck, C. A.: *The Reformation and the Anti-reformation in Bohemia,* London, 1845, 2 vols. Trans. from the German. An account of the sufferings and persecutions endured by Bohemian

Protestants in the Counter-Reformation and the emigration of many of these to other lands.

Reichel, Gerhard: *Die Anfänge Herrnhuts,* Herrnhut, 1922. Presented by the directors of the Brethren's Unity at the two hundredth anniversary of the founding of Herrnhut.

Reichel, L. T.: *The Early History of the Church of the United Brethren, commonly called Moravians, in North America, A. D. 1734-1748,* Nazareth, Pa., 1888. In addition to the early history of the Brethren in America, this work gives an account of the moral and religious conditions of the Germans in Pennsylvania and the relation of the various religious sects.

—— *The Moravians in North Carolina,* Salem, N. C., 1857.

Reichel, William C.: *Historical Sketch of Nazareth Hall from 1755-1869,* Phila., 1869.

—— *A History of the Rise, Progress and Present Condition of the Bethlehem Female Seminary with a Catalogue of its Pupils 1785-1858,* Phila., 1858.

—— *Memorials of the Renewed Church,* 1870. "A series of memorials treating of the varied activity of the Moravian pioneers in this country, as missionaries, as evangelists, and as educators of youth, of their religious and social organization, of the life they led, and the spirit by which they were actuated, of their relation to each other as members of one body pervaded by a common purpose, and of the relation they sustained to those by whom they were surrounded."

Ritter, Abraham: *The Moravian Church in Philadelphia,* Phila., 1857. Giving an account of its founding by Zinzendorf, items of local interest, together with the old Moravian customs, with the aim "to call up the spirit of our fathers, to chasten our own waywardness, to simplify our manners, to imbue us with their faith and faithfulness."

Schwarze, William N.: *History of the Moravian College and Theological Seminary, founded at Nazareth, Pa. October 2, 1807, reorganized at Bethlehem, Pa., August 30, 1858,* Bethlehem, 1910.

Stocker, Henry Emilius: *A History of the Moravian Church in New York City,* New York, 1922.

Unttendörfer and Schmidt: *Die Brüder,* Gnadau, 1914. A panoramic view of the Renewed Church and its related activities as the missionary and Diaspora work, and brief sketches of the leaders and their thoughts.

II. Doctrine and Church Constitution.

An Account of the Doctrine, Manners, Liturgy and Idioms of the Unitas Fratrum, London, 1749. "Taken from, and comprising the supplement, dedicated to the Church of England of the vouchers to the report of the committee of the honourable, the House of Commons concerning the Church of the Unitas Fratrum."

Barbyzche Sammlungen, Alter und Neuer, Lehr-Principia, Sitten-Lehren, und den vorigen und itzigen gang der Öconomie Gottes und ihrer Diener illustrirender Stükke; wie auch theils gedrukter, theils ungedrukter kleinerer Schriften des dermaligen ordinarii der Brüder, Barby, 1760. Gives information of the constitution of the Brethren's Church, from the writings of Zinzendorf and extracts from the Conferences and Synods from the years 1726-1753.

Becker, Bernhard: *Zinzendorf im Verhältnis zu Philosophie und Kirchentum seiner Zeit,* Leipzig, 1866. Sets forth Zinzendorf's theological conceptions and his views of the Church.

Book of Order of the Moravian Church in America, Northern Province, Bethlehem, 1911. A codification of the laws of the Church.

Catechism of the Moravian Church, Bethlehem, 1896. Published by order of the Provincial Synod of 1893.

Concise Historical Account of the Present Constitution of the Protestant Church of the United Brethren, adhering to the Confession of Augsburg, Manchester, 1815. Trans. from the 4th German ed. This account contains "a list of all the countries and places where the Congregations and missions of the Brethren are settled at present" and "a description of the internal and external constitution of the Brethren's Unity."

Enchiridion das ist Haupt—Summa der ganzen Heil Schrift, in ein Hand-Büchlein gebracht, mit möglichster Beybehaltung der Worte des Buchs, London, 1752. A compendious systematic theology in 40 pages, based on the Old Testament.

Extracts of the Twenty-one Doctrinal Articles of the Augsburg Confession, London, 1793. Particularly for children in the Brethren's congregations. Also contains some litanies for the children.

Hagen, F. F.: *Old Landmarks: or Faith and Practices of the Moravian Church, at the time of its revival and restoration in 1727, and twenty years after,* Bethlehem, 1886.

Handbook of the Moravian Congregation at Bethlehem, Pa., Bethlehem, 1890. Contains the Brotherly Agreement, the By-laws, rules and regulations, the act of incorporation, etc.

Henry, James: *Sketches of Moravian Life and Character*, Phila., 1859. "A general view of the history, life, character and religious and educational institutions of the *Unitas Fratrum*."

Kurze, Zuverläszige Nachricht von der unter dem Namen der Bömisch-Mährischen Brüder bekannten Kirche Unitas Fratrum herkommen, Lehr-begriff, äussern und innern Kirchen-Verfassung und Gabräuchen, aus richtigen Urkunden und Erzälungen von einem Ihrer Christlich Unportheiischen Freunde heraus gegeben und mit sechzehn Vorstellungen in Kupfer erläutert, 1762.

Lieberkühn, Samuel: *Der Hauptinhalt der Lehre Jesu Christi zum Gebrauch bey dem Unterricht der Jugend in den Evangelischen Brüder gemeinen*, 2nd ed., Barby, 1778. Trans. into English as *Summary of the Doctrine of Jesus Christ to be used for the instruction of youth in the congregations of the United Brethren*, Phila., 1818.

Manual of the Doctrine or a Second essay to bring into the form of question and answer as well the fundamental doctrines, as the other scripture knowledge, of the Protestant congregations who for three hundred years past have been called the Brethren, London, 1742. Trans. from the German. Contains 1,710 questions and answers and an introduction by Bishop David Nitschmann, and a letter by Daniel E. Jablonsky.

Moravian Manual, Bethlehem, 1901. Published by the authority of the Provincial Synod of the American Moravian Church, North. Sets forth very briefly the Church constitution, rules of discipline, and doctrines.

Nachricht von dem Uhrsprung und Fortgange und hauptsächlich von dem gegenwärtigen Verfassung der Brüder-Unität, Halle, 1781. An explanation of the composition and constitution of the Moravian Church.

Probe eines Lehr-Büchelgens vor die sogenannten Brüder-Gemeine zu mehrer deutlichkeit und Gründlichern Verstande unserer heiligen Wahrheit in diesen form gebracht, Büdingen, 1740. A catechism, containing many brief questions and answers.

Örter, M. F.: *The Doctrinal Position of the Moravian Church*. A paper read at the synod of the second district, held at Lancaster, Pa., October 5-7, 1897.

Ratio Disciplinae Unitas Fratrum—oder: Grund der Verfassung der

Evangelischen Brüder-Unität Augsburgischer Confession, Barby, 1789. Sets forth the history of doctrine, Church order and customs of the Ancient and Renewed Church.

Schultze, A.: *Essentials of the Christian Faith,* Bethlehem, 1903. Pamphlet published by order of the Synod.

—— *Christian Doctrine and Systematic Theology,* Bethlehem, 1909. "The pages of this volume contain the substance of lectures on Systematic theology which have been given by the writer for nearly forty years to successive classes of students at the Moravian College and Theological Seminary at Bethlehem, Pa."

—— *What do Moravians Believe?,* Moravian publication office, 1876. Tract.

—— *Why I am a member of the Moravian Church,* Moravian publication office, 1876. Tract.

Spangenberg, A. G.: *Idea Fidi Fratrum oder kurzer Begrif der Christlichen Lehre in den evangelischen Brüdergemeinen,* Barby, 1779. Trans. from the German by Benjamin La Trobe as *An Exposition of Christian Doctrine.*

—— *Kurzgefaszte historische Nachricht von der gegenwärtigen Verfassung der evangelischen Brüderunität Augsburgischen Confession,* Frankfurt and Leipzig, 1774. A very compendious work of the rise, progress, doctrine, and customs of the Moravians.

Stocker, Harry Emilius: *Moravian Customs and other Matters of Interest,* 3rd ed., Bethlehem, 1928. Contains short accounts of the past and present customs and constitution.

III. Sermons and Addresses.

Spangenberg, A. G.: *Das Wort vom Kreuz ist eine Thorheit denen die verloren werden; die wir selig werden ist es eine Gottes Kraft,* Barby, 1791. Trans. from the German as *The Preaching of the Cross is to them that perish foolishness but unto us which are saved it is the power of God,* Phila., 1793.

—— *Einige Reden an die Kinder gehalten in verschiedenen Brüdergemeinen, Zweite Sammlung,* Barby, 1799. A collection of 22 short sermons to children.

—— *Vergebung der Sünde,* Barby, 1792. A sermon on sin and forgiveness.

Zinzendorf, N. L. von: *Auszüge aus des Seligen Ordinarii der Evangelischen Brüder-kirche Rede über Biblische Texte nach Ord-*

nung der Bücher heiliger Schrift gefertiget und herausgegeben von Gottfried Clemens, Barby, 1763-1765, 3 vols.

Zinzendorf, N. L. von: *Des Ordinarii Fratrum Berlinische Reden, in Druck gegeben von Gottlieb Clemens*, London and Barby, 1758.

—— *Des Ordinarii Fratrum Öffentliche Reden von dem Herrn, der unsere Seligkeit ist, und über die Materie von Seiner Marter*, 3rd ed., London and Barby, 1760. A collection of nine sermons preached by Zinzendorf as pastor of the Lutheran Church in Philadelphia and two additional sermons in the appendix.

—— *Der Offentlichen Gemein-Reden im Jahre 1747*, first part 1748, second part 1749.

—— *Des Ordinarii Fratrum Reden Über die Litaney des Lebens, Leidens und der Wunden unsers Herrn Jesu Christi, gehalten vom ende April bis in den August, 1747*, 2nd ed., Barby, 1759. A commentary or exposition on the Litany of the Wounds.

—— *Einige der letzten Reden des seligen Grafen Nicolaus Ludwig von Zinzendorf*, Barby, 1784. A collection of 27 sermons dealing almost exclusively with Christ as Redeemer.

—— *Einiger seit 1751 von dem Ordinario Fratrum zu London gehaltenen Predigten in zwei Bände*, London and Barby, 1756.

—— *Jeremias ein Prediger der Gerechtigkeit*, 2nd ed., Berlin, 1830. Jeremiah is here held up as an example for ministers in the evangelical churches.

—— *Marienborn Reden*, place and date of publication not given. Some addresses made in the years 1744-1746.

—— *Maxims, Theological Ideas and Sentences, out of the Present Ordinary of the Brethren's Churches, his Dissertations and Discourses from the year 1738 till 1747*, London, 1751. Extracted by J. Gambold.

—— *Nine Public Discourses upon Important Subjects in Religion, preached in Fetter-Lane-Chapel at London in the year 1746*, London, 1748. Trans. from the German.

—— *Reden über die vier Evangelisten, herausgegeben von Gottfried Clemens und Jacob Christoph Duvernoy*, 1766-1792.

—— *Sammlung Einiger von dem Ordinario Fratrum wärend seines Aufenthalts in den Teutschen Gemeinen von Anno 1755 bis 1757 gehaltenen Kinder-Reden*, Barby, 1758. A collection of 84 addresses to children.

—— *Seven Sermons on the Godhead of the Lamb; or the Divinity of Jesus Christ*, London, 1742. Trans. from the German ms.

—— *Sixteen Discourses on Jesus Christ our Lord*, London, 1751.

Trans. from the German. "Being an exposition of the second part of the creed preached in Berlin."

Zinzendorf, N. L. von: *Sixteen Discourses on the Redemption of Man by the Death of Christ. Preached at Berlin, by the right reverend and most illustrious Count Zinzendorf, Bishop of the Ancient Moravian church, with a dedication to the archbishops, bishops and clergy, giving some account of the Moravian Brethren,* London, 1740. Trans. from the German.

—— *Zwey und Dreysig einzele Homiliæ oder Gemein-Reden in den Jahren 1744, 1745, 1746,* place and date of publication not given.

—— *Twenty-one Discourses or Dissertations upon the Augsburg Confession which is also the Brethren's Confession of Faith; delivered by the Ordinary of the Brethren's Churches before the seminary to which is prefixed a synodal writing relating to the same subject,* London, 1753. Trans. from the German by F. Okeley.

—— *Des seligen Grafen Nicolaus Ludwig von Zinzendorf Gedanken über verschiedene evangelische Wahrheiten, aus dessen Schriften zusammengezogen,* Barby, 1800. Twenty-five short discourses setting forth the theology of Zinzendorf.

IV. BIOGRAPHIES.

Benham, Daniel: *Memoirs of James Hutton, comprising the annals of his life, and connection with the United Brethren,* London, 1856.

Burkhardt, G.: *Zinzendorf und die Brüdergemeine,* Gotha, 1866. A biography of Zinzendorf in relation to his connections with the Moravian Church.

De Schweinitz, E. A.: *Life and Times of David Zeisberger,* Phila., 1870. A detailed account of his labors and travels among the Indians.

Duvernoy, Jacob Christoph: *Kurzgefaszte Lebensgeschichte Nicolaus Ludwig, Grafen und Herrn von Zinzendorf und Pottendorf,* Barby, 1793.

Erbe, Hans Walter: *Zinzendorf und der fromme hohe Adel seiner Zeit,* Leipzig, 1928. A critical and analytical account of the life of Zinzendorf in relation to the pietism of his time.

Ledderhose, Charles T.: *Life of Augustus Gottlieb Spangenberg,* London, 1855.

McMinn, Edwin: *Life and Times of Henry Antes,* Moorestown,

N. J., 1886. An account of the activities of Henry Antes in connection with the religious movements in Pennsylvania, and more particularly with the Moravians.

Müller, J. George: *Zinzendorf's Leben*, Winterthur, 1822.

Reichel, Gerhard: *August Gottlieb Spangenberg, Bishof der Brüderkirche*, Tübingen, 1906. A very valuable biography.

Reichel, Gottlieb B.: *Leben des Grafen von Zinzendorf, stifters der Brüdergemeine*, Leipzig, 1790.

Risler, Jeremias: *Leben August Gottlieb Spangenberg, Bishop der evangelischen Brüderkirche*, Barby, 1794. A very complete biography.

Rondthaler, Edward: *Life of John Heckewelder*, Phila., 1847. An account of his missionary activities among the Indians.

Spangenberg, A. G.: *Leben des Herrn Nicolaus Ludwig Grafen und Herrn von Zinzendorf und Pottendorf*, 1773-1775, 8 vols. Sets forth the activities of Zinzendorf from childhood, and his connection with the Brethren year by year until his death in 1760. An abridged translation by Samuel Jackson appeared in 1836 (London) called: *The Life of Nicolaus Lewis Count Zinzendorf*.

Verbeek, John William: *Des Grafen Nicolaus Ludwig von Zinzendorf Leben und Charakter in kurzgefaszter Darstellung*, Gnadau, 1845.

Von Schrautenbach, L. C. F.: *Der Graf von Zinzendorf und die Brüdergemeine seiner Zeit*, Gnadau, 1851. A narrative of Zinzendorf's labors in connection with the Moravian Church.

V. PUBLICATIONS OF HISTORICAL SOCIETIES.

Pennsylvania Archives.

Proceedings of Pennsylvania German Society, 38 vols.

Pennsylvania Magazine of History and Biography, 54 vols.

Transactions of the Moravian Historical Society, Whitefield House, Nazareth, Pa., 1876-1917, 10 vols. These volumes contain valuable historical and biographical information of the early and later period of the Moravian Church.

VI. PERIODICALS.

Germantowner Zeitung, edited by Christopher Saur and established Aug. 20, 1739. Until 1745 it was called *Der Hoch-Deutsch Pennsylvanische Geschicht-Schreiber*. At first issued every three months but in 1741 changed to a monthly. From October

1745 to June 1746 the title was changed to *Hoch-Deutsch Pennsylvanische Berichte*. From 1746 to 1762 it was called the *Pennsylvanische Berichte*, being at first a monthly then a semi-monthly. Later it was called the *Germantowner Zeitung*.

Der Brüder Bote, 1862-1891. Historical and missionary information.

Missionary Intelligencer, 1822-1849, 10 vols. (Quarterly.)

Moravian Church Miscellany, 1850-1856, 6 vols. (Monthly.)

The Moravian, 1857-. (Weekly.) A continuation of *Moravian Church Miscellany*.

The Moravian Messenger, 1850-, published in England. First called *Fraternal Messenger*, then *Fraternal Record*, then *The Messenger*, and now *The Moravian Messenger*. "Contains characteristical, historical and biographical sketches."

Moravian Missions, 1903-, published in England.

Periodical Accounts, 1790-. A missionary journal.

VII. Missions.

Buckner, J. H.: *The Moravians in Jamaica*, London, 1854. An account of the moral and religious state of the island, the climate, the slavery conditions, and the coming of the missionaries.

Crantz, David: *The History of Greenland: containing a description of the country and its inhabitants; and particularly, a relation of the mission carried on for above these thirty years by the Unitas Fratrum, at New Herrnhuth and Lichtenfels, in that country*, London, 1767, 2 vols. "Translated from the High-Dutch, and illustrated with maps and other copper plates."

Geschichte der Mission in Süd Amerika, Barby, 1805. A description of the country and the people and of the beginning of Moravian Missions there.

Heckewelder, John: *A Narrative of the Mission of the United Brethren among the Delaware and Mohegan Indians from the year of its commencement in the year 1740 to the close of the year 1808*, Phila., 1820. "All the remarkable incidents which took place at their missionary stations during that period interspersed with anecdotes, historical facts, speeches of Indians and other interesting matter."

Holmes, John: *Historical Sketches of the Missions of the United Brethren for Propagating the Gospel among the Heathen, from their commencement in the year 1817*, 2nd ed., London, 1827. A narrative of the many Moravian missions with remarks on the geographical situation, the climatic conditions and other interesting particulars about the natives.

Herbert, A. B., and Schwarze, W. N.: *David Zeisberger's History of the Northern American Indians,* Ohio State Archeological and Historical Society, 1910.

Hutton, J. E.: *A History of Moravian Missions,* London, 1922. A large volume touching upon all the missions of the Brethren, their achievements and losses, the Moravian Missionary ideals, methods and principles, and the method of support and administration.

Hutton, S. K.: *Among the Eskimos of Labrador,* London, 1912. "A record of five years' close intercourse with the Eskimo tribes of Labrador." Illustrated with 47 pictures and two maps.

Instructions for Missionaries of the Church of the Unitas Fratrum or United Brethren, by the Mission Department of the Elders' Conference of the Unity, trans. from the German, 2nd ed., London, 1840. Contains general rules for the conduct of missionaries, the care of their health, the doctrine and manner of preaching, and the conversion of the heathen.

La Trobe, C. I.: *Journal of a Visit to South Africa in 1815 and 1816 with some account of the missionary settlements of the United Brethren near the Cape of Good Hope,* New York, 1818. A narration of the settlements, of travels through the wilderness, of the Hottentot clans, of their desire to hear the missionaries, of the wild beasts, and of the brutality of some of the Boers.

Loskiel, George H.: *History of the Mission of the United Brethren among the Indians in North America,* trans. from the German by Christian Ignatius La Trobe, London, 1794. A large work in three parts giving an account of the manner of life and customs of the Indians and the establishment of the missions amongst them.

Rice, W. H.: *David Zeisberger and his Brown Brethren,* Moravian Pub. Concern, Bethlehem, 1902.

Schneider, H. G.: *Working and Waiting for Tibet,* London, no date. Trans. and revised by Arthur Ward. An account of the Tibetans, their country, their social and religious life, and how the mission work is carried on.

Schulze, A., and Gapp, S. H.: *World-wide Moravian Missions in Picture and Story,* Bethlehem, 1926. A bi-centenary publication 1732-1932. Contains brief sketches with pictures of Moravian missions in Greenland, Labrador, West Indies, South Africa,

Alaska, North American Indians, Nicaragua, East Central Africa, Tibet, Dutch Guiana, and among the Lepers.

Spangenberg, A. G.: *An Account of the Manner in Which the Protestant Church of the Unitas Fratrum or United Brethren preach the gospel and carry on their missions among the heathen,* London, 1788. Trans. from the German.

Thompson, A. C.: *Protestant Missions, their Rise and Early Progress,* New York, 1894. A study of the growth of the missionary ideal and practice since the Reformation.

VIII. HYMNS AND LITANIES.

Christliches Gesang-Buch der Evangelischen Brüder von 1735 zum drittenmal und durchaus revidirt, 1741, 972 hymns. Based upon the earlier edition of 1725 called *Sammlung Geistlicher und Lieblicher Lieder.*

Anhang als ein Zweiter Theil zu dem Gesang-Buche der Evangelische Brüder-Gemeinen, no place of publication. Contains 12 supplements. Hymns 973-2156. Of these supplements the first eight appeared in 1737, the ninth and tenth in 1741, and the eleventh and twelfth in 1745.

Zugaben I-IV, no place of publication. These are four additional supplements in the year 1749. Hymns 2157-2357.

Hirten Lieder von Bethlehem, zum gebrauch vor alles was arm ist, was klein und gering ist, Germantown, 1742. This little hymnal of 360 hymns was compiled by Zinzendorf for general use when he visited America in 1742. J. M. Levering states that to his knowledge there are only two copies in existence (*Hist. of Bethlehem,* p. 97). A copy in the Bethlehem Archives.

Alter und Neuer Brüder-Gesang, London, 1753. A second part: *Das Evangelischen Lieder-Buchs unter dem Titel Brüder-Gesang,* London, 1754. These hymns were collected by Zinzendorf after the evacuation of Herrnhaag. Many of these hymns reflect this period.

A Collection of Hymns of the Children of God in all Ages . . . designed chiefly for the use of the congregations in union with the Brethren's Church, London, 1754. Contains 1,155 hymns which are largely translations of the edition of 1753 and 1754. For their early theology I have used these two editions, since in these hymnals Zinzendorf purposely deleted every thought and expression which seemed to him extravagant and related to the spirit of the "Sifting Time."

Das Liturgien Büchlein nach der bey den Brüder dermalen haupt-sächlich gewöhnlichen Sing-Weise von neuem revidirt und in dieser bequemen Form ausgegeben von dem Cantore Fratrum Ordinario, 4th ed., Barby, 1757. This edition was translated into the English as: *The Litany Book according to the manner of singing at present mostly in use among the Brethren*, London, 1759.

Das Kleine Brüder-Gesang-Buch, in einer Harmonischen Sammlung von kurzen Liedern, Versen, Gebeten und Seufzern bestehend, 2nd ed., Barby, 1761. Contains 2,397 hymns.

Gesangbuch Zum Gebrauch der evangelischen Brüdergemeinen, Barby, 1778. The 1,750 hymns of this edition were collected by Christian Gregor and distinctly mark the saner theology of the Spangenbergian era over against that of the Zinzendorfian.

Gesangbüchlein für die Kinder in den Brüdergemeinen, Barby, 1789. Consists of verses selected from their large hymnology, arranged sytematically under subject heads.

Liturgien für die Chöre in den evangelischen Brüdergemeinen aufs neue revidirt und vermehrt, Barby, 1791. Containing Choir litanies for the children, Single Brethren, Single Sisters, married Choir, widows, and widowers.

Gesangbuch zum Gebrauch der evangelischen Brüdergemeinen, Barby, 1802. Contains 1,750 hymns.

Litaneien und Liturgien zum Gebrauch in den Gemeinen der Amerikanischen Provinz der Brüder Kirche, Bethlehem, 1890.

Hymnal and Liturgies of the Moravian Church, Bethlehem, 1920, published by authority of Provincial Synod. The hymnal now in use.

Historische Nachricht von Brüder-Gesangbuche des Jahres 1778, Gnadau, 1835. Gives a history of Moravian hymnology until 1778.

IX. CONTROVERSIAL.

Duyckinck, G.: *A Short Tho' True Account of the Establishment and Rise of the Church So Called Moravian Brethren, under the protection and administration of Nicholas Lodewyck Count of Zinzendorf; by which it plainly appears that they are not of that church of the Ancient United, Moravian and Bohemian Brethren. The same is taken out of their own writings and some observations on it*, New York, 1744.

Finley, Samuel: *Satan striped of his angelick Robe; being the sub-*

stance of several sermons preached at Philadelphia, January 1742-1743 from II Thessalonians 2:11, 12, shewing the strength, nature and symptoms of Delusion, with an application to the Moravians, Phila.

Fresenius, Johann Philip: *Bewärte Nachrichten von Herrnhutischen Sachen,* Franckfurt a. M., 1747. A study of the activities and movements of the Brethren by the minister of the St. Peter's Church in Frankfurt am Main.

Hutton, James: *An Essay towards giving some just ideas of the personal character of Count Zinzendorf; the present Advocate and Ordinary of the Brethren's Churches; in several letters written by eye-witnesses to the man,* London, 1755. A letter from Gambold to Spangenberg; by Mr. Hutton and others to set forth the true character of Zinzendorf.

Kulenkamp: *Treu-Vätterlicher Hirten-Brief an die Reformirte Gemeine der Stadt Amsterdam auf Veranlassung der Entdeckten und Gefährlichen Irrthümen der Zinzendorf und Herrnhuthischen Brüderschafft, zur Warnung geschrieben von denen Predigern und Ältesten des Amsterdammer Kirchen-Raths,* Amsterdam, 1739. A letter from the Classis of Amsterdam warning against the heresies of Zinzendorf and the Brethren, declaring that Zinzendorf and his followers were not to be associated with the Ancient Bohemian-Moravian Brethren.

Lavington (Bishop of Exeter): *The Moravians Compared and Detected.* From the preface: "The filthy dreamers have been so evidently detected, their immoralities and impieties so manifested unto all men that their shame is sufficiently conspicious, and no serious and good person, no sincere Christian especially can look upon them in any favorable light."

Rimius, Henry: *A Candid Narrative of the Rise and Progress of the Herrnhuters commonly called Moravians or Unitas Fratrum,* London, 1753. Dedicated to the Archbishop of Canterbury. This work is a warning against the heresies and political intrigues of the Brethren.

—— *A Solemn Call on Count Zinzendorf, the Author and Advocate of the Sect of Herrnhuters, commonly called Moravians, to answer all and every charge brought against them in the Candid Narrative, with some further observations on the spirit of that sect,* London, 1754.

—— *A Pastoral Letter against Fanaticism addressed to the Mennonites of Friesland, by Mr. John Strinstra, one of their ministers at Harlingen,* London, 1753. Trans. from the Dutch. "Which may serve as an excellent antidote against the principles and fanaticks in general, and the Herrnhuters or Moravians in particular."

Rimius, Henry: *Aufrichtige Erzälung von dem Ursprung und Fortgang der Herrnhuter, nebst einer Kurzen aus ihren Schriff gezogenen Nachricht von ihren Lehren, wie auch einige Anmerkungen über ihre weltliche Absichten und ehemaliges Betragen in der Grafschaft* Büdingen, Coburg, 1753. The author depicts the Brethren as a dangerous sect, a menace to the state and society.

Tennent, Gilbert: *Some Account of the Principles of the Moravians: chiefly collected from several conversations with Count Zinzendorf; and from some sermons preached by him at Berlin, and published in London,* London, 1743. "Recommended by the Reverend Dr. Colman, and other ministers of Boston. With a preface offering some reasons for this publication."

—— *The Necessity of Holding Fast the Truth, represented in three sermons on Rev. 3:3 preached at New York, April 1742. With an appendix, relating to errors lately vented by some Moravians in those Parts. To which are added, a sermon on the priestly office of Christ, and another on the virtue of Charity, together with a sermon of a Dutch Divine on taking the little foxes; faithfully translated,* Boston, 1743.

—— *The Examiner,* Boston, 1743. Phila., re-printed and sold by B. Franklin. "Containing a confutation of the Rev. Mr. Gilbert Tennent, and his adherents; extracted chiefly from his own writings and formed upon his own plan of comparing the Moravian principles, with the standard of orthodoxy, in distinct columns."

Spangenberg, A. G.: *Darlegung richtiger Antworten auf mehr als dreyhundert Beschuldigen gegen den Ordinarium Fratrum,* Leipzig and Görlitz, 1751. Contains answers to over 300 accusations against Count Zinzendorf.

—— *Schlusz-Schrift worinn über tausend Beschuldigungen gegen die Brüder-Gemeinen und ihren zeitherigen Ordinarium nach der Wahrheit beantwortet werden,* and a second volume called: *Apologetische Schlusz-Schrift, zweiter Theil worinn einige Beylagen nebst dem Register über beyde Theile enthalten sind,* Leipzig and Görlitz, 1752. This work in question and answer form attempts to clear the Brethren of all libels and calumnies.

The History of the Moravians from their first settlement at Herrnhaag in the county of Büdingen, down to the present time, London, 1754. "The whole intended to give the world some knowledge of the extraordinary system of the Moravians and to show how it may affect both the religious and civil interests of the state." It is a warning to other states against "being ever involved with the Moravians in the manner the illustrious House of Büdingen was."

The Representation of the Committee of the English Congregations in Union with the Moravian Church, place and date of publication not given. Dedicated "to his grace the Archbishop of York, primate of England." A defense by the committee representing the English Brethren, clearing them and Zinzendorf of the calumnies against them.

Zinzendorf, N. L. von: *Acta Fratrum Unitatis in Anglia,* London, 1749. "Report from the committee to whom the petition of the deputies of the United Moravian Churches, in behalf of themselves and their United Brethren was referred; together with some extracts of the most material vouchers and papers contained in the appendix of the said report." Contains a statement of their doctrine, manner of preaching, the rationale of their liturgies, and extracts from the synods.

—— *An Exposition of the Matters Objected in England to the People Known by the Name of Unitas Fratrum,* London, 1755. This work in two parts is an answer to the accusations against the Brethren.

—— *Naturelle Reflexiones über allerhand Materien, nach der Art, wie er bei sich selbst zu denken gewohnt ist. Denenjenigen verständigen Lesern, welche sich nicht entbrechen können, über ihn zu denken, in einigen Sendschreiben bescheidentlich dargelegt,* in 12 parts and 9 supplements. These are reflections by Zinzendorf justifying his thoughts and practice. These appeared in periodical form in the years 1746-1749. On the title page in Greek are the words: "I am not mad, but speak forth words of truth and soberness." (Acts 25: 26.)

—— *Preemtorisches Bedencken or the Ordinary of the Brethrens' Churches . . . remarks on the way and manner wherein he has been hitherto treated in controversies and what reasons dissuade him from descending to minuter answers . . . translated from the High Dutch with a preface by John Gambold,* London, 1753.

—— *The Plain Case of the Representatives of the Unitas Fratrum,* London, 1754. An answer to the controversial writings and a defense of the Brethren.

—— *Theologische Bedencken welche Ludwig Graf von Zinzendorf zeitheriger Bischoff Böhmisch und Mährisch Evangelischen Brüder, seit 20 Jahren entworfen,* 3rd ed., Büdingen, 1742. Sketches from the theological thinking of Zinzendorf to set the Brethren's doctrine in a true light.

X. MISCELLANEOUS.

August Gottlieb Spangenberg's kurzegefaszte Nachrict von der gegenwärtigen Verfassung der evangelischen Brüder-Unität Augspurscher Confession mit Anmerkungen begleitet von einem ungenannten, welcher sich acht Jahre in verschiedenen Brüder-Gemeinen aufgehalten, Berlin, 1786. Contains critical anecdotes by an unknown author to the above-mentioned work by Spangenberg.

Benham, Daniel: *Comenius' School of Infancy with a Sketch of his Life,* London, 1858. A treatise on the education of youth in the first six years. Contains also a sketch of the life of Comenius.

Büdingische Sammlung Einiger in die Kirchen-Historie Einschlagender Sonderlich neuerer Schriften, 1740-1745, 18 parts in 3 vols. Contains speeches, letters, and historical accounts with the aim of making the Brethren better known to the public.

Chronicon Ephratense, enthaltend den Lebens-lauf des ehrwürdigen Vaters in Christo, Friedsam Gottrecht, weyland Stiffters und Vorstehers des geistl. Ordens der Einsamen in Ephrata in der Grafschaft Landcaster in Penn., Ephrata, 1786. A very interesting account of the origin, doctrines, and customs of the sect known as the Seventh Day Baptists (*Siebentäger*) or also Ephrata Brethren, settled at Ephrata, Pa., of which Conrad Beissel was the founder.

Die Welt der Stillen im Lande, Berlin, 1922. *"Bilder aus zwei Jahrhunderten Herrnhutischer Geschichte und Brüderischen Lebens, herausgegeben von S. Baudert und Th. Steinmann, mit dreizehn Federzeichnungen, sieben mehrfarbigen und fünfundzwanzig einfarbigen Bildtafeln nach bisher meist unveröffentlichten Vorlagen."*

Fisher, Sydney George: *The Making of Pennsylvania,* 8th ed., Phila., 1908. "An analysis of the elements of the population and the formative influences that created one of the greatest American states."

Geistliche Gedichte des Grafen von Zinzendorf, Stuttgart and Tübingen, 1845. A large volume containing excerpts from the fertile pen of the Count; selected by Albert Knapp.

Hasse, E. R.: *The Moravians*, London, 1911. Deals with the contributions of the Moravians to the eighteenth-century revivals.

Hutton, J. E.: *The Moravian Contribution to the Evangelical Revival in England, 1742-1755*. Owen College Historical Essays, 1902.

Keith, Charles P.: *Chronicles of Pennsylvania from the English Revolution to the Peace of Aix-la-Chapelle 1688-1748*, 2 vols., Phila., 1917.

Kriebel, Howard Wiegner: *The Schwenkfelders in Pennsylvania*, Lancaster, Pa., 1904. A reprint from vol. XIII of *Proceedings of the Pennsylvania German Society*.

Loosungen or Daily Texts, 1731-1932. These are texts from the Bible for every day in the year, printed yearly in book form in all the languages of the countries where the Brethren are to be found. These texts are used in their private and group devotionals.

Menzel, Wolfgang: *History of Germany*, trans. from the 4th German ed. by Mrs. George Horrocks, Bohn's *Standard Library*, vol. III.

Meyer, H. H.: *Child Nature and Nurture according to Count Ludwig von Zinzendorf*, New York, 1928. A study of the educational ideas and practices of Zinzendorf.

Moravians in New York and Connecticut, Phila., 1860. "An account of the dedication of two monuments, erected by the Moravian Historical Society, on the sites of once flourishing Moravian stations among the New England Indians in New York and Connecticut."

Ogden, John C.: *An Excursion into Bethlehem and Nazareth in Pennsylvania, in the year 1799; with a succinct history of the society of United Brethren commonly called Moravians*, Phila., 1805. A description of these settlements as a visitor sees it.

Pfister, Osker: *Die Frömmigkeit des Grafen Ludwig von Zinzendorf*, Leipzig and Vienna, 1910. *"Ein Psychoanalytischer Beitrag zur Kenntnis der Religiosen Sublimierungsprozesse und zur Erklärung des Pietismus."*

Sachse, Julius Friedrich: *The German Sectarians in Pennsylvania*, Phila., 1899-1900, vol. I, 1708-1742; vol. II, 1742-1800. A very valuable study of the Pennsylvania sectarians and of their relationships.

Twelve Views of Churches, Schools and Other Buildings erected by the United Brethren in America, with brief descriptions annexed, New York, 1836.

INDEX

Ancient Church, 7

Antes, Henry, 21, 29, 44, 51, 55, 59, 86, 184 f., 210

Apostolic Succession, 6, 227 f.; see Episcopacy

Archives, Bethlehem, 88

Atonement, 112, 139, 142, 161, 173

Augsburg Confession, 27, 137, 138, 219

"Bands," 98, 120

Baptism, 217

Baptist Church, 56, 211

Baumanites, 47 n.

Bechtel, John, 21, 49 n., 55, 59

Beissel, 30 n., 35 n., 39, 42

Benezet, Stephan, 83, 84 n.

Bethlehem, 19, 20, 21, 37 n., 72, 75, 80, 171, 188 ff., 198, 213

Bethlehem Steel Corporation, 92

Bethelsdorf, 9, 12

Böhler, Peter, 11, 53, 68 n., 76 f., 121, 144, 153, 185

Böhn, John Philip, 69

Brotherhood, holy, 79, 93 ff.

Brotherly Agreement, 84 f., 193 f.; see Appendix A

Buildings, 89, 161, 191

Cammerhoff, John Frederick, 171, 183 f.

"Choir" Houses, 75, 81, 89, 93 f., 97, 104, 160, 197, 203, 213 f., 215

"Choirs," 19, 31, 93 f., 97 f., 112, 198; Boys, 81, 114; Children, 82, 94, 96 f., 112 f.; decadence of, 81, 201 ff., 204; economic expedient, 93 f., 97; educational device, 96; Girls, 81, 115; Married, 81, 97 f., 117 f., 191; origin of, 95 ff., religious institutions, 94, 98; Single Brethren, 81 f., 91, 93, 97, 104, 117, 202; Single

Sisters, 81 f., 93, 97, 116, 202; Widowers, 97, 119 f.; Widows, 97, 118 f., 202; see Festivals, Discipline

Christiansbrunn, 82, 90 f., 194, 198

Christology, 144 ff.

Church, conception of, 209 ff.; established in America, 20, 53, 76; extended, 14, 15, 62, 72, 207, 214; Invisible, 25 f., 28 f., 53, 62, 210, 213; loyalty impaired, 206 f.; relationship to other denominations, 24, 83, 84, 142, 225 f.; see Diaspora, Ecclesiola in Ecclesia, Government, Membership, Settlement

Church of God in the Spirit, 21 ff., 27 ff., 40, 83; failure of, 48, 59, 61 ff.; meaning of, 24

Church-village, 198 f., 206

Colonization, 15 f., 21, 72

Comenius, John Amos, 5

Communism, religious, 76 f., 79, 80 f., 85; abolition of, 194, 196, 213; family life, 99; see General Economy, Government, Settlements

Confirmation, 217

Creed, 27, 107, 137, 138, 219, 223; see Doctrines

Czecho-Slovakia, 224

"Daily Texts," 62, 108

David, Christian, 10, 156

Devotions, 106 ff., 120 ff., 137

"Diaspora," 24 f., 213

Discipline, 198 f., 201

Dober, Leonard, 143

Doctrines, 100, 138, 220, 222; see Atonement, Christology, Church, Creed, Faith, God, Holy Spirit, Jesus, Sin, Soul, Theocracy, Theology, Total Depravity, Trinity, Wound Theology

261

144, 153 f., 157, 183; Christology, 8, 112, 220 f.; death of, 194, 219; in Denmark, 13; enemies, 13 f., 14 n., 158 f.; fanaticism, 157; work among Germans in Pa., 21, 138; at Halle, 7, 144; accused of heresy, 64 ff.; hymnologist, 112 f., 120 f., 216 f.; Lutheran clergyman, 25 f., 40, 63, 82; missionary career, 17 f.; opposition to him in America, 63 ff.; patron of Moravians, 9, 11, 13; pietism, 142, 144, 157; reorganizer of Moravian Church, 6 f.; at the Saxon Court, 8, 12 f.; travels among the Indians, 21, 59, 83; at Wittenberg, 8, 144; on church, 26 f., 206; on creeds, 138; on the Lutheran Church, 41; on regeneration, 142; on the Trinity, 144 ff., on the Wounds of Jesus, 140

VITA

Jacob J. Sessler was born in Aplington, Iowa, June
30, 1899. He received the degree of B.A. from Central College, Pella, Iowa, in 1925. In 1928 he finished
a three-year theological course in the Seminary of the
Reformed Church in America, in New Brunswick,
N. J., and in the same year received the degree of B.D.
from Rutgers University.